# Daniel Calparsoro

Manchester University Press

# Spanish and Latin American Filmmakers

*Series editors:*
Núria Triana Toribio, University of Manchester
Andy Willis, University of Salford

*Spanish and Latin American Filmmakers* offers a focus on new filmmakers; reclaims previously neglected filmmakers; and considers established figures from new and different perspectives. Each volume places its subject in a variety of critical and production contexts.
The series sees filmmakers as more than just auteurs, thus offering an insight into the work and contexts of producers, writers, actors, production companies and studios. The studies in this series take into account the recent changes in Spanish and Latin American film studies, such as the new emphasis on popular cinema, and the influence of cultural studies in the analysis of films and of the film cultures produced within the Spanish-speaking industries.

# Daniel Calparsoro

Ann Davies

Manchester University Press

Manchester and New York

*distributed exclusively in the USA by Palgrave Macmillan*

Published by Manchester University Press
Oxford Road, Manchester M13 9NR, UK
and Room 400, 175 Fifth Avenue, New York, NY 10010, USA
www.manchesteruniversitypress.co.uk

Distributed in the United States exclusively by
Palgrave, 175 Fifth Avenue, New York,
NY 10010, USA

Distributed in Canada exclusively by
UBC Press, University of British Columbia, 2029 West Mall,
Vancouver, BC, Canada V6T 1Z2

British Library Cataloguing-in-Publication Data
A catalogue record for this book is available from the British Library

Library of Congress Cataloging-in-Publication Data applied for

ISBN 978 0 7190 7364 9 hardback

First published 2009
18 17 16 15 14 13 12 11 10 09          10 9 8 7 6 5 4 3 2 1

Typeset in Scala with Dax display
by Koinonia, Manchester
Printed by the MPG Books Group in the UK

# Contents

# List of illustrations

# Acknowledgements

My first thanks must go to Daniel Calparsoro himself, who willingly and generously agreed to meet me and talk about his work. Thanks also to his production company who arranged the meeting. I am also grateful for the assistance given to me by the Filmoteca Española, Madrid, particularly Marga Lobo; and by the Euskadiko Filmotegia, Donostia/San Sebastián, particularly Peio Aldazabal and María Carmen Ausan.

Colleagues at Newcastle University who gave support and encouragement include Elizabeth Andersen, Rosaleen Howard, the late Vanessa Knights, Sarah Leahy, Florence Myles, Phil Powrie, Brian Stimpson. A particular note of thanks must go to my PhD student Rebecca Naughten, who generously shared some of her copious material on the current state of Spanish cinema. Colleagues and friends elsewhere who also gave assistance and encouragement include Mark Allinson, Jackie Collins, Chris Perriam, Rob Stone, Núria Triana-Toribio.

Work on this book was facilitated by a grant from the Arts and Humanities Research Council that supported a period of leave.

I am fortunate to be able to count on my family and many friends who gave informal support and guidance while I wrote this book. One of the foremost of these is my sister Cheryl. I dedicate this book to her.

Arts & Humanities
Research Council

**To my sister Cheryl**

**PART I**

# The context

# 1

# Introduction

The purpose of this study is essentially twofold, although one element will appear more immediate than the other. It is in the first place to consider the work of a contemporary Spanish film director, Daniel Calparsoro, and to do so arguably in auteurist terms. The reasons for doing so are theorised more explicitly below, although anyone picking up this book might assume the approach to be already implied by taking a single director as a focus of study. That this study does not take auteurism for granted is suggested by the second element of its overall purpose, to relate the work of one director to his (in this case) specific context, the Spanish industry within which he makes his films. And in doing this it is not a question of simply enlarging the auteurist frame to take in more of the background – the auteur as dominant voice in a chorus, rather than as solo singer. It is to suggest the director as a nexus, a crossing point, of interrelated threads that go to make up the contemporary Spanish cinema scene. In this light, a study of Calparsoro should tell us something not only about Calparsoro's films but also about Spanish cinema of today and the ways in which it is studied, written about and presented. The present study aims to make explicit some of the ways in which certain films and production processes are implicitly deemed more desirable, more worthy of attention by academics, critics and audiences (with the recognition that these groups are not always distinct from each other: they may find themselves embodied in the selfsame individual). It does so first by studying Calparsoro within his industrial context. Part I of this book offers an overall presentation of Calparsoro and his total corpus of work to date in relation to trends and traditions within Spanish cinema, serving to problematise these. Thus Calparsoro is discussed against the background of specific developments in

Spanish cinema since 1995, how both the film industry and critics perceived these developments, and how perceptions changed (or not) after Spanish cinema arguably fell into crisis from 2002. It also considers Calparsoro as part of ongoing efforts on the part of some scholars to distinguish a specifically Basque cinema from Spanish cinema more generally, and within this the director's oeuvre as part of a more particular debate linking Basque cinema to the representation of violence as an example of the complexities of attempting to determine a Basque national cinema. Part I continues with a consideration of the overlap that can occur between director/auteur and another element of film industry and culture that has risen to prominence more recently in film studies, the star, and how the star can impinge on our perception of the director (and vice versa). The argument here is then placed within a wider framework, that of Calparsoro's use of female characters in his films in relation to trends of the depiction of women more generally in Spanish cinema. Following this overview of Calparsoro's interaction with the cinematic context around him, the study then proceeds in Part II to a more detailed discussion of Calparsoro's individual films with the intention of teasing out still further the interrelation of director and industrial/cultural context.

The overall twofold purpose of this study – the dialogue between auteurism and film industry and culture, and in particular the way in which film is critiqued – makes Calparsoro a particularly apt choice for the simple reason that, as I will argue, his specific styles and themes are at present at odds with preferred forms of filmmaking, and ways of interpreting filmmaking, so that his own films seem anachronistic in contemporary Spanish cinema. In fact, as I hope to demonstrate, Calparsoro's films suggest greater continuity with some aspects of Spanish film today than such a notion implies. Nonetheless, I would claim that the overall perception of Calparsoro at the moment is very much one of a director against the grain, and this perception tells us as much if not perhaps more about prevailing values within the Spanish film scene as about Calparsoro himself or his own films. Calparsoro formed part of a new vanguard of directors that appeared in the mid-1990s. This resurgence is widely thought to have derived to a great extent from the slicker commercial values synonymous with Hollywood cinema, induced not only by a growing difficulty in obtaining government funding for films (in contrast to government support in the 1980s) but also by a new generation of Spanish directors who had grown up not only without the impulse to resist the ideologies of the dictatorship of 1939–75 but with the desire to make films like the ones they themselves enjoyed, which tended to be the Hollywood ones. Such an interpretation of the contemporary Spanish scene is of course reductive; earlier directors were not all necessarily interested in resistance to dictatorship and some were indeed looking for box-office success (mostly through comedy, a trend that persists today), nor have directors today necessarily dispensed with the desire to critique ideologies and values simply in order to churn out Hollywood imitations. In addition, the perception of the resurgence in terms of Hollywood carries the danger of neglecting the nuances that pertain in the Hollywood industry itself, which does not consist simply of box-office blockbusters. Nonetheless, the sense of a creeping Hollywoodisation haunts discussion of contemporary Spanish cinema, a perception that Spanish cinema is more closely aligned to commercial and high production values commonly associated with Hollywood.

In contrast to a simplistic assumption that Spanish directors today are moulded by US production values, Calparsoro has struck out on his own individual path ever since his debut feature film of 1995, *Salto al vacío* (Jump into the Void). In the process he has demonstrated the intricacies, conflicts and ambiguities that link a debatable national cinema (Spanish, Basque), the values of other cinemas both Hollywood and European, and also auteur style. Calparsoro's corpus of work, particularly the early films, is reminiscent of the older style of Spanish auteur with links to the *cine social* that recurs not only within Spain but European cinema more generally; but his style and themes suggest a contemporary figuration of auteurist cinema that includes his recent move in the direction of the war film with *Guerreros* (Warriors, 2002) and the growing corpus of contemporary Spanish horror with *Ausentes* (The Absent, 2005), thus suggesting that the director is neither totally divorced from current filmmaking trends nor confined to older forms of Spanish filmmaking. It is for these reasons that Calparsoro merits a more detailed and systematic study than he has hitherto received in either Spanish or Anglo-American scholarship. While he might not have the national and international status of other Spanish directors, his work garnering less attention than the commercial big hitters of Spanish cinema such as Pedro Almodóvar and, more recently, Alejandro Amenábar, he is nonetheless an important exemplar of Spanish cinema from and beyond the upsurge of 1995. Calparsoro can arguably be claimed as one of the

1995-plus generation (at the risk of saddling Spanish culture with another generational label to match those that pertain in literature): this generational conceptualisation is highly implicit in the two major works by Carlos Heredero, whose writings on the new generation of directors are now, according to Núria Triana-Toribio (2003: 147), generally accepted by Spanish academics and critics. Francisco María Benavent (2000: 12) is less enamoured of the notion of a generation, since he believes that the new directors might share the same age but not the same interests). Heredero's *20 nuevos directores* (1999) showcases the work of those directors who are comparatively new to Spanish cinema but whose films suggest the potential for prominence on the Spanish scene. Heredero's heftier *Espejo de miradas* (1997) provides lengthy interviews with these and other directors. Calparsoro is included in both volumes, which has done something to maintain a continued scholarly interest in his work. More will be said about this notion of the new generation of film directors in a more detailed discussion of the Spanish cinema scene below; at the moment it is sufficient to note the importance of the concept in discussion of contemporary film. Now that just over a decade has passed since that upsurge it is time to begin to look in more detail at what has endured into the new century; and looking at the corpus of work of a director such as Calparsoro is one contribution to this process.

This becomes more timely as the original impetus that heralded 1995 fades away and attitudes towards the upsurge – and the directors involved in it – change with the benefit of a certain amount of hindsight (in particular the failure in promise of some of the newer directors) and, as we shall see in Calparsoro's case in particular, a certain amount of exasperation that some members of the new generation could not settle down to either commercial success or a smooth transition to arthouse cinema. While Calparsoro's first film was hailed as evidence of raw talent, enthusiasm gradually gave way to impatience from some critics and reviewers with his style. Although academics have not been quite so quick to criticise, they have nonetheless devoted their attention to the very early work of Calparsoro while neglecting the latter (see, for example, Ballesteros (2001), Rodríguez (2002a)). The present volume will draw on these earlier insights, but will expand on them – in conjunction with my own ideas on Calparsoro's early work – to cover the later work as well, and trace the development of a contemporary director in the contemporary Spanish scene.

The stress I have placed hitherto on Calparsoro's positioning within contemporary cinema should not, however, obscure his links – whether intentional or not – to other, more established trends in filmmaking in Spain and Europe more generally. I have in mind here the strand of filmmaking that deliberately addresses local social realities – known as *cine social* in the Spanish context. A particular subgenre of the *cine social* has become prevalent in Spanish and European filmmaking, what I term the 'marginalised urban youth' genre. This involves films that revolve around the frustrations of young people in deprived urban settings with the lack of resources and opportunities in their environment. Calparsoro's first four films exemplify this genre, but what makes him unusual in this group in his emphasis on female protagonists and female subjectivity, as opposed to the sense of woman as other, as just one more unattainable and incomprehensible thing in a sphere of general frustration. Very few other directors in Spanish *cine social* do this. This offers another and very urgent reason for the study of Calparsoro's work.

The resurgence of Spanish cinema at the end of the twentieth century should not obscure the continuities with earlier forms of Spanish cinema more generally, of which *cine social* is one vital part. Although the marginalised urban youth genre may have become prevalent in contemporary *cine social*, it was not new. Carlos Saura made a notable contribution to the genre with his early film *Los golfos* (Hooligans, 1962) and later *Deprisa deprisa* (Hurry, Hurry, 1981), while Luis Buñuel provided perhaps the classic example with his Mexican film *Los olvidados* (The Young and Damned, 1950). It is significant that these are major directors in Spanish film history; previously *cine social* coincided with the height of auteurism in Spain, facilitating a distinction between cinema as high art – or at the very least social comment – and cinema as entertainment. This dichotomy between the two forms of cinema can be condemned as oversimplistic, not least because it frequently led to a devalorisation of popular and commercial vehicles. But the recent swing in Spanish film scholarship towards popular cinema, welcome as it is, should not blind us to the fact that this division is still with us and that we have not left behind the desire to make difficult cinema. The challenges to interpretation of arthouse cinema mean that academics, despite the turn towards the popular, are unlikely to leave arthouse alone for long. The disadvantage for now is that those directors deemed less accessible to audiences get less of the attention lovingly devoted to earlier directors who offered similar problems. Currently, directors who do not fit the popular or populist model run the risk of neglect due to a dismissal of older models of film critique. Calparsoro's style of filmmaking does not approach the surrealism of Buñuel (though there are still some continuities, as we shall see in the discussion of his second film *Pasajes* (Passages, 1996)); nonetheless, his early films are not so slick or easily digestible as the works of other directors. Entertainment has filtered into contemporary *cine social* with films that offer heart-warming stories alongside a dissection of specific social issues; notable examples include *Solas* (Alone, Benito Zambrano, 1999) and *Flores de otro mundo* (Flowers from Another World, Iciar Bollaín, 1999). Calparsoro does not seek to entertain. His stories are not tied up with neat bows at the end: the early films – *Pasajes* above all – end rather abruptly. The sheer noise of some of the films, the incomprehensible dialogue, the sense of bleak annihilation and despair; all these are not easy to absorb.

For the above reasons, then – all of which will be elaborated further in the course of this book – a study of Calparsoro's films can tell us not only about the work on an individual director and the potential for auteurism in Spanish cinema today but also something about the wider national industry and culture and the ways in which they are perceived and interpreted, indicating that the auteur is neither a thing apart from a more pervasive cinema culture and industry nor subordinate to it or absorbed by it. I hope in the course of this study to explore in depth the intricacies of Calparsoro's films but in so doing to say something not just about him but about his context.

## Calparsoro, theories of auteurism and the Spanish context

Why discuss Calparsoro in auteur terms at all? Mark Allinson notes that Hispanists have preferred to use an auteurist approach to film, while critics in Spain have preferred a historical approach, both of which ignore the transformation of the Spanish film industry by the market and by an increasing preference for genre (Allinson, 2003: 143–4). Yet he also observes that this does not in fact mean the death of the auteur but reformulations of the notion: 'Young, hip Spanish directors are keen to exploit constructions as auteurs commercially while creating increasingly genre-based films' (151). This description of the contemporary Spanish director fits Calparsoro neatly as he moves from social realist film to the war and horror genres. It is reflected in the critique of his work which, as I shall discuss in the following chapters, insists on assessing him in quasi-auteurist terms (in slight contradiction of the historical perspective perceived by Allinson). But while Calparsoro has recognisable links with the generation of 'young, hip directors' within which he is customarily included, his works have elements that either distinguish him from or problematise prevailing trends in Spanish cinema. In particular, the fact that since approximately 2002 and the putative new crisis in Spanish cinema (of which more below) he appears to be at odds with the main contemporary strand of Spanish film scholarship and critique allows us to consider the value of discussing the work of an individual director in terms of the cultural and industrial context. It is interesting, although probably coincidental, that the upsurge of Spanish cinema came towards the end of a revival of auteurist theory within film studies, which earlier fell out of favour because of its separation of the director from the collaborative production context within which he (and it nearly always was he) worked. The concept of the auteur has, however, proved a little too useful or convenient to disappear completely, and the 1990s saw a revamped concept of the auteur proposed, one that included crew, production, industry and socio-historical context as part of the field of study, but recognising that a director is not necessarily simply subordinate to these concerns. In particular, the auteur was allowed to claim both commercial and artistic success. Calparsoro himself has argued that the denigration of the concept of the auteur is a fear of, a way to ensure control over, the young director (Heredero, 1997: 260): the revival of the concept has neatly coincided with Heredero's figuring of contemporary Spanish cinema through the figure of the director, giving it – and giving the directors of the contemporary Spanish scene – continued critical power.

Timothy Corrigan argues for the contemporary auteur as 'a commercial performance of *the business of being an auteur*' (Corrigan, 1991: 104; italics in original) and goes on to comment:

> In the cinema, auteurism as agency thus becomes a place for encountering not so much a transcending meaning (of first-order desires) but the different conditions through which expressive meaning is made by an auteur and constructed by an audience, conditions that involve historical and cultural motivations and rationalizations [...] the commercial status of that presence [of the auteur] now necessarily becomes part of an agency that culturally and socially monitors identification and critical reception. (Corrigan, 1991: 105)

Corrigan is writing primarily about US cinema, and there the word 'commercial' as applied to cinema has a different resonance from the European context. How does Corrigan's notion of the contemporary auteur fit in the Spanish context where very few directors have the commercial success of the Almodóvars and the Amenábars? In a cinema where commerce does not have quite the same power as in the USA – where funding comes primarily from coproductions, government cultural bodies and the like – how applicable is Corrigan's analysis for the Spanish context? Calparsoro may not have the financial clout of his fellow generation member Amenábar, yet he nonetheless obtains money to make his films, and thus has in the last decade succeeded in establishing a reasonable corpus of films (larger than Amenábar's in fact). The number of films in a resumé may depend on other factors as well as finance, but we can posit that Calparsoro is 'commercial' enough to continue making films. In any case, within Spain as elsewhere, the division between auteurism and commercial cinema is increasingly blurred. Peter Evans (1999: 2–3) observes that in Spain successful cinema of the last two decades of the twentieth century has tended to be associated with recognised auteurs. He also observes (3) an increasing convergence of auteurist or arthouse cinema with popular cinema, drawing on audience awareness of the codes of the latter. Thus Spanish auteurist films 'incorporate elements of the popular in texts that transcend postmodernist abolition of aesthetic boundaries in their pursuit of more thorough treatment of subjects that in popular cinema often proved for various reasons – say, commercial or ideological – too difficult' (4).

Corrigan suggests that auteurs fall into two broad groups. He first posits the commercial auteur, with whom 'the celebrity of their agency produces and promotes texts that invariably exceed the movie itself, both before and after its release' (Corrigan, 1991: 107). In the Spanish context, Almodóvar is an obvious example of such an auteur: his name functions as a brand label (and his films carry his name as a label in precisely this way: the title credit is immediately followed by the caption 'an Almodóvar film'). Amenábar, too, functions in such a way: his name is key in promoting his work. This chimes with Corrigan's suggestion of the auteur as star:

> auteurs have become increasingly situated along an extratextual path in which their commercial status as auteurs is their chief function as auteurs: the auteur-star is meaningful primarily as a promotion or

recovery of a movie or group of movies, frequently regardless of the
filmic text itself. (Corrigan, 1991: 105)

It is tempting to place Calparsoro into this first group, since arguably
his name functions as label for his particular style and he, too, uses
his name as a label in the opening credits much as Almodóvar does.
He is, however, an oddity alongside the auteurs that Corrigan cites
in this first group (Spielberg, Lucas, Woody Allen, to offer but three
examples: Almodóvar might, however, fit here). But in Corrigan's
second category we have the auteur of commerce: a filmmaker who
'attempts to monitor or rework the institutional manipulations of the
auteurist position within the commerce of the contemporary movie
industry' (Corrigan, 1991: 107). Auteurism here works precisely
to destabilise rather than offer coherence, but it is not necessarily
separate from mainstream cinema, in line with the blurring of boundaries that Evans observed. The '95 generation, in one sense, functions
to auteurise the upsurge in the Spanish film industry without taking
away from its commercial success, such as it is. I would claim Calparsoro as an auteur in this second sense: he destabilises current conceptions of Spanish – and Basque – cinema, while insisting on his own
particular cinematic ideas of style, plot and character. His position as
auteur is, moreover, a tool for this very destabilisation process even as
he works within the Spanish film industry. He is in fact the auteur that
Carlos Losilla seeks and fails to find in his diatribe against contemporary Spanish cinema (1997a: 40), the ideological and aesthetic dissident committed to his own solitary war but doing so within rather
than separate from the contemporary scene.

Corrigan has received some criticism for his theories, notably that
of Dudley Andrew, who argues that Corrigan views the auteur 'not
as an individual with a vision or even a program but as a dispersed,
multi-masked, or empty name bearing a possibly bogus collateral in
the international market of images, a market that increasingly trades
in "futures"' (Andrew, 1993: 81). Andrew's comment might be valid for
the US case; it is harder to see its validity in the Spanish case, where
the industrial and cultural context is small enough for some meaning
at least to attach to the actual person to whom the auteur name corresponds: even while Almodóvar's auteurist style is becoming more
diffuse (and abroad problematically equated with Spanish cinema in
its entirety), the importance of Almodóvar as an embodied individual
functioning with the Spanish production circle cannot be denied.

Likewise with Calparsoro: a good part at least of the meaning of his name still attaches to himself as an individual artist.

James Naremore concludes his theorisation of authorship and auteurism with a brief summary of the contemporary tensions surrounding the concept: 'auteurism ... mounted an invigorating attack on convention, but it also formed canons and fixed the names of people we should study' (Naremore, 1990: 21). Naremore then goes on to observe:

> these tensions are inescapable, if only because writing about individual careers is necessary to any proper sociology of culture. Such writing helps us to understand the complicated, dynamic relation between institutions and artists, and it makes us aware of performance, theatricality, and celebrity. (Naremore, 1990: 21)

Hopefully, this study of Calparsoro will go at least some way to teasing out the intricacies of the relationships between the different component parts of the Spanish film culture and industry, and shedding some light on the dynamic between its own institutions and artists.

How does the process of auteur as destabilisation work? It is now time to consider that by looking in depth at Calparsoro's context and his films. But first there is one further introduction to be made, and that is to Calparsoro himself. We need to know who it is we are analysing and of his resumé to date – the raw data, as it were, of the forthcoming analysis.

## Background

Daniel Calparsoro López-Tapia was born in 1968 in Barcelona, of Basque parentage. He grew up in San Sebastián in a comfortable and artistic environment: his mother was an artist, while his father was a schoolfriend of Iván Zulueta, best known for his film *Arrebato* (Rapture, 1980), an exploration of the world and of the filmmaking process as seen through heroin use – a film which subsequently gained a cult following. A school dropout, Calparsoro got involved in gangs and even one or two hold-ups, and was expelled from four schools. In his interview with Carlos Heredero (1997: 25) he talks of having survived a period in his life at a time when some of his contemporaries were falling by the wayside, from drugs, AIDS or crime. His parents, appearing to despair somewhat of their errant son, eventually persuaded him to study politics, drawing and filmmaking in Madrid. After working on the production of *Ander eta Yul* (Ander and Yul,

Ana Díez, 1988), he went to New York and began to study film more seriously. While in the USA he worked on the New York set of *Sublet* (Chus Gutiérrez, 1992) and began to make video shorts, including *W.C.* which he brought back to Spain to exhibit. On his return to Spain he began to seek funding for his first feature-length film. The eventual result, *Salto al vacío*, was released in 1995 and had a great impact in that key year, including exhibition at the Berlin Film Festival. The international film festival circuit was also open to Calparsoro's next two films, *Pasajes* at Cannes and *A ciegas* (Blindly, 1997) at Venice. These three films all have the Basque Country as their setting and thus function as a form of Basque trilogy. Of the three films, *Salto al vacío* remains the most critically acclaimed, but the trilogy as a whole earned Calparsoro notice as part of the burgeoning cinema scene of the mid- to late 1990s, to say nothing of his inclusion in Heredero's clutch of new hopefuls. From his next film, *Asfalto* (Asphalt, 2000), we see a move away from the Basque Country to a more heterogeneous sense of setting and style, which continued with *Guerreros*, a virtually unique example of the contemporary war film in Spanish cinema, and set in Kosovo; and *Ausentes*, a horror film set in a Madrid suburb. *Guerreros* and *Ausentes* also suggest a move towards genre film – the war film and horror and away from the emphasis on urban youth that characterised the first four films.

Although Calparsoro's films always gained a mixed reception, from *Guerreros* there is a noticeable disenchantment with the films on the part of critics, although Calparsoro continued to garner newspaper interviews at the time of release of each film, indicating that a new Calparsoro film was still something of an event, if not quite the major event implied by the release of other films by directors who by now had made it bigger than Calparsoro had.

Calparsoro's venture into horror, however, has sparked interest in the USA, and the website IMDb (Internet Movie Database) Pro records that the director is now in pre-production of his first American film, a horror offering currently titled *Incident at Sans Asylum*, and in addition is slated to direct two more horror films for 2009, a remake of his own *Ausentes* and another, set in Kansas, called *Anvil*. The success of these ventures remains to be seen, but Calparsoro has clearly embarked on a new phase of his career, joining an increasing number of foreign directors making English-language films and making films in the US film industry. His fortunes in the US industry may modify our perception of him as director and as auteur in the future. For now, as the Spanish phase of his career is put on hold at the very least, the present study should act as a summary study of this phase.

## The Spanish context

What of the context within which Calparsoro has worked? We have already observed that the Spanish film industry is generally credited with a resurgence in terms of both box-office success and entertainment value in the mid-1990s, around the time that Calparsoro began making films (see, for instance, Jordan and Morgan-Tamosunas, 1998: 4–5). The new resurgence, generally tagged as a drift towards the commercial (certainly by older generations of directors who felt sidelined: see Benavent, 2000: 12), followed a downturn at the beginning of the 1990s after the dissolution of the government cinema policy of the 1980s, under the supervision of Pilar Miró. Miró's policy was to support films with high production values that appealed to notions of high art, resulting in glossy costume dramas and literary adaptations that delighted the elite end of the cinema market but which lacked box-office clout. The increasing lack of available funds for such productions, exacerbated by high budgets and some squandering of government subsidies (including grants awarded to films that were then never released), led to a reversal of government policy in 1990 under the direction of Jorge Semprún and a further law under Carmen Alborch in 1994, both of which insisted on government subsidy only after the event, ensuring that subsidies went to films that were actually screened and that subsidies were linked to box-office takings. Such laws pushed film funding closer towards commercial values, and these policies were confirmed with the change of government from the left-wing PSOE (Spanish Socialist Workers' Party) to the right-wing Partido Popular or PP (Popular Party) in 1996, who embraced neo-liberal attitudes to culture in that the latter must stand on its own two feet without government support. There is some indication that, with the return to power of the PSOE, the industry and the critics are looking to change the emphasis again, away from the overtly commercial and the 'bad taste' films of directors such as Alex de la Iglesia and Santiago Segura.[1]

The new emphasis under the PP on films succeeding or failing above all in terms of the box office was not by itself enough to guarantee the appearance of new directors or stars, or the emphasis on youth culture and stories for contemporary young people that duly emerged under the new aegis. One reason to connect the two phenomena might be that the newer directors, unfamiliar with the systems of government subsidies and the old ways of working, were better able to adapt to the new requirements and thus more aggressive in seeking out funding. Another factor is that newer directors had on the whole not grown up under the Franco dictatorship and had no real memories of it; they therefore did not experience the same impulse to use film as a form of oblique resistance to Francoism. They did not have the same compulsion to revisit the past, a fact that has worried José Castro de Paz and Josetxo Cerdán, who lament this divorce from the past as an erroneous move (2003: 36); their opinion being perhaps an example of a possible backlash against the new cinema discernible amidst the later talk of a crisis in Spanish cinema (which I discuss below). In 1995 new filmmakers preferred to make films about contemporary problems and stories, and they hired the actors appropriate to the newer roles rather than more established actors. Hence we have the appearance of a new generation emerging at that time, and the resurgence of Spanish cinema has become virtually synonymous with it. The sense that Heredero gives in his books (1997, 1999) of a new generation (despite his protests that the new directors are too heterogeneous a group to be labelled so neatly: Heredero, 1999: 15) reflects to some extent the breath of fresh air provided to the industry from younger directors not hidebound by the traditions of older Spanish filmmaking. Heredero posits that the increasing ability of young directors to penetrate the Spanish film industry has given the latter renewed hope for the future, perhaps almost too much so (Heredero, 1999: 15). Their tradition, if they had one, was the Hollywood one, as Heredero notes:

> Quizás la dimensión más interesante y novedosa de este proceso resida en la combinatoria que se ensaya entre algunos de los géneros habituales del cine americano ... y ciertos moldes o tradiciones de profundas raíces en el cine español [...] muchos de los nuevos cineastas confiesan que vuelven sus ojos hacia determinados cauces genéricos, que son habituales en la producción americana, como arsenal del cual extraer la vitalidad que echaban de menos en el cine español de la década anterior, y cuya ausencia – según ellos – tanto les alejaba de sus imágenes y sus propuestos. (Heredero, 1999: 23)

> (Perhaps the most interesting and novel dimension to this process lies in the effort to combine some of the usual American genres ... and certain models and traditions of Spanish cinema [...] many of the

new filmmakers confess to turning their gaze towards specific genres, common in American film production, as a resource from which to obtain the vitality they found lacking in Spanish cinema of the previous decade, the absence of which – according to them – alienated them from their images and ideas.)

According to this, Spanish strands of filmmaking were not entirely left behind; and the use that Heredero makes of the word 'confiesan' (confess) might suggest that somebody at least feels a little guilty about the turn towards Hollywood. We can perceive from Heredero's comment an impulse both on his part and on that of the unidentified directors to retain some stamp of Spanishness on their work. If they maintained any Spanish roots it seemed that at least the political turn of earlier years had been abandoned: the new directors shunned filmmaking with overt political messages or attempts to change hearts and minds, but an ethical viewpoint was often still implicit, suggesting an ambivalent attitude (Heredero, 1999: 21). Núria Triana-Toribio (2003: 144–5) observes that the new generation as presented by Heredero facilitated a discourse about Spanish cinema as diverse, a notion that coincided with the policies of the government and of cultural institutions, but as she herself goes on to observe 'not all the "cinemas" inside the tent of the national are equal or equally desired. The discourse on plurality, prima facie, disavows what is really at work within the articulation of the [Spanish] national cinema' (147). Directors such as Calparsoro may thus function as an alibi for diversity in the discussion of contemporary Spanish cinema and thus be tolerated if denied access to the centre of the discourse.

Not everyone accepted the idea of a new generation with the same enthusiasm as Heredero. Carlos Losilla, in an article that implies Spanish cinematographers to be damned whatever they do, accuses Spanish cinema of lacking and being unable to create a true tradition (Losilla, 1997a: 36), being out of touch with reality (37) and obsessed with creating a US-style industry (40). One of the dangers of this last point is, he believes, precisely the danger of the disappearance of the dissident auteur:

> la industria que se está creando, si es que así sucede, se basa en la desaparición de los autores, con todo lo que ello conlleva, entre otras cosas la eliminación del derecho a la disidencia estética e ideológica – que es, casi siempre, la más creativa, como demostraron incluso los mejores cineastas del Hollywood clásico – y la cada vez mayor imposibilidad de hacer la guerra en solitario. (Losilla, 1997a: 40)

(the industry being created, if it turns out this way, is based on the disappearance of the auteur, with all that that entails, among other things the
elimination of the right to aesthetic and ideological dissidence – which
is nearly always the most creative, as even the great classic Hollywood
directors demonstrated – and the increasing impossibility of carrying
out a solo war.)

Losilla's article is keener to find fault than to offer alternative suggestions but it does sketch out a notion of an auteur cinema based on a
strong tradition and steeped in Spanish reality (although Losilla does
not define what the latter might be). Although he readily dismisses
Calparsoro (38) – who by this stage had made only two films – I believe
that Calparsoro does coincide to some extent with what Losilla was
looking for in 1997, a dissident auteur with links to a Spanish tradition of *cine social* but also rooted in contemporary Spanish realities,
while not neglecting elements of Hollywood filmmaking. Losilla's
critique is hardly fair to the '95 generation, who at this stage (1997)
had hardly had sufficient time to establish a body of work sufficient
to garner the label of auteur. Losilla is, however, indicative of some
Spanish critics who seem never to be satisfied regardless of what their
cinema produces; thus the auteurs they are looking for go unnoticed.
In a similar move, Losilla accuses directors of being out of touch with
reality, but, as we shall see in Part II, only certain realities qualify as
'real' and the poor *barrios* of the Basque Country in Calparsoro's films
are dismissed by critics as simply a figment of Calparsoro's imagination. But, above all, Losilla demonstrates how debate about contemporary Spanish cinema revolves primarily around some concept of the
auteur, a construct necessary in order to talk about Spanish cinema's
new generation.

When singling out 1995 as a year of upsurge in Spanish cinema,
the dual emphasis on a rapprochement with Hollywood and the new
generation works to partly obscure the continuation and continuity
with, in particular, the *cine social*. Many of the '95 generation have
made films that could be described thus, and Calparsoro's work
arguably belongs to this social-realist cinema which, Triana-Toribio
argues, is still seen as the most legitimate form of filmmaking within
the Spanish industry (Triana-Toribio, 2003: 155–6) and which reflects
a Europe-wide belief that European cinema's *cine social* is the most
effective counter to the fantasy worlds of Hollywood (156). As she
goes on to observe, films prized by the Goya awards at the turn of
the century include an emphasis on alcoholism and domestic abuse

(*Solas*), teenagers in deprived urban areas (*Barrio* (Neighbourhood),
Fernando León de Aranoa, 1998), parental abuse (*El bola* (Pellet),
Achero Mañas, 2000). We could also note in this context the success
of the gloomy *Lunes al sol* (Mondays in the Sun, Fernando León de
Aranoa, 2002) about male unemployment, as well as the excellent
film about domestic violence, *Te doy mis ojos* (Take My Eyes, Iciar
Bollaín, 2003). Amenábar, too, has drawn closer to this genre after
his commercial successes with *Mar adentro* (The Sea Inside, 2004),
a well-made if occasionally sentimental version of the story of real-
life paraplegic Ramón Sampedro and his campaign for the right to
die; although this was something of a departure for Amenábar after
his previous three films in the thriller genre, his previous commercial and critical success was nonetheless a factor in *Mar adentro*'s
own success (the film won an Oscar in 2005 for Best Foreign Film).
Within *cine social* lies the more specific genre of marginalised urban
youth films referred to above, and exemplified in *Barrio* and *El bola*,
two critical successes in the genre. Jordan and Morgan-Tamosunas
(1998: 96–101) acknowledge juvenile delinquency and drug culture as
a prevalent theme of filmmaking in Spain (and they cite Calparsoro's
*Salto al vacío* as an example of this: 101). This coincides with what
Carlos Losilla felt to be the easy way out for Spanish cinema of the
1990s: the avoidance of metaphorical filmmaking in favour of 'un
cine pobre, humilde, desnudo, que indague en la trastienda moral de
nuestro tiempo y saque a la luz sus miserias, sus sueños rotos' (a poor,
humble, denuded cinema which investigates the moral underside of
our time and exposes its miseries and broken dreams: Losilla, 1997a:
42). Jesús Palacios, however, found in Calparsoro's films the saving
grace of an otherwise mediocre collection of Spanish offerings on
urban youth:

> Quizá el único joven director (o ya puestos, director a secas) que ha sido
> capaz de trazar una poética coherente y hasta fascinante de la juventud
> desesperada y rebelde o, mejor dicho, desesperada a secas, durante los
> años 90, haya sido Daniel Calparsoro. (Palacios, 2006: 378)

> (Perhaps the only young director in the 1990s (or the only director,
> young or not) capable of delineating a coherent and even fascinating
> poetics of desperate and rebellious – or simply desperate – youth has
> been Daniel Calparsoro.)

Palacios sees in Calparsoro's first four films a mythical and poetic
dimension lacking in most other urban youth films in which all too

1   *Salto al vacío* as cine social

often the juvenile delinquent is incorporated tamely into society. The only comparable film, in Palacios's opinion, is Ray Loriga's *La pistola de mi hermano* (My Brother's Gun, 1996), and this film as well as Calparsoro's work reveals a capacity for myth and poetry that distinguishes the true artist (379).

## A cinema in crisis?

With the hindsight of a decade or so, it seems clear that some but not all of the promise of the '95 generation has been fulfilled. Benavent (2000: 12) suggests that more people were going to see Spanish films in the latter half of the 1990s, but they were not necessarily going to see a wide variety of Spanish films; instead, they went for the top Spanish box-office successes. His comment reminds us that the mantle of resurgence is quite small and does not necessarily apply across the board. By 2002, according to Castro de Paz and Cerdán, Spanish film was in crisis with reduced production and distribution and calls for the return of protection measures (Castro de Paz and Cerdán, 2003: 28). Not everyone would agree with the crisis label: Pau Raussell (2003), for instance, argues that Spanish cinema's portion of the Spanish film market has never been that great. He acknowledges the years between 1994 and 2001 to have seen a rapid rise in feature film production (up 140%), audiences (up 260%) and box-office takings (up 460%). All that has happened is that in 2002 figures dropped away from the dizzy heights of 2001, a year which accounted for the box-office success of Amenábar's *The Others* and Santiago Segura's *Torrente 2: misión en Marbella* (Torrente 2: Mission in Marbella). These two films were dominant in terms of 2001 box-office takings; the fact that no similar films appeared in 2002 accounted for much of the downslide. 2001 was thus simply an unusual year, and 2002 is no worse than can be expected. Or one might take the very extreme notion of Josep Lluis Fecé and Cristina Pujol that there is no crisis in Spanish cinema because Spanish cinema does not in fact exist, being simply a construct of the industry and the academics rather than of the cinema-going public (Fecé and Pujol, 2003: 164–5). At any rate, what does seem clear is that the notion of the '95 generation appeared to allow for a certain degree of consensus about Spanish cinema (which clusters around the figure of the director), and a positive one at that (albeit one that masks contradictions and neglect, as Triana-Toribio observes above). This consensus is now fragmenting as critics dispute whether or not Spanish cinema has fallen (back?) into crisis; and as the consensus crumbles, we can detect an element of backlash against the cinema of '95.

It is interesting to compare the sense of the '95 generation as critics saw it at the turn of the century, drawing on Heredero's work, and, for example, listings of the most lauded Spanish directors today, in lists such as that provided by the film magazine *Cinemanía* for October 2005. This film magazine offers two brief listings of successful Spanish directors under the categories 'fenómemos nacionales' (national phenomena) and 'generación española' (the Spanish generation). In the former category are what we might regard as the big, established names – so Almodóvar appears there but so does Amenábar, Fernando León de Aranoa and Santiago Segura, all of whom arguably come from the '95 generation and who have thus made a fairly rapid transition to the premier league. The 'generación española' might be considered to be those 'bubbling under' the big time, and covers many of the names from Heredero's earlier listings (including, rather curiously, Julio Medem, whose status by now should surely have taken him into the other category), but Calparsoro is absent, despite having made (and thus having been able to secure funding for) six films altogether (the most recent film, *Ausentes*, having been released shortly before). It is valuable to compare Calparsoro's case to that of one of the directors in the generations list, Juan Carlos Fresnadillo, whose resumé is very sparse but marked by international success. As the *Cinemanía* listing reminds us, he received an Oscar nomination for best short film with *Esposados* (Handcuffed, 1997), but also obtained cult international success with *Intacto* (Intact, 2001). Since this was Fresnadillo's only feature film to date at the time of the article (he has since directed *28 Weeks Later*, 2007), it would seem that *Cinemanía's* list prioritises international recognition rather than a solid resumé that is nonetheless confined to the national sphere as is Calparsoro's work to date. Similar reasons might be deduced for the presence of Isabel Coixet, who makes films with predominantly American actors and in English, and of Iciar Bollaín, whose films also get an international release. Commercial success back home is nonetheless also valued; hence the presence in the list of Javier Fesser for his box-office success *La gran aventura de Mortadela y Filemón* (Mortadela and Filemón's Big Adventure, 2003) ('Directores: los que gritan "¡Acción!"', 2005: 204–5).

One should not, of course, read too much into these listings. But lists such as these may tell us something of the ways in which the industry – and the press that form a part of it – views which directors are 'in' and which are not. In this sense, by now, we can more than suspect that Calparsoro is no longer 'in'. On the other hand, it is worth noting that he is still able to make films in an era when, as Castro de Paz and Cerdán observe, a proportion of film professionals cannot find work (Castro de Paz and Cerdán, 2003: 30), suggesting in turn that Calparsoro's earlier cult success still counts for something when it comes to finding backers for his films. Unlike others who started making films in the mid-1990s but, because of lack of work, have not formed a reputation and thus still count as new (ibid.), Calparsoro has passed this stage and is himself now more established, without quite having the status to qualify as a 'national phenomenon'.

Heredero (1997: 247) describes Calparsoro's work in the following terms: 'Completamente ajeno a las tradiciones estéticas y narrativas del cine español, su obra bucea con pasión iconoclasta en la exploración de un universo desgarrado que esconde la herida de un romanticismo enfermizo' (Completely alien to Spanish cinema's aesthetic and narrative traditions, his work delves with iconoclastic passion into a world in tatters that hides the wound of a sickly romanticism). The key word here is 'iconoclastic', which I believe is a basis of Calparsoro's style much more than that of other directors, some of which may have wished to break away from the styles and subjects of more established directors, but not necessarily with the purpose of being more challenging. Calparsoro's iconoclasm extends in a more attenuated form even to the later films where he appears to immerse himself in genres strongly linked to Hollywood; he breaks the taboo against tackling contemporary war films, and then pays due homage to horror while simultaneously breaking some of its tenets. As Heredero also posits, the iconoclasm hides a wounded romanticism which I believe to be a key element in Calparsoro's filmmaking and which I will discuss in terms of the melodramatic thread in his Basque trilogy, though I am less in agreement that Calparsoro totally eschews a Spanish tradition in terms of style and narrative, as his links to *cine social* attest. If Calparsoro seems at odds with prevailing trends in Spanish cinema of the last ten years, this is perhaps only to be expected from his comments to Heredero in an interview that Spanish cinema of the 1980s acted to make the spectator feel comfortable above all. He argues that younger directors want to convey ideas by making the viewer uncomfortable, generating more dynamic and nonconformist sensations (Heredero, 1997: 257). Calparsoro's comments apply well to himself, perhaps less so to the directors around him. The question of comfort or discomfort is especially problematic given trends towards the commercial, towards light comedy and towards sentimentality even in *cine social* (Amenábar's *Mar adentro* and Benito Zambrano's *Solas* exemplify this trend neatly). While Calparsoro incorporates a melodramatic thread into his Basque trilogy (as I discuss in the next chapter), his work has avoided simple sentimentality.

Calparsoro's style makes the critics uncomfortable, suggesting that, regardless of his own putative roots in an earlier Spanish cinema, his deviation from the increasing convergence of Spanish *cine social* and slick commercialism has irritated the critics, indicating in turn that their expectations, if not his, have changed. While rarely condemning his work out of hand, time and again they accuse him of poor scripts, mumbled dialogues and a sense of his work as rough and unfinished. Initially critics were prepared to put this down to youthful inexperi- ence, but by the time of his later films there is now apparently less excuse. It is as if, since we are talking of a new generation of younger directors, that Calparsoro is the child that refuses to mature in the way his elders and betters would like, and his youthful failings that once were understandable and forgivable in his early days are not so acceptable now that he is no longer 'young'. Calparsoro's screenplays come in for the worst criticism; and this, too, has its counterpart in discussion of the Spanish context more generally. Carmen Arocena's diatribe against the poor screenplays that, in her opinion, typify contemporary Spanish cinema appears to be aimed directly at Calparsoro himself, although he is never named in her article. She blames the scriptwriters for not writing the sort of films that audiences want to see and for not taking the audiences into account, and argues that reality does not simply consist of poverty, drugs and unemployment (Arocena, 2003: 92). Arocena also cites Juan J Gómez's interview with Fernando Méndez-Leite, in which the latter says that many films are implausible, inconsistent, badly made, noisy and interminable (cited in Arocena, 2003, p. 90). These two descriptions appear to have some relation to Calparsoro's work, though the comments of Arocena and Méndez-Leite in fact come across as caricatures of what is currently going on in some sectors of the Spanish cinema scene. They also indicate some of the expectations placed on Spanish directors today – for either works of art or slick, easily digestible films that do not provoke or disturb the audience. And if these criticisms seem directly aimed at Calparsoro, whether Arocena and Méndez-Leite intended it or not, this implies that Calparsoro is not readily going to fit into the critically desired panorama of contemporary Spanish film. But we must remind ourselves that it is what some sectors of the field *desire*; it does not automatically equate to what is actually going on – after all, despite these observations, Calparsoro still makes films and somebody is giving him the funds to do so. Instead, what we can observe is the aptness of Triana-Toribio's earlier observation that some films are more welcome under the diversity umbrella than others – and, if we only consider those films that merit the demands for quality of Arocena and Méndez-Leite, then our perception of contemporary Spanish cinema is going to be more than usually partial.

Calparsoro's films nonetheless receive due coverage in the press, and increasingly he can draw on fairly major actors on the Spanish scene to act in his films, notably Eduardo Noriega in *Guerreros* and Ariadna Gil and Jordi Mollà in *Ausentes*. In itself this does not prove Calparsoro a great director; it may show simply that in an industry that is small compared to the dominant US one, a director or anyone else in the industry can gain a comparatively large amount of – even begrudging – recognition. After all, cinema critics for the newspapers and magazines have a compulsion to cover Spanish films simply because they are critics in Spain and only so many of the films released are Spanish. Nonetheless, in an era where funds are competitive and hard to come by, where subsidies are in short supply and much of the promise of some directors has only been fulfilled in part at best (including some of *Cinemanía*'s Spanish generation), and where the most successful options for directors are bland or bad-taste comedy, slick commercial thrillers or sentimentalised versions of social-realist cinema, Calparsoro's persistence is remarkable.

A consideration of Calparsoro, then, needs to include at the least a questioning of the insistence of contemporary reviewers on the weak points of Calparsoro's work in the context of what is currently happening in the Spanish film industry. This is not automatically to deny the possibility that the critics are correct, but the issue does point to the presupposition of specific criteria that prevail today concerning what is a good film and what is not. It seems that there is now less place for experimentation within the new generation of Spanish directors; while the label of auteur nonetheless grants an alibi to older directors whose work can still be thought complex in an arthouse fashion, Calparsoro is not allowed the same licence, precisely because he belongs to the '95 generation that was supposed to have moved away from the older styles. Thus one of the most overriding problems of the generational concept is revealed: although it functions as a useful shorthand for the resurgence of Spanish cinema in the mid-1990s, it serves to preclude certain types of film from the debate, and ways of perceiving film and directors that go back beyond this resurgence are also precluded precisely because they are supposedly dispensed with.

## Calparsoro and Basque cinema

In his early career Calparsoro was also confronted with the label of Basque film director, given that he comes from the Basque Country and his first three films use the Basque Country as a setting. Heredero detects roots in Basque cinema of the subsequent upsurge in cinema production by new directors (including Calparsoro), when in the early 1990s the quartet of directors, Julio Medem, Alex de la Iglesia, Enrique Urbizu and Juanma Bajo Ulloa brought a new impetus to Basque film (Heredero, 1999: 12). Joseba Gabilondo (2002: 265) includes Calparsoro in a group of Basque filmmakers recognised as crucial to the Spanish film industry (along with the usual four suspects mentioned above plus Iciar Bollaín and Arantxa Lazcano). This builds on the earlier prominence of Basque cinema in the 1980s, of which the director Imanol Uribe was at the forefront.

The question of Basque cinema, as distinct from Spanish cinema more generally, has become bound up with the question of Basque identity as a whole. The issue as to whether or not there is such a thing as a separate Basque cinema is hard to disentangle from a desire to promote a distinct Basque identity that thus merits recognition as a nation – and thus, eventually, a nation-state – as opposed to one of many regional identities under a Spanish umbrella. The application of the label 'Basque cinema' to those directors who come from the Basque Country may be regarded at one level as simply a convenient marketing tool, underscored by the fact that the Basque regional government of the 1980s was a major source of funding of such cinema. But it was also a chance to promote a culture, a region and a history that had been oppressed during the Franco era and thus perhaps also to hint at the idea of an essential Basque identity distinct from a Spanish one. The prevailing party of government in the Basque Country throughout the democratic era – and thus the funders of Basque filmmaking – has been the Basque Nationalist Party (Partido Nacionalista Vasco, or PNV), a party specifically created to promote the Basque Country as a separate nation. The rise of Basque cinema, then, has always carried an implicit link to questions of Basque identity – questions which some directors have not wished even to attempt to answer – and these questions surface prominently in efforts to theorise Basque cinema. Although Uribe has been the Basque director most active in addressing the Basque situation, others have seen the Basque label as a trap, a potentially restrictive ghettoisation, and have either drifted away from the Basque Country both literally and in terms of subject matter, or used the Basque Country as simply incidental setting, or have avoided Basque elements of style and theme altogether. Calparsoro himself argues that a Basque identity is not possible in a climate of fear of the future and of modernisation, and is concerned about the possibility that nationalism can be restricting: an artist should not feel confined in this way (Heredero, 1997: 255). His remark that insisting on a Basque identity ensures that cinema is stuck in the past offers a link to the perception more generally and noted above that Spanish cinema also neglects the past in favour of the present.

Calparsoro, in fact, is one of very few directors of Heredero's generation that has given specific and sustained attention to the Basque Country with his first three feature-length films. While Calparsoro's trilogy does not profess any specifically nationalist vision – even though the third film, *A ciegas*, has a Basque terrorist as protagonist – the fact that the director is telling us something about the Basque Country (its urban deprivation as a result of the falling off of earlier industrial and commercial success) is undeniable. In one interview Calparsoro insisted that the economic situation and unemployment are equally as crucial as nationalism in understanding the Basque Country (Rubio, 1996). So why does Calparsoro deny the label of Basque director? His denial may appear to chime in with the concept of Basque cinema posited by Jaume Martí-Olivella: 'Basque cinema seems to constitute itself by its (paradoxical) opposition to its own existence' (Martí-Olivella, 1999: 205). There have to some extent been attempts to package films by Basque film directors as 'Basque cinema', which has in turn led some directors deliberately to look outside of the Basque setting for inspiration, in a fear of ghettoisation. Martí-Olivella cites Calparsoro's denial of the existence of Basque cinema and comments on the director's remarks as a refusal to be imprisoned, ghettoised, in 'reductive identity politics' (206). Martí-Olivella compares this move to that of Spanish women writers and filmmakers who fight shy of being identified with feminism. But he views the director's remarks also in terms of the inability of Basque cinema to ever 'go home': Basque cinema, like Basque culture more generally, cannot find its own home territory because that territory is understood as either too violent or non-existent. In this sense, Martí-Olivella argues, Basque cinema is a 'migrant cinema', estranged from itself (208).

Calparsoro is perhaps rather unfairly singled out, as other directors have either expressed similar concerns or demonstrated it in their filmmaking. Directors such as Alex de la Iglesia have rejected the Basque Country as setting, while others show ambivalence; Medem moved well away from the Basque setting before returning with a vengeance to make the documentary about Basque violence *La pelota vasca* (Basque Ball, 2003: the controversy aroused by this film demonstrates the dangers in attempting to go home), while Uribe has vacillated after his early work on Basque separatism. But if, as Martí-Olivella suggests, Basque cinema is always migrant and estranged to itself, what does this say about the interaction of Basque cinema with the Spanish cinema that overlaps it, and both held in the potentially suffocating embrace of US cinema? Martí-Olivella's concept of Basque cinema appears to exist in an international cultural vacuum. Calparsoro, however – and he is not alone of Basque directors in doing this – responds either instinctively or overtly to traces of other cinemas, as is very clear in terms of his most recent, genre-modelled films. Martí-Olivella was, however, particularly unlucky when discussing a possible execution by the Basque terrorist group ETA at the end of *Salto al vacío*, which Calparsoro at the time denied was a direct reference to the terrorist group. Martí-Olivella offered this as an example of Calparsoro's tendency to deliberate self-estrangement from his own local reality by a refusal of local politics (Martí-Olivella 1999: 217); unfortunately, his argument does not take into account Calparsoro's *A ciegas*, which overtly acknowledges ETA.[2] Martí-Olivella's criticism of Calparsoro also neglects another, very real possibility in tackling Basque problems within cinema, the threat of a permanent sacrifice of individual identity at the service of national identity: Calparsoro received ETA threats while making *A ciegas*.

Gabilondo (2002: 266–7) prefers to describe Basque cinema in terms of the Freudian uncanny: 'uncanny identity is a negative identity, an othered identity that, in its negativity, returns to haunt the attempt to repress its being' (266). And 'Basque identity and its visibility recur with a violence that is clearly uncanny: familiar in its effect and yet frightening' (267). Gabilondo's theory of Basque cinema as uncanny refers to the Freudian concept of the uncanny as 'unheimlich' or literally unhomely, implying in turn a putative concept of home that also exists in Martí-Olivella's migrant cinema. This notion of home that underlies both concepts of Basque cinema threatens to subsume the latter under questions of an essential Basque identity once again. On this reading, by denying the label of Basque cinema Calparsoro and others may simply be denying the possibility of the Basque land as homeland. What the director demonstrates with his trilogy is precisely the fact that the Basque Country itself functions not as a home but a prison for his characters. The use of the term 'home' as a basis for these theories of Basque cinema does not take into account the fact that home can mean different things to different people, in particular women, for whom home may entail work, responsibility and entrapment.

These theories of Basque cinema ignore the possibility that has been posited by other critics such as Fecé and Pujol, mentioned above, that Spanish cinema itself does not exist. But they also ignore Calparsoro's own belief that such cinema is very much tied up with the past, and is thus a trap. The Basque Country in his films is all past and no future, revealed in the dereliction of former industrial glory within which today's youth cannot find any work and can only rebel against those in authority, that authority being precisely symbolic of the Basque land and the Basque law. The only way of acquiring a future is to abandon the Basque Country and the search for an authentic identity as suggested by the abandonment by the protagonist of *A ciegas* of ETA's armed struggle and her departure for a new life. Calparsoro is not so much denying a Basque identity as simply demonstrating its irrelevance to solve contemporary problems. Hence he can make films about the Basque Country while denying the label of Basque cinema, if the latter entails laying claim to an essential Basque identity. Perhaps we should not be talking in terms of the migrant and uncanny but simply of the alienated, which sounds less theoretically elevated but, I believe, comes nearer to the truth as far as Calparsoro's cinema is concerned.

I do not want here to imply necessarily that there is no such thing as Basque cinema or that films from or about the Basque Country are simply a subset of a more general Spanish cinema. In terms of putative national cinemas, I believe there is a need to explore further the attempt to carve out a Basque cinema over and against a Spanish cinema. In the Basque debate, Spanish cinema is itself a term that remains undefined and uncontested at a time when the very existence of a Spanish national cinema is coming under question elsewhere (see Triana-Toribio, 2003: ch. 6). While this question cannot be addressed adequately within the scope of the present study, it is pertinent here to ask how this slippage between purported cinemas positions the director. What does it mean when Martí-Olivella highlights what Gabilondo would describe as Calparsoro's active denial of a repressed, subconscious Basque identity that supposedly haunts him? At the very least it suggests the intended subordination of the director to a national cinema: any director who denies the pertinence of such a cinema would thus require the therapeutic recovery of the national buried within his or her subconsciousness. If previously auteurist theory in its more traditional conceptualisation ran the risk of overestimating the contribution of the individual director to the cinematic process while ignoring the cultural context, such a rigid definition of national cinema takes us too far in the opposite direction. The auteur can never be entirely separate from his or her cultural and industrial context, but it seems to me highly problematic to assume that the auteur must be totally subject to it in order to be discussed

within the national cinema project. The need of a national cinema
for the director is made clear with another comment of Martí-Olivella
on Calparsoro's work (in this case *Salto al vacío*): this film 'becomes
another powerful example of Basque cinema's shining paradox: to
render visible its own invisibility' (Martí-Olivella, 2003: 112). This
comment reminds us that a national cinema still requires films in
order to exist, and for that to happen it needs directors, too. Perhaps
the fear underlying the theories of Basque cinema outlined above is
its very dependence on directors, without whom it cannot exist – a
dependence that, as demonstrated by directors such as Calparsoro, is
by no means mutual.

## Violence in Basque and Spanish cinema

One particularly germane question that illuminates some of the difficulties in positing a specifically Basque cinema is that of the representation of violence. The struggle over Basque identity has been and
at the time of writing continues to be sometimes violent: there is a
currently indelible association of Basque identity with violence, fairly
or not, and that trace of violence has in turn figured within discus-
sions of Basque cinema. Gabilondo discusses violence in Basque
cinema, arguing that it is not confined to terrorism, and the 'Basque
cinema does not represent violence but rather *performs the violence of
the process whereby its identity is represented as other*' (Gabilondo, 2002:
268, italics in original), though this conceptualisation of violence
once again relies on too narrow a link of Basque cinema with the
Basque nation, and ignores the possibility that Basque directors may
take their cues from elsewhere. Gabilondo posits violence purely in
terms of the axis of Basque identity and the Spanish state (276–7); in
itself this hypothesis neglects the possibility that the Basque nation
(or certain elements of it, anyway) can itself 'other' people through
violence, but violence is implicit in any unequal relationship and is
not confined to the state.

Violence in contemporary Basque cinema has been noted by Barry
Jordan and Rikki Morgan-Tamosunas as a particular trend among
contemporary Basque filmmakers such as Juanma Bajo Ulloa and
Alex de la Iglesia; and they remark:

> among some of the younger Basque directors of recent times, we find
> a certain fascination with the excesses of screen violence and what
> might appear to be a knowing, self-conscious indulgence in physical

injury and cruelty. In some cases, such truculence forms part of a wider parodic intent, the impact of which is lessened by its very explicitness, exaggeration and excess, all of which tends to distance the spectator. In other cases however, the violence sometimes becomes transformed into a sensationalist visual spectacle. Blood and gore are fully and explicitly displayed for the specular delight and delectation of the audience, the horrors of aggression and physical injury are given a deliberately graphic, shocking treatment. Needless to say, the boundaries between the filmically warranted portrayal of the terrible effects of violent behaviour and screen violence as an aestheticised visual spectacle in itself tend to become seriously blurred. (Jordan and Morgan-Tamosunas, 1998: 191)

The question of violence is of particular import when it comes to discussing Calparsoro's work because violence is a paramount element within it and has been identified by critics as such, right from the opening scene of *Salto al vacío* with its apparently pointless killing of a policeman by a gang who themselves find self-expression difficult except through violent means. Violence is a recurrent motif in the Basque trilogy and *Asfalto* as part of living life on the margins. Violence in a war film such as *Guerreros* is in itself a defining generic characteristic, while it remains a latent possibility in all horror and thus in *Ausentes*. The issue of violence in Calparsoro's films has relevance in relation to the discussion of him as a putative Basque director, but also to Spanish cinema more generally and the '95 generation specifically; and thus it serves as a demonstration of how confining Calparsoro to the Basque camp is detrimental to our understanding of his own work. For violence has also been identified as characteristic of Spanish cinema.

Mark Allinson perceives the use of violence in recent Spanish film as an imitation of violence in US cinema, a way of catching up with the latter and a move away from 'years of introspective, politically engaged or otherwise commercially unpopular manifestations of violence' (Allinson, 1997: 315). Allinson comments of this historical trajectory that nonetheless 'most of these violent films are firmly rooted in a Spanish context, historical or contemporary, many telling stories which can be seen as being necessary to tell. There is almost an element of catharsis in their expression of repression, fratricide and torture, a kind of national purification of Spain's *leyenda negra*' (Allinson, 1997: 319). Calparsoro's use of violence can, however, be seen as a throwback to the earlier notion of violence as introspective and politically engaged – more reminiscent of the violence of some of

Carlos Saura's films such as *Los golfos* (1961), *La caza* (The Hunt, 1965) and *Llanto por un bandido* (Lament for a Bandit, 1964), as well as the excessive violence of films of the Spanish transition to democracy.

This is not to say that Calparsoro's work can be seen as a contrast to a simple series of American film clones, as Allinson makes clear when he refers to specifically Spanish cultural references that may be present or absent in different films. It seems clear that Calparsoro's films do participate in forms of cinematic violence that touch on the generic as well as the national. The violence in these films serves purposes related to the depiction of specific and localised issues (urban alienation in the Basque Country and Madrid, the apparently purposeless violence of warfare), but it also makes use of a more generalised presence of violence to imply that these specific cases are linked to violence as an endemic and pervasive form of expression and communication. It may also allude to some American films: references to Tarantino are commonplace in early reviews of Calparsoro, while individual films may also quote particular American films or genres (the contemporary war film, for example, in relation to Calparsoro's *Guerreros*: I say more about this example in chapter 7).

On the other hand Calparsoro's work does not fit with the grotesque, esperpento style of films such as Alex de la Iglesia's *El día de la bestia* (The Day of the Beast, 1995), with its approach of parody and black humour. In this I disagree to some extent with Allinson who argues that Calparsoro's first film *Salto al vacío* is another interesting blend of socially inspired conflict (though internalised) with an almost esperpentic aesthetic in the lack of sympathy for its protagonists' (Allinson, 1997: 329). The term 'esperpentic', suggesting as it does the grotesque, seems inappropriate for the violence we find in these films. The violence may be excessive but is rarely funny or parodic; it certainly suggests blackness but there is no humour within it. This accords better with *cine social* films about urban youth; the violence, arising from the frustrations of deprivation, is too seriously grim to include the least element of humour.

One of the key theorists writing about violence in Spanish cinema is Marsha Kinder in her groundbreaking *Blood Cinema: The Reconstruction of National Identity in Spain* (Kinder, 1993). Kinder posits two theories with which to analyse violence in Spanish film: René Girard's theories of sacrificial violence (Kinder, 1993: 140–50), and the Oedipal narrative (197–200). While some cinematic violence may certainly operate in this way in the Spanish context, there is nothing to say that all film violence has this function, and, while Kinder nowhere claims her theories to be exhaustive, it is nonetheless a lack that there is no sustained link between violence and urban deprivation. By the time of the '95 generation, with democracy well established, it is harder to see how violence in these films serves as sacrificial ritual or Oedipal narrative beyond the notion of Spanish youth as the scapegoats of economic policies in Spain and elsewhere, policies decided by their elders without reference to them. But violence in contemporary cinema has also on another level reflected moves in some quarters away from the use of violence as a metaphor for Francoist repression and also towards a use of violence more closely aligned with Hollywood. Kinder commented of the situation up to the time of writing (1993):

> this oppositional system of violent representation developed against a double hegemony: domestically, it had to be distinguished from the conventions of the Counter-Reformation (particularly as remolded by the Francoist aesthetic), where violence was eroticized as ritual sacrifice; globally and commercially, it had to be distinguished from Hollywood's valorization of violence as a dramatic agent of moral change. (Kinder, 1993: 138)

But this system has become more diffuse since then, and directors such as Amenábar in particular and those who make horror films have produced representations of violence more akin to that of mainstream US cinema as Allinson argues (which may also function as spectacle as much as dramatic agent of moral change). On the other hand, as Kinder also observes, violence has historically been linked with Spanish auteurism (137), and this way of viewing the use of violence still persists. This would appear to persist in Calparsoro's case at least: critics quickly perceived violence as a specific trade-mark. The continuity with the cinema of the Franco era may help us to rethink the violence of the earlier cinema not simply in terms of opposition to Franco (though it certainly enacts this). But violence also expresses other ways in which the social fabric has been torn, and therefore forms a more generic element of *cine social*. Yet Calparsoro's use of violence also reflects the more nihilistic tendencies of some US cinema, thus problematising a split in the consideration of violence between Spain and Hollywood.

Calparsoro himself argues that the whole cinematic process is violent:

te metes en una sala oscura y te asaltan. Cuando colocas la cámara delante de un actor, con veinticinco personas mirándolo y el director dándole órdenes, estás ejerciendo violencia sobre él. Todo lo que se mueve para cambiar las cosas también es violento, pero lo que me interesa es la violencia como motor, no como regodeo. (Heredero, 1997: 269)

(you go into a dark room and are assaulted. When you place the camera in front of an actor, with twenty-five people looking at him and the director giving him orders, you are doing violence to him. Anything that moves to change things is violent, too, but what interests me is violence as motivation rather than pleasure.)

He continues by saying that he is more interested in conveying the true experience of death and the internal effects of violence rather than violence as spectacle (Heredero, 1997: 270). For Calparsoro, then, violence is an inherent part of any form of cinema so that, while it may explicitly express localised forms of violence, violence and cinema are more universally related. Although the comparison to Tarantino suggests an excessive use of violence for sheer spectacle, the director declares himself more concerned with audience empathy: we are to experience the violence that the characters undergo as directly as possible, to enter into it, rather than sit back and view it as entertainment. Of course, this goal is a utopian one, as our experiences of filmic violence can never be immediate but must always be mediated; and the impossibility of this aim induces in us a sense of frustration

2   Chino gets violent in *Asfalto*

and bewilderment to match that of many of Calparsoro's characters. Calparsoro's use of violence, then, has some connection with
the earlier Spanish auteurist use of violence in cinema before 1995,
and also with the desire to expose the contradictions in contemporary
Basque and Spanish society, but it is not obvious that the violence
functions in metaphorical terms as Kinder proposed, simply a symbol
of something else. Calparsoro's violence is 'pure' in the sense that
it stands above all for itself: it does not represent anything else – it
simply *is*. Calparsoro tells us of violence, rather than using violence
to tell us of something else.

To conclude, the motif of violence in Calparsoro's films can be
perceived within more than one framework, and the use of it by
contemporary directors indicates some of the problems raised by
attempting to distinguish Basque violence, within Basque cinema,
from Spanish violence and Spanish cinema. Gabilondo's hypothesis,
outlined above, does not take into account the pressure placed on
both cinemas by the dominance of US filmmaking, the interrelation
between traditions and trends in Spanish and Basque filmmaking and
the fact that violence is not confined to the Spanish state. This is not
to say that cinema can never reflect the 'othering' process perpetrated
by the Spanish state on Basque identities as Gabilondo posits: such
a process does indeed go on. Nor is it to say that theoretical frameworks should not be attempted within which to discuss a specifically
Basque cinema. It is to say, however, that such frameworks run the
risk of being out of step with cinematic trends in the Iberian penin-
sula, of neglecting the overlap with Spanish and other cinemas and of
constricting the interpretation of a director's work. In the latter case,
the simultaneous awareness of an auteurist framework can help to
counteract this, as this brief discussion of Calparsoro in the light of
Basque/Spanish cinematic violence should make clear. Calparsoro's
films might well conform to Gabilondo's hypothesis of the othering
process of the Spanish state but, as we shall see in the chapters on the
individual films, there are other ways of looking at the question.

## Notes

1 Conversation with Núria Triana-Toribio, 2 March 2006.
2 *A ciegas* may not have been released at the time Martí-Olivella was writing,
   although it had been released before publication.

## 2

# Najwa Nimri: the interaction of director and star

One central reason why the original conceptualisation of the auteur has been challenged and reformulated is the fact that the director, however distinctive his or her individual cinematic vision, rarely if ever works alone. Critics and scholars increasingly recognise the contribution of others involved in the filmmaking process: actors, camera operators, costume designers, musicians and so on. This chapter starts from that very premise: that Calparsoro has not made his six films unaided, that others participated in his work and have collaborated to a greater or lesser extent. Calparsoro has drawn on the abilities of others in making his films: the swooping steadycam of early cameraman Kiko de la Rica that gave the dizzying sense of claustrophobia to *Salto al vacío* and *Pasajes* and the more polished camerawork of Josep María Civit in the genre films; the haunting music of Carlos Jean that garnered praise for the later three films and developed Calparsoro's style on from the aggressive rock and choral chords of *Salto* and *A ciegas*. In the earlier films, too, Calparsoro gathered together a group of regular actors such as Alfredo Villa, Ion Gabella and Mariví Bilbao. In addition there is the incalculable contribution of Calparsoro's sister Carla, who played roles in some of the films and took on other tasks such as working with the child actors of *Ausentes*. But one collaboration overarches all of these, being the most noted by the critics and arguably having the most impact in collaborative terms beyond Calparsoro's own work and into the wider field of Hispanic cinema: that of Calparsoro and the actress Najwa Nimri. This chapter will discuss this collaboration both in terms of its significance for Calparsoro's own work but also in terms of how an individual director's work leaches into and interacts with other aspects of the Spanish film scene, in this case the Spanish star system. Such discussion does not, clearly, exhaust the implications of collaboration on Calparsoro's work, but it does help to clarify the director's position as auteur in the light of the overview of contemporary auteurism outlined in the intro-duction. The chapter then expands to a consideration of the presenta-tion of women in his films, particularly the Basque trilogy, ultimately linking this debate back to the role of Nimri in Calparsoro's work.

Chris Perriam makes a strong case for the ability to discuss contem-porary Spanish stars at all:

> the significance, resonance and prominence of the best-known Spanish actors means that there now exists a matrix of production and consump-tion of Spanish stars within Spain and beyond ... the number of active performers in demand by the industry, their filmographies ..., their quickly consolidated careers, and the volume of printed and electroni-cally mediatised coverage of their lives and roles ... all argue if not for a Spanish star 'system' exactly, then certainly for a strong and specifi-cally determined supporting matrix of image production, deals, outlets, tailored scripts, and simple star vehicles. (Perriam, 2003: 2–3)

Nimri certainly has her place within this matrix. Although, as Barry Jordan and Mark Allinson caution (2005: 122–3), we cannot talk of Spanish stars in the same way that we do stars from Hollywood, they go on to argue that actors can still be perceived as stars precisely through their performance in film, regardless of any immersion in a celebrity culture that would be more familiar in the USA. Although Nimri's personal life (the fact that she was married to Calparsoro) has impinged on the perception of her star persona, the latter is founded primarily on the roles she has undertaken. As Jordan and Allinson put it: 'even the most performance-orientated actors still carry with them a "baggage" which is the sum of their portfolio of roles (and the extent to which these have been personification and/or impersonation-led) and their celebrity star status' (130).

Nimri forms part of a new stable of Spanish stars that arose along-side the emergence of new directors in the mid-1990s. Some of these stars had appeared prior to the key year of 1995, such as Javier Bardem, Penélope Cruz and Jordi Mollà, but consolidated their position with the mid-1990s upsurge that offered more and better opportunities. Likewise, from 1995 onwards new actors came to prominence in a cinema that arguably emphasised youth, such as Eduardo Noriega, Juan Diego Botto, Paz Vega and Ernesto Alterio. Nimri forms a part of this latter group, gaining attention as she did in 1995 with *Salto al vacío*. Calparsoro's films contributed to her viability as a star, but

3   Nimri as Nuria in *Abre los ojos*

she also began to develop a repertoire separate from that of Calparsoro's work, starting with *Abre los ojos* (Open Your Eyes, Alejandro
Amenábar) in 1997. To date she has not gained the larger profile of the
likes of Cruz, nor has she yet managed to break into English-language
cinema to the same extent that Cruz and Bardem have done (alongside
Latin American actors such as Gael García Bernal); although she has
made it as far as a cameo role in *Before Night Falls/Antes que anochezca*
(Julian Schnabel, 2000). Nonetheless, she is reasonably established
as a leading actress within the Spanish scene, and in the early days
of her career she found work with both Medem and Amenábar: some
of these films are rightly becoming contemporary classics of Spanish
film. Since the turn of the century the quality of the films she has
appeared in has become patchier; but she was nonetheless able to
top the billing alongside Eduardo Noriega in the recent *El método*
(The Method, Marcelo Piñeyro, 2005). Angel Quintana describes
Nimri (along with the actress Silke) as an example of a 'certain level
of postmodern eccentricity', part of the star system of the 1990s, as
opposed to the ordinary-looking stars of the early twenty-first century
Spanish cinema (Quintana, 2005: 20).

## The fragility of Nimri's characters

Jordan and Morgan-Tamosunas comment that the influx of new Spanish female stars:

> has ... been crucially important to the construction of positive representations of female identity. [Work by these stars] articulates the very different formative cultural experience and concerns of a generation of young women born into the postmodern and postfeminist Spain of the democratic period. The simplicity and naturalness of their acting styles and the *despreocupación* (nonchalance) which characterises many of their roles, marks a visible distance from the more dramatic and traumatic roles of the older generation, weighed down with the personal baggage of Francoism. These actors consistently represent young women who are socially, professionally and sexually independent and, whilst still having to negotiate conflict and contradiction, do so with a greater sense of confidence and self-sufficiency. (Jordan and Morgan-Tamosunas, 1998: 128)

Much of this is clearly true of Nimri, who in the trilogy and elsewhere plays roles that provide a portrait of an independent woman working her way through various levels of conflict, much of which has been imposed upon her. Although Jordan and Morgan-Tamosunas's comment bears a middle-class predisposition that is unsurprising given the lack of coverage of women in lower classes (as I will discuss below), it applies to some extent to the three protagonists of Calparsoro's Basque trilogy of *Salto al vacío*, *Pasajes* and *A ciegas*. Above all, Calparsoro posits his women as desiring subjects rather than desirable objects; this is a crucial contribution to more positive representations of women in Spanish cinema, and Nimri as the star of these films plays a significant part in her turn within this contribution. However, we can also easily detect a vulnerability and a neediness which is overt in the trilogy but also within other films; a fragility which is enhanced by her large eyes, of which Calparsoro makes much, particularly in *Pasajes* by way of heavy kohl pencil and in *A ciegas* by the eyeholes of Marrubi's mask. When Julio Medem later came to make his film *Los amantes del círculo polar* (Lovers of the Arctic Circle, 1998), he intended from the start that Nimri should play the central female role precisely because of her eyes (Ángulo and Rebordinos, 2005: 241). Her role as Nuria in *Abre los ojos*, dependent on the love of César (Eduardo Noriega) to the point of self-destruction, demonstrates this neediness and vulnerability beyond Calparsoro's work. In this vulnerability Nimri shows a star persona not unlike some of Penélope Cruz's characters, in which sassiness masks a search for a father figure, as Peter Evans has suggested (2004: 54–63), again hinting at neediness and dependence. The potential comparison to Cruz might imply that there are other qualities looked for in some Spanish actresses beyond postmodern independence: the potential for greater freedom does not preclude dependence on others.

Calparsoro's trilogy suggests the reliance of Nimri's characters on melodramatic desires which goes against a sense of self-sufficiency. Heredero describes Nimri in the following terms:

> Su [i.e. Calparsoro's] gran personaje, casi su 'alter ego' cinemato-gráfico, es una mujer pequeña y frágil, pero extraordinariamente fuerte de carácter, generalmente perdida en lo más profundo de un mundo sórdido y violento, capaz de alimentar y, en última instancia, de poner en marcha el sueño de una vida mejor. (Heredero, 1997: 246–7)

> (His major character, virtually his cinematic alter ego, is a small, fragile woman with nonetheless a very strong personality, generally lost in the depths of a sordid and violent world, capable of nurturing and ultimately realising the dream of a better life.)

I will return to the notion of Nimri as Calparsoro's alter ego below, as well as to the question of melodrama as a motif within Calparsoro's films. But the perception of Nimri as fragile pervades many of the reviews of Calparsoro's early work. Thus Jordi Costa, for instance, compares the Nimri of *A ciegas* to 'una mena de Bambi femení perdut en el més inclement dels universos' (a sort of feminine Bambi lost in the harshest of worlds; Costa, 1997). Carlos Losilla, in his own review of *A ciegas*, talks of the film as a mixture of incompetence and daring of which the greatest symbol is Nimri as Calparsoro's muse, who moves us with her pathetic, stuttering inability to express herself (Losilla, 1997b: 14). Losilla is rather unkind in his suggestion of Nimri as the embodiment of all that is wrong (in his opinion) with Calpar-soro's work, but his comment on her ability to inspire sympathy with her hesitant attempts to communicate echoes not only the perception of Nimri as fragile and childlike but also the attraction that it has in its capacity to inspire emotion. (Losilla's comment also hints at diffi-culties in understanding Nimri's speech, a question to which I will return). This image of Nimri as tough on the outside but childlike and fragile beneath the surface recurs in much of her work with other directors: *Abre los ojos* as we have seen, but also the warm but vulner-able nurturer of *Lucía y el sexo* (Sex and Lucía, Julio Medem, 2001) or the cameo of the childlike prostitute in rabbit ears of *20 centímetros* (20 Centimetres, Ramón Salazar, 2005). Even in *El método* her character Nieves comes across for most of the film as a strong, hard-headed businesswoman but retains a weakness for romantic memory that ultimately undoes her. There are other matches between the way Calparsoro perceived Nimri and her roles and the way in which other directors have seen her since. Cristina Pujol Ozonas talks of Nimri's character Elena in *Lucía y el sexo* as lyrically sensual (Pujol Ozonas, 2005: 103); and later remarks that all three female characters of the film – thus including Elena – live for others 'to serve, care for and protect the people around them' (107n). The comment reminds us readily of Alex in *Salto al vacío*, as we see in Part II: she cares for her family and in particular tries to look after her junkie brother Juáncar. Similarly with *Los amantes del círculo polar*, Nimri's character of Ana remains throughout dependent on Otto, the man who she has loved since childhood, to the extent that she waits for him in the Arctic Circle in the expectation that fate will bring him to her, a romantic desire carried to extremes that reflects the romantic desires of the protagonists of the Basque trilogy. (It is worth observing in passing that Ana comes to desire Otto in the first place because she believes

4   The dependent Nimri: Ana and Otto in *Los amantes del círculo polar*

he is the reincarnation of her dead father, an indication of the need for protection that forms a part of Nimri's own persona). At the time of the release of *Los amantes del círculo polar* Nimri herself talked about Alex in *Salto* as a hard character, suggesting by implication that her character of Ana is softer ('Najwa Nimri', 2000). The film *Fausto 5.0* (Faust 5.0, Álex Ollé and Isidro Ortiz, 2001) takes a somewhat different tack in positioning Nimri as Julia, a character who functions as the Marguerite figure in this updated version of the Faust story. Unusually, Nimri takes up a position as desired object rather than desiring subject of the story; the conception of Julia/Marguerite as desirable precisely because she is pure and thus in need of protecting still draws, however, on Nimri's trademark fragility. In *Piedras* (Stones, Ramón Salazar, 2002) Nimri rounds out her persona with the ditziness of her character Leire, probably the neediest of all her characters to date, descending into histrionics when her boyfriend Kun leaves her. This film also reprises a taste for outlandish shoes that Calparsoro introduces in *Pasajes* as discussed in more detail in the chapter on that film: Leire steals exotic shoes from the store in which she works.

Calparsoro's work has clearly contributed to an overall persona of Nimri as a hard cookie with a soft centre, the softness coming a little more to the fore as Nimri moved away from the ambience of violent urban youth that typified the director's early films. How far this can be attributed to the director and how far to the actress will be debated below. There is, however, one element of Nimri's persona of vulnerability which I would argue has directly contributed to a negative reception of his films. As we shall see Calparsoro has devoted his early work as a virtual homage to Nimri, and the reviewers have for the most past followed suit in finding Nimri fascinating as a heroine. But if, as I cited earlier, they have observed her fragility, they have on the whole not noted how much her whispering voice has contributed to this. Nimri rarely speaks above a murmur, which reinforces the childlike patina that encases her persona. Yet many critics have noticed how mumbled the dialogue of Calparsoro's films is. Having listened attentively to the dialogue, I have to conclude that this complaint must be laid primarily at Nimri's door. Hers is the only dialogue that I find occasionally unintelligible (most notably in *A ciegas*: a crucial exchange with Aiztpea after the shooting of Eneko is virtually swallowed whole). It is intriguing that critics did not take Nimri to task specifically for this, rather aiming their complaints at the films as a whole. The quiet, breathy voice may have formed a vital part of Nimri's attraction for

Calparsoro; but whether or not he originated this tone of voice she has kept it since. Most of her roles with other directors employ this voice. It works well enough when she plays the *femme fatale* Nuria in *Abre los ojos*, adding to her attempts to seduce César; and to some extent also in *Los amantes del círculo polar* in which Ana remains on one level the little girl she originally was when she first fell in love with Otto. This relationship stemming from childhood never really allows her to grow up, and the voice underscores this idea. However, by the time of *Piedras*, one reviewer had clearly lost patience and castigated her for her poor diction (Barredo, 2002: 286). Nimri retains her breathiness right up until and including *El método*, the most recent of her films available for viewing at the time of writing.

It is hard to say how far Calparsoro was responsible for this Nimrean trait, since it appears in most of Nimri's work without any apparent correction by any director. This voice may simply be the only register she has, which contrasts with a reasonable flexibility of performance that she brings to other aspects of her acting: Nimri also has a singing career, and her voice has the same breathiness there. As Calparsoro avowed more interest in the visual aspects of film rather than the dialogue, he may simply not have been that bothered about a comparatively poor diction, which coincides rather uncomfortably with the aggressive criticism that stems particularly from the 2002 crisis in which good diction and polished scripts seem to form part of that perennial ideal which Spanish cinema can never reach. Nonetheless, what is, I believe, beyond dispute is that Nimri's voice supplies an essential ingredient to her star persona, and that persona in turn has impacted on the reception of Calparsoro's films. It is an essential ingredient of her little-girl-lost image, suggesting that the move towards depictions of independent women noted by Jordan and Morgan-Tamosunas does not mean the consequent abandonment of notions of women as needy and infantile. The two ideas can coexist in the same persona. Unfortunately, one cannot hold out too much hope for the independent woman of Spanish cinema if she cannot be heard.

## Nimri as muse

Reviews of Calparsoro's work refer time and again to the idea of Nimri as Calparsoro's muse. The word 'muse' reads uncomfortably in the Anglo-American tradition of scholarship, implying as it does the passivity of the woman whose sole purpose is simply to exist in order to inspire the male artist. Nevertheless, the term appears frequently and indiscriminately in Spanish reviews, where 'muse' can refer to any actress who works with a director more than once. If European cinema might be more inclined to favour the director as both auteur and artist, there may be a corollary inclination to attach a muse, in the style of Buñuel (Catherine Deneuve, Silvia Pinal) and Saura (Geraldine Chaplin), to say nothing of French directors such as Jean-Luc Godard (Anna Karina). 'Muse' in the field of Spanish cinema thus appears to be a more throwaway term than it would be in English-language cinema criticism. The working relationship between Calparsoro and Nimri nonetheless carries the potential to reinvest the term with meaning. Calparsoro's work has become so deeply associated with Nimri that even as late as *Ausentes* Calparsoro must explain why she was not involved in the film, saying that her lack of participation was not pre-planned (Galindo Frías, 2005), even though by now she has clearly moved on from their collaboration. This insistence on Nimri occurs despite the fact that the director and actress, who married each other shortly after *Salto al vacío*, split up subsequent to *Asfalto* (although Nimri collaborated for the music of *Guerreros* as part of the musical duo Najwajean). For now, Nimri remains a ghost that haunts Calparsoro's more recent work.

There seems little doubt that the first four films reveal Calparsoro's obsession with Nimri, as Palacios lyrically describes:

estamos ante una trilogía que no deja de ser una especie de poema épico de Daniel Calparsoro a Najwa Nimri y, a través suyo, a las fuerzas femeninas, tanto creadoras como destructoras, de la Naturaleza, tan presentes siempre en el inconsciente colectivo del pueblo vasco ... romántica musa del director, que la sigue fascinado con su cámara a través de todas sus encarnaciones, haciendo que sea para él lo que su cámara desea [...].

Enamorada, la cámara de Calparsoro sigue y persigue a Najwa Nimri, vistiéndola de harapos, desnudándola, maquillándose ante el espejo [...] ha conseguido articular toda una forma personal de hacer cine, con su propia mitología incorporada ... pero que gira alrededor de una figura central, la de Najwa Nimri, diosa a quien estuvieron consagradas todas y cada una de las mejores locuras cinematográficas de Daniel Calparsoro. Y la locura sagrada honra siempre a quien la sufre. (Palacios, 2006: 380)

(We are looking at a trilogy which continues to be a sort of epic poem from Daniel Calparsoro to Najwa Nimri and thereby to the feminine forces of Nature, both creative and destructive, always so very much present in the collective unconsciousness of the Basque nation ... the romantic muse of the director, who, fascinated, follows her with his camera through all her incarnations, making her all that his camera desires [...].

Calparsoro's loving camera follows and pursues Najwa Nimri, dressing her in rags, stripping her clothes off as she puts on make-up in front of the mirror [...] it has managed to articulate a whole personal way of filmmaking, incorporating its own mythology ... but which revolves around a central figure, Najwa Nimri, a goddess to whom all Daniel Calparsoro's best cinematic insanities were dedicated. And sacred madness always does honour to the one who suffers it.)

This lyricism has been quoted at some length because I believe that the cumulative effect serves to encourage the reader to fall in love equally with the spectacle of Nimri, but also because the critique offers insight into perception of both actress and director. As we see, the term 'muse' is here, in conjunction with the concept of woman as nature both beautiful and terrible, thus recuperating some rather retrograde stereotypes of women that are at odds with the notion of Calparsoro's women as desiring subjects, or indeed of the more positive portraits of contemporary women recognised by Jordan and Morgan-Tamosunas above. (The equation between woman as nature and the collective unconsciousness of the Basque Country suggests Palacios's perception of the latter as just as much an alien other as women are). Nimri, in Palacios's view, is clearly the object (and not the subject) of the gaze, while the camera aggressively pursues her. But while this implies Nimri as passive, Calparsoro for all his pursuit is equally weak, unmanned through his desire for Nimri, which Palacios describes as a sacred madness.

All this, then, is potentially recuperated by the notion of the muse as a label for Nimri. And yet is this really what is going on? Although Nimri undoubtedly has inspired Calparsoro, some, at least, of his cinematic conception predates her. Nimri was discovered by casting director Sara Bilbatúa when she was looking for a supporting actress for the film *Justino, un asesino de la tercera edad* (Justino, an Old-Age Assassin, Santiago Aguilar and Luis Guridi, 1994). Although Nimri was unsuccessful when auditioning for the part, Bilbatúa subsequently recommended her to Calparsoro for the part of Alex (Taberna, 2006: 36). Although Nimri may subsequently have had a hand in shaping the depiction of Alex that we have today, some concept of the character existed in Calparsoro's mind before she came along and, if Bilbatúa understood the original conception of the character accurately enough, then she suggested Nimri for the part precisely because of the fit between the two. In a later interview Nimri talks of her character Alex as being created by Calparsoro (and thus not her) and emphasises the character's hardness, as if this comes from the director and not herself ('Najwa Nimri', 2000). This comment might result from the changing relationship between the director and the star – as I shall go on to discuss below, there is evidence that after a while Nimri began to pull away from Calparsoro's sphere. But it reinforces the argument that the director and not Nimri was the original creative source for the character. If describing an actress as a director's muse carries the danger of disempowering her, then we also have to beware the opposite danger of presuming the director's vision to be totally subordinate to the actress – the dual dangers that Palacios's description encapsulates.

Interviews with Calparsoro and Nimri over the course of their working relationship also reveal a more complex structure than the stereotype of passive muse and active artist. Not that this tradition is totally absent: at the time of starting to work on *Pasajes* Calparsoro refers to Nimri in terms of an artist's model, saying that all painters need one and that he has found his model in her. Nimri reciprocates by saying that for now she wants to stay with the same director (Gómez, 1995: 2). Six months later, however, there is a suggestion of greater creative tension between the two. Sara Torres reports Calparsoro as saying that 'With [Nimri] I feel I can write what I want, whatever I feel like, because she'll be capable of understanding and interpreting it, even if she doesn't agree with me'. And Torres adds that Nimri is not simply Calparsoro's appendage but has her own ideas about the film (*Pasajes*) and the role (Gabi) (Torres, 1996: 127). Although one should be careful in taking these comments at face value, this being the image of their working relationship that the duo wish to present to the world, nonetheless we can perceive a more complex notion of this working relationship beyond the star as muse.

Hesitation in accepting interview comments at face value does not disguise Nimri's increasing assertion of herself as independent of Calparsoro. At the time of *Los amantes del círculo polar* she remarked that her personality was unformed like a baby when Calparsoro discovered her ('Najwa Nimri' 2000). This indicates Calparsoro's role in forming her, 'determining' her, but also hints at the possibility that he exploited her innocence. This, taken together with the discrepancy over her perception of Alex in *Salto* as hard, already referred to above, suggests by this time that Nimri no longer fits the role of passive muse but is instead expressing a desire to distinguish herself from Calparsoro's female protagonists and perhaps also the grungy image associated with a character such as Alex. Her self-assertion becomes more pronounced subsequently, in an interview on the occasion of *Asfalto*. She talks of the possibility of extending her profile and filmography, with the implication that by now Calparsoro might be restricting her: she argues that she wants to be more available and that if she puts her mind to it she could play any character or style. She would like the chance to work with Almodóvar, someone from the Dogme stable or even a James Cameron blockbuster. She would also like to work again with Medem (which she subsequently did) and Amenábar (which to date she has not). All these comments, taken together, indicate a keenness to work in a sphere wider than that offered by Calparsoro. It might even imply that she sees herself as, by now, bigger than Calparsoro (Ángulo, 2000: 33).

Another way of looking at this relationship is to consider Nimri in terms of an alter ego for Calparsoro, as we saw earlier with Heredero's description of the actress in these terms. Calparsoro at an early stage talked of the autobiographical quality of his work (at this stage, *Salto* and pre-production of *Pasajes*) (Gómez, 1995: 2). This idea tends to support Heredero's suggestion of Nimri – or at least her roles, which contribute to her star persona – as Calparsoro's other self: they indicate his own personal investment in these roles, and by extension Nimri's portrayal of them. It also coincides with a similar notion that women are all the same, as Palacios suggests: 'Dejando de lado los diversos nombres y aspectos que adopta ... no hay duda de que nos encontramos siempre ante el mismo personaje' (Leaving aside the different names and characteristics adopted ... there is no doubt that we are looking at the same character; Palacios, 2006: 38). This notion is mitigated by an interview with Calparsoro after the release of *Pasajes* but before *A ciegas* went into production: the director notes that while Alex and Gabi were based on himself, the character of his next film would be based on Nimri herself (Rozas, 1996: 12). Other critics implicitly posit the concept of a more equal partnership than the actress's simple reflection of the director's personality. In an admittedly fulsome report on production of the film *Pasajes*, Torres compares the Calparsoro/Nimri partnership with other such cinema couples such as Rossellini/Bergman, Fellini/Giulietta Masina and above all Leos Carax/Juliette Binoche (Torres, 1996: 127), suggesting that we cannot but think of director and actress together. Roberto Cueto also notes the Calparsoro/Nimri partnership as the only exception to the general state of affairs within Spanish cinema where women are notably lacking in films about juvenile delinquents: he talks of the powerful and rounded characters created by the duo of Calparsoro and Nimri (Cueto, 1998: 15).

Taken together, these ideas suggest a move away from an earlier conception of the director/actress role in which the latter acts merely as a blank canvas for the former to another of negotiation and collaboration, wherein the director's work may still be perceived in terms of the actress but where the actress reveals her independence of the director while nonetheless bearing the traces of his work on her persona. This may well destabilise the older sense of auteurism in that he does not have the power over his creation and vision: the star persona he helped to form has a life of its own, but one that also betrays his presence.

## Emotion and women

Bound up with the use of Nimri in his work is Calparsoro's emphasis on a female point of view and on women as a conduit of emotion. Emotions and atmosphere are to Calparsoro more important than plot and character:

> El sentido profundo de una película no es tanto contar una historia como narrar la experiencia vivida en esa historia ... no se trata de que la historia hable de la emoción, sino de que la emoción como experiencia sea el objetivo de la película. Estoy hablando de un cine emocional, donde las emociones sean expresadas visualmente por la iluminación, por el decorado, por la cámara, por la interpretación o por la puesta en escena en su conjunto. Las películas no están para llevarte al entendimiento de algo ... sino para provocar dudas o generar emociones. (Heredero, 1997: 261)

> (The deeper meaning of a film is not so much to tell a story as to tell of the lived experience within the story ... it is not that the story deals with emotion but that the experience of emotion is the aim of the film. I'm talking about an emotional cinema in which the emotions are expressed visually through light, set, camera, interpretation or *mise-en-scène* as a whole. Films aren't there to make you understand ... but to provoke doubts or generate emotions.)

For this reason he expresses a wish to escape from the text as a trap that leads to closure. Ideally the viewer should be stirred to think about the emotions induced by the images, rather than the story (262). A text should not pose a question and then offer an answer, thus leading to increased knowledge. The divide Calparsoro appears to place here between knowledge and experience (the sensation of emotion) is a problematic one, but it reinforces the way in which to him cinema is above all a question of experience per se, as with violence. The director goes on to comment on his need to draw out the maximum amount of emotion from each scene, as if face to face with pure reality (Heredero, 1997: 274). This adds a new dimension to social-realist cinema in that for Calparsoro emotion is as real as the gritty urban surroundings in which we find it. The emphasis placed on emotion as a fundamental cinematic element has, however, the potential to problematise what might be considered Calparsoro's most notable characteristic: his tendency to use women as subjects rather than objects in his films. This tendency would be enough of itself to merit more attention for his work, particularly the Basque trilogy: the marginalised urban youth film normally focuses on the frustrations of young men, while women as object and other, often as a symbol of the young men's frustrations. Calparsoro offers us a rare female viewpoint on urban marginalisation. The potential problem comes, as we will see in the more detailed discussion of the following chapters, with the traditional link between women and the emotions.

Although Jordan and Morgan-Tamosunas (1998: 100–1) suggest that several contemporary films have emphasised women as protagonists in marginal social settings, in fact the only major director they mention in this regard is Calparsoro himself with *Salto al vacío* and *Pasajes*, the only two of his films released at the time that Jordan and Morgan-Tamosunas were writing. (Jordan and Morgan-Tamosunas also mention just one other film in this regard, *Antártida* (Antarctica) of 1994, directed by Manuel Huerga). Roberto Cueto observes that, as regards Spanish films about juvenile delinquents, the presence of women is a notable gap all the more remarkable in an era when the number of female directors is on the rise. He cites only one exception: the powerful, rounded characters created by the partnership of Calparsoro and Nimri (Cueto, 1998: 15). It is fair to state, however – as Jordan and Morgan-Tamosunas do (1998: 126) – that while Calparsoro appears almost unique in his focus on women in films about marginalised urban youth, his films also form part of a wider emphasis in

Spanish cinema on women as active subjects, though I would add that
the wider trend stresses the more obvious female-centred vehicles of
the melodrama and the romantic comedy (though they are also active
agents in thrillers such as Amenábar's *Tesis* (Thesis) of 1995). Jordan
and Morgan-Tamosunas also note that representations of women as
active agents in underprivileged surroundings are far more rare than
an emphasis on middle-class career women: they quote the sparse
examples of the earlier *¿Qué he hecho yo para merecer esto?* (What Have
I Done to Deserve This?, Almodóvar, 1984) and a film more contemporary with Calparsoro, *Nadie hablará de nosotras cuando hayamos muerto*
(No One Will Talk About Us Women When We're Dead, Agustín Díaz
Yanes, 1995) (Jordan and Morgan-Tamosunas, 1998: 130–1). In contrast
to a focus on female solidarity and overt efforts to counter patriarchal
structures in many Spanish films (Jordan and Morgan-Tamosunas,
1998: 133) I do not think we have the same sense in Calparsoro's films
of women working together to subvert patriarchy, partly because most
of his films have one dominant female protagonist and consequently
less opportunity to form female teams. Where the women in his films
do get the chance to interact with other women, they often seem at
odds with each other, and – the example of Carmina in *Pasajes* notwithstanding (because of her desire to assimilate herself into the patriarchal structures of marriage and motherhood) – patriarchy seems for
the most part ultimately irrelevant in Calparsoro's early work. Yet, as
I will argue when discussing Calparsoro's Basque trilogy, the characters also sink back into the female-dominated private sphere in search
of meaning for their lives, in true melodramatic fashion. Calparsoro's
stress on emotion and his characters' thoughts and feelings facilitates
this move.

The possibility of such a move does not, however, automatically
define Calparsoro as a traditionalist in his attitudes to women: indeed,
of all the directors emanating from the 1995 generation (including
those who are women), Calparsoro is one of those who have done
most to depict women as complex subjects rather than simple objects
(and this applies even to secondary characters such as Balbuena in
*Guerreros*). He sees women as more multi-faceted than men, able
to portray more complex ideas and emotions while nonetheless
maintaining coherence – and thus better able to bear subjectivity. He
comments that:

> Ningún hombre es capaz de generar esa riqueza. Las mujeres, en
> cambio, tienen esa capacidad de desplegar facetas diferentes sin que

ninguna resulta incoherente con las otras. Por mi parte, como hago un
cine basado en figuras principales, que son como retratos de una idea,
para que la película no se quede pequeña necesito que ese personaje
sea lo más amplio posible, incluso contradictorio a ratos, y para eso
no encuentro mejor salida que imaginármelo como mujer. Incluso yo
mismo, si pudiera imaginarme como un personaje de cine, sería una
mujer para poder dar una gama más variada de matices y de registros.
(Heredero, 1997: 270)

(No man is capable of generating that richness. Women, on the other
hand, have a capacity to display different facets without them seeming
contradictory. For me, as I make films based on central characters who
embody an idea, I need that character to be as broad as possible, even
contradictory at times, in order that the film isn't too small in scale, and
for this there's no better solution for me than imagine the character as
a woman. Even I myself, if I could imagine myself as a film character,
would be a woman in order to be able to give a greater range of nuances
and registers.)

He continues by commenting on his trilogy that the women of those
films are 'tres mujeres que aspiran a vivir en un mundo mejor o que
sueñan con tener otra vida. Esto nace de un sentimiento puramente
autobiográfico, pero creo que también es una aspiración universal'
(three women who aspire to live in a better world or dream about
a better life. This derives from purely autobiographical feeling, but
I think it's also a universal desire; Heredero, 1997: 270). He also
observes (271) that these women refuse to resign themselves to
the lives they are leading. As I shall observe in more detail when
discussing the trilogy, this approach lends itself to a melodramatisa-
tion of plot as well as an understanding of women's aspirations in
primarily emotional terms. But Calparsoro's attitudes to women are
more complex than a simple retreat into emotions. They participate
in the increasing depiction within Spanish cinema of women as active
subjects, capable of complexity, capable of carrying a story.

The intricacy of the positioning of Calparsoro's female characters
is demonstrated by their relation to both the gaze of the active subject
and the style of the film, within which the female characters become in
turn objects of the spectator's gaze as part of the overall style. Calparsoro aims to produce a cinema that prioritises the gaze (Heredero,
1997: 257). This might remind us of the adverse criticism of his screenplays and dialogues to which I have already alluded; while they could
be simply a blind spot for the director, a more positive possibility lies
in Calparsoro's emphasis on vision and the visual (rather than the

verbal) as an integral part of his style. The possibility is reinforced by his preference for female protagonists, who cast their own gaze on the world around them and find it more than a little wanting. The emphasis on the gaze is of a piece with the emphasis on women as active subjects: in order for us to understand the women, Calparsoro ensures that as far as possible we adopt their gaze.

Such an approach adds a further dimension to the interrelationship between director and star in that the complexity of the depiction of women as subject is bound up with this interrelationship. Calparsoro places an emphasis on women as better able to express the emotions than he, a man, can: thus Nimri proves essential to his ability to express emotion and the intricacy with which this is done speaks to the acting capacity of Nimri and the directorial capacity of Calparsoro himself. The star thus empowers the director. This does not, however, preclude some problematic traces of older gender stereotypes reappearing in Calparsoro's work, as we can perceive from considering the director's touches of melodrama in his first three films.

## The Basque trilogy: a tendency to melodrama

In conjunction with his concentrated focus on Nimri in the first half of his career to date, Calparsoro's first three films are dominated by one central female character, in a way which would not happen with Calparsoro's later films until *Ausentes*. Unlike many films that focus on the frustrations of urban youth, Calparsoro's trilogy takes women as central characters and considers the ways in which women in particular suffer from, and attempt to come to terms with, their existence in marginalised cultures. On the other hand the trilogy can be understood on one level as a distorted form of melodrama and 'woman's film', and viewing the films in this way brings in its wake the potential for conservative readings that recycle all too familiar images of women as orientated towards the family and emotional relation-ships: meaning is, in fact, bestowed on them primarily in these terms. Discussing the trilogy using the framework of melodrama might at first glance appear perverse, given the emphasis throughout Calpar-soro's work on violence and on marginalised youth in grim urban surroundings, using plots, characters, *mise-en-scène* and a frenetic style seemingly far removed from the concerns of film melodrama, widely tagged as treating bourgeois problems and possibly reinforcing bourgeois ideology. It contradicts Crumbaugh's contention that *Salto*, the first film of the trilogy, can be understood in terms of tragedy (2001: 48). All three films, however, have at their centre a female protagonist who, despite her rebellion and rage against a dysfunctional social order, attempts to establish a form of private domestic space to counteract the collapse of the public sphere around her – acting almost as a postmodern homemaker. The dream of retreat into the private refuge is, however, frustrated. This is the stuff of melodrama and the woman's film. This is not necessarily to say that the trilogy falls neatly into the category of film melodrama, which might seem at odds with the Calparsoro's use of *cine social*, but it is to say that the trilogy bears a strong melodramatic vein that coincides with an increasing tendency to blur cinematic genres, and which has occurred elsewhere in *cine social*, as mentioned in the previous chapter.

The marginal wastelands of the Basque Country that form the backdrop for Calparsoro's trilogy, to say nothing of its cynical and hard-bitten central characters, seem far removed from the more traditional loci of melodrama, such as the nineteenth-century French theatre and novel that provide the foundation for Peter Brooks's seminal theorising on the melodrama, or the middle-class Americana of the 1950s films of Douglas Sirk. I would nonetheless argue that the three heroines of Calparsoro's trilogy demonstrate the impulse to reveal the 'moral occult' of submerged ethical value to which Brooks refers (1995: 202), even if, in the apparently amoral urban wasteland where each person seems to be for only him- or herself, attempts to rise above this often seem half-hearted and doomed to fail. In Calparsoro's trilogy the three protagonists seek to reinstate some sort of moral value into an amoral environment; and the moral values that are prized are closely linked to the traditional spheres and responsibilities of women, often enshrined in the so-called 'woman's film'. These moral values are those that emphasise the family and personal relationships. In addition, the closed worlds of the American woman's film are, ironically perhaps given their basis in middle-class suburbia, not so far removed from the closed worlds of the Basque trilogy in that there appears to be no escape for the women from a claustrophobic existence in which their desires are frustrated. Many symbols in the trilogy of escape and movement elsewhere – roads, bridges, rails – merely serve to underscore the entrapment of the central characters.

Nonetheless, the three protagonists are those characters who seek a meaning beyond the mindless violence that surrounds them (and in which they participate), and they reflect those critics of Sirk's films who argue that in this case melodrama insists on the need for the mundane to be 'equal to the demands of the imagination for a heightening of existence, a more interesting psychic engagement of the ordinary transactions of urban and suburban life' (Brooks, 1995: ix). Their insistence on the importance of personal relations reveals the poverty, both in emotional and material terms, of their environment, coinciding with Thomas Elsaesser's reflection (1987: 62) that: 'In melodrama, violence, the strong action, the dynamic movement, the full articulation and the fleshed-out emotions ... become the very signs of the characters' alienation, and thus serve to formulate a devastating critique of the ideology that supports it'. Calparsoro's trilogy thus to some extent contradicts Geoffrey Nowell-Smith's assumption that melodrama is inherently a genre arising from and dealing with the concerns of the bourgeois (Nowell-Smith, 1987: 70–1), and suggests that indeed melodrama offers a chance to recuperate a sense of hope, and of prospects for the future, in the bleakest of marginal environments, although some of the desires of Calparsoro's characters could themselves be perceived in terms of bourgeois aspiration. It also simultaneously suggests, however, the frustration of that hope. The melodramatic desire to rise above a sordid environment, through the personal relationships of family and romantic attachments, is unsurprising but also unrealistic. The social crisis of alienated youth is thus personalised in a move typical of melodrama and links the problem to dysfunctional family and personal relationships, which the central female character must try and repair. Calparsoro is simultaneously conservative in his bestowal of traditional feminine feelings on his heroines, while perhaps more radical in suggesting that these feminine feelings are the main locus of hope in these terrible environments. This ambiguity is arguably reinforced by the use of the same actress, Najwa Nimri, to play all three central characters in the films. Nimri's striking gamine appearance reinforces the ambiguities in terms of both sexuality and gendered power to be found in the three protagonists of the trilogy. In turn, the melodramatic thread of the trilogy contributes to to Nimri's ultimately vulnerable star persona.

Thus Calparsoro's trilogy reflects the contradiction of the melodramatic enterprise, which may critique the prevailing order of things and suggest that things could be different, but simultaneously entraps women through their responsibility for personal relationships which is dictated by the selfsame prevailing order. The trilogy demonstrates both the need for change in women's lives and the impossibility of it, because of the insistence on both change and preservation which is part of this emotional burden. They can improve their own lives by making things better for those they love, but these very people are the ones that prevent change and entrap them. This reinforces the point made by Mary Ann Doane when she argues that the woman's film 'functions quite precisely to immobilise' (1987: 296) (which Doane discusses in terms of the problematisation of Laura Mulvey's male gaze that the woman's film induces). And Elsaesser comments of melodrama:

> The discrepancy of seeming and being, of intention and result, registers as a perplexing frustration, and an ever-increasing gap opens between the emotions and the reality they seek to reach. What strikes one as the true pathos is the very mediocrity of the human beings involved, putting such high demands upon themselves trying to live up to an exalted vision of man, but instead living out the impossible contradictions that have turned the proverbial American dream into its nightmare. (Elsaesser, 1987: 67)

The miserable world of the industrial Basque country is far removed from the American dream: the nightmare has already been conjured up into existence (though in both cases the context is derived from the capitalism that undergirds the American dream). But in all other respects Elsaesser's comments appear all too apt for the women of Calparsoro's Basque trilogy – living out the impossible contradictions of melodramatic desire while attempting to aspire beyond a sordid industrial wasteland. Calparsoro's melodrama is ultimately a circle that is vicious in more ways than one.

Heredero describes the three heroines of the trilogy in the following terms:

> Alex, Gabi y Marrubi ... no son más que distintas facetas de la misma mujer: un ser de apariencia frágil, pero de fuerte determinación interior, de talante y modales andróginos, de ambiguo atractivo sexual y con hondas raíces en un universo violento del que sueña con escapar para recuperar la vida, el amor y la estabilidad propias de una existencia que nunca ha conocido. (Heredero, 1999: 99)

> (Alex, Gabi and Marrubi ... are no more than different sides of the same woman: of fragile appearance but with a strong inner resolve, androgynous habits and tendencies, an ambiguous sexual attraction and deep roots in a violent world from which she dreams of escaping in order to claim the life, love and stability belonging to an existence she has never known.)

Heredero's description of the women as simply three faces of one woman suggests the notion of individual identity as subsumed under the generic identity of woman – a common conservative move that sees women as all the same, indistinguishable, and thus lacking the unique character and skills with which to confront and tackle the problems that face them. In one sense this description ignores the fact that the three women of the trilogy possess differing personalities. But it is apt enough in terms of the situation within which Calparsoro positions them and the way in which they attempt to escape. It is also another aspect to the Calparsoro/Nimri axis: the repeated use of Nimri facilitates a more reductive reading that coincides with early perceptions of her star persona in terms of the fragile Bambi-like figure mentioned above – indeed, the two overlap.

We can garner a more intricate consideration of Calparsoro's melodramatic subjectivity from a more detailed study of his trilogy, and it is to the first film of this trilogy that we now turn.

# PART II

# The films

# 3

# *Salto al vacío*: opening up the void

Of all the films in Calparsoro's oeuvre, none has had more impact or been more discussed than his first feature-length film *Salto al vacío*. It has received the most academic attention hitherto, including a role as case study in two of the most significant monographs of contemporary Spanish (Ballesteros, 2001) and Basque (Rodríguez, 2002a) cinema. Its blunt and visceral style also served to gain critical attention from the industry and the press at a time when Spanish cinema was coming into full ferment: according to Justin Crumbaugh it received great acclaim from directors such as Steven Spielberg at its premier at the Berlin Film Festival (Crumbaugh 2001: 40). To get such attention its impact needed to have been swift; there were, after all, other new directors clamouring for attention. In contrast to those slicker directors who served to give Spanish cinema a better reputation as a commercial rather than an art product, Calparsoro achieved this precisely through a rough, unfinished and awkward style combined with a strong visual impression. The shot of the back of the head of protagonist Alex (Najwa Nimri) with the word 'void' shaved into the back of her neck, used in much of the film's publicity, has become virtually iconic of contemporary Basque and urban cinema, and above all iconic of Calparsoro's work as a whole. This imperfect style may in fact have come about as a result of financial difficulties that Calparsoro encountered as he made the film (in the end respected director and producer Fernando Colomo intervened in order to ensure the film's post-production, itself an endorsement of the film). Calparsoro had only enough money to film half his original script, which he then stripped down to its basic components, which for him were the characters (Heredero, 1997: 263). This necessity may or may not have been the impulse behind the director's attitude to the script as a trap

(Heredero, 1997: 262), something that insists on closure; at any event the sense of a lack of finish in terms of style, dialogue and plot would rapidly become trademarks in the films immediately following *Salto* and prior to his later move towards genre cinema, and also targets for the critique of the reviewers.

On the DVD commentary on the film, Calparsoro speaks of the experience of making this, his first feature-length film, and compares the title to his own situation, launching himself (and others working on the film, many of whom had no previous experience) into a cinema void. He discusses the difficulties of filming with a combination of lack of money and of experience. A notable example was the absence of a fight instructor, with the result that the actor playing the policeman of the early scenes suffered two cracked ribs during a fight. In the subsequent scene where the policeman is shot, the part was taken over by Calparsoro himself (wearing a hood) while the original actor recovered. All the principal actors, with the exception of Karra Elejalde in the part of Alex's brother Juáncar, were inexperienced, and Calparsoro contrasts the different approach taken with the latter, where many key scenes such as those in the car and Esteban's (Alfredo Villa) caravan were improvised in terms of both dialogue and movement, while scenes with Elejalde, notably the night-time conversation with Alex, were planned and scripted in detail beforehand. The improvisation aimed at authenticity, a crucial motif for Calparsoro; in support of such authenticity the actors lived beforehand in Sestao, a suburb of Bilbao, where the action was filmed, going out at night and mixing with the people of the area. The sets, too, are authentic: crumbling houses in Sestao that were due to be pulled down to make way for luxury housing.

Reviews of the film observe in Calparsoro the potential to be a great filmmaker but with much still to learn. The criticisms that would turn more sour and pointed with later films are here comparatively benign, as to a young hopeful. As Calparsoro persists in these elements of style and plot, we can later sense an exasperation on the parts of the critics of the refusal of this precocious talent to learn and to mature (perhaps also at his refusal to profit from their advice?), but for now the press and the industry were willing to indulge the newcomer and forgive him his supposed faults. Angel Fernández Santos (1995) is typical of this approach in his review, describing the film as 'una torpísima y abrupta tacada de cine salvaje, pero con la semilla de talento, el dolor y la originalidad bajo sus balbuceos' (a very clumsy and abrupt hit of rough cinema, but with a grain of talent, pain and originality beneath its babble). He later comments: 'El filme es un castillo de naipes sobre el vacío, pero inexplicablemente se sostiene' (The film is a house of cards over the void, but inexplicably it remains standing). Likewise, E. Rodríguez Marchante (1995) argues for Calparsoro's potential, but believes that the performance of Najwa Nimri in the central role is crucial to this, the other characters only existing in relation to her. Rodríguez Marchante was not alone in finding Nimri/Alex the main pivot of interest: Augusto M. Torres (1995) also finds Alex's character the most striking element of a film that shows evidence of talent as well as a lack of experience and money, arguing that the film is strongest when it does away with violence and concentrates on Alex's personal relationships (a point that hints at the film's use of melodrama). More scathingly, Jose Luis Martínez Montalbán describes Nimri as the only redeeming feature of a film with a thin story and a poor screenplay, and then only intermittently (s.d.: 493). Nimri's performance in fact garnered her awards at festivals in Valencia, Geneva, Moscow and Angers, while the Spanish daily *El Mundo* awarded her a prize for best Basque actress. In interview Calparsoro expressed a preference for working with stars who are yet to be discovered rather than established actors (Leyra, 1995a). At this stage in his career this might have been a necessity rather than a preference (though Calparsoro's difficult experience in working with the established actress Charo López in his next film might have confirmed his preference). With *Salto al vacío* we see nonetheless a phenomenon of director and star coming into prominence together.

Calparsoro acquired a reputation for violent cinema very rapidly; almost immediately the press began to compare his work with that of American director Quentin Tarantino to the extent that Calparsoro's denial of the comparison headlined some reviews and interviews, as in, for example, the review by Manuel Montero (1995). As this article emphasises, Calparsoro does not resort to the humour and irony with which Tarantino's film are shot through, but stresses the reality of what we see – which irony and humour would tend to undercut. This indicates the point made in the introductory chapter that Calparsoro does not want to mitigate the cinematic experience of violence for the viewer. Torres (1995) argues that one of the film's biggest problems is its obsession with North American culture in terms of crude violence and music, a criticism that, in terms of violence if not of its musical accompaniment, neglects a history of violent Spanish cinema (see

Kinder, 1993). Martínez Montalbán (s.d.: 492) uses his review of the film to launch an extended attack (that takes up half his review) on the use of violence by the current crop of film directors, claiming that violence has become not so much a mechanism to drive the plot along or the response to certain situations but simply an end in itself. Calparsoro himself argued that the film is not as violent as it first appears, with only four or five violent scenes, and that while some scenes may upset people, the film is in fact a story of tenderness (Leyra, 1995b: 357). The violence is for him the excuse for telling the story rather than the other way about. With *Salto* he aimed to depict violence as a documentary effect rather than as spectacle, believing that the usual images and techniques of contemporary cinema serve to create a sense of unreality that in fact protects us (Leyra, 1995b: 356). With his raw and rough images of violence, then, the director works to strip away the protective screen (in more than one sense) offered by much cinematic violence. Nonetheless, Calparsoro does not connect such violence with specific situations. In defiance of the tag of Basque director that would come to haunt him (as discussed previously) Calparsoro argued that the violence of the film could occur anywhere, Madrid or Seattle (Montero, 1995: 600); and indeed the possible execution of Juáncar, while in itself a climatic event, is subordinate to the more general level of violence that is needed simply to survive on the margins. Ironically for Calparsoro's claims, however, Montero's article also reports an incident at the film's screening in the Berlin Film Festival wherein the poster of Alex's shaven head had to be removed for fear of an association of this image with German Neo-nazis (Montero, 1995: 600), thus indicating that the local specificities of violence can still have an impact.

We shall return to the question of violence in *Salto* below. At this point in the argument I wish to use this question as part of a consideration of the interaction of Calparsoro's work with the Spanish context that surrounds it. As regards violence, as we have seen, there has been a tendency to perceive and to critique the film primarily in terms of US cinema (particularly through the Tarantino tag), rather than the graphic violence that has also featured in Spanish cinema (and specifically arthouse cinema): films such as *El crimen de Cuenca* (The Cuenca Crime, Pilar Miró, 1980) and *Furtivos* (Poachers, José Luis Borau, 1975). The press rushed to pigeonhole Calparsoro in this way, while he has resisted this (whether he specifically resents the precise comparison to Tarantino or to US cinema more generally is not clear).

This tells us of the readiness with which writers on Spanish cinema can view cinematic output in US terms even though a Spanish framework potentially exists. A more specifically Basque framework for violence is also barely considered. As Calparsoro continues to make films, however, his work will be interpreted much more on his own terms rather than in terms of a particular cinema, suggesting that the critics implicitly absorb a sense of Calparsoro as auteur. The Tarantino tag will disappear. What will persist is the disappointment and irritation with poor screenplays and dialogue, with less indulgence than the newcomer receives here.

## Alex as melodramatic heroine

Although the *mise-en-scène* of *Salto al vacío* is gritty and sordid, it nonetheless contains at least the twisted trace of romantic desires, in keeping with Heredero's description of Calparsoro's cinema as the exploration of wounded romanticism (1997: 247). Calparsoro himself perceived the heroine of his film as a princess without a throne, of a seductive tenderness (Leyra, 1995a). It is hard at first blush to perceive Alex as anything remotely like a fairytale princess. She forms part of a gang of violent young men, resorts to violence and drug dealing in order to survive, and has what is traditionally a very unfeminine appearance, with her shaven head into which the English word 'void' has been worked. In the opening scene in the confined space of the car, it is hard initially to mark her out as female until she speaks. But as we learn more about Alex we can view her as a sort of distorted Cinderella, dreaming of an ideal world amidst a miserable reality. For Calparsoro, as he says on the DVD commentary, the central story of *Salto* is that of a girl who wants to be loved while living in a terrible environment. The hardness of her demeanour is superficial, covering a tenderness beneath.

While it appears that she has a lot of power and control in her ability to sort out problems (within the gang as well as within her family), I think there is also a case for a more conservative reading in terms of the woman's film. Her ultimate aims are more traditionally feminine and nurturing: keeping her dissolute and rather dreadful family together and securing romantic commitment, in echo of – if not quite in the style of – the woman's film. In relation to the idea of Alex in a 'women's film', Crumbaugh notes (2001: 46) that 'Her most original and active expression of autonomy ... is her struggle to weld together a sense of solidarity despite the odds' and then immediately goes on to discuss her function as principal carer and breadwinner of the family. She is also the one who sorts out family quarrels such as the one between her father and her uncle (although she resorts to violence to do so by holding a gun to her father's head), providing nurture, particularly to her brothers and to some extent her drunken mother as well. As her mother says, when Alex is not there everything is reduced to chaos. A small vignette highlights Alex's role: while the family watch a video of the uncle's fighting dog, Alex is adding up the family finances on a notepad (the word 'gastos' (expenses) appears on the pad). The lollipop she sucks as she adds up the figures might imply a childish nature, indicating in turn the oppression of taking on responsibility for the family at such a young age. Alex's family always make demands of her and give nothing back. Even her youngest brother, who she treats with care and reassurance, starts and ends his conversation with her by demands to be given something. Calparsoro wanted to suggest in Alex a saint or an angel living in hell, but that hell had to be internal as well as external, hence creating a family that is suffocating in its constant need.

Alex's burdens are primarily emotional ones, and indeed she seems to be responsible for maintaining personal relationships – as always, the traditional task of the woman. If, as Crumbaugh argues, Alex is looking 'to forge a degree of self-definition and a sense of autonomy' (2001: 46), then there is a certain irony in that she does this through her attempts to sustain relationships with others. This comes across clearly in the scene where she talks to her brother Juáncar about her relationship with Javi (Roberto Chalu), one of the gang members. Her dreams about Javi seem ultimately conventional, as in her comment to her brother Juáncar that 'I want him to love me and to tell me so many times, and to kiss me and stroke me, and for us to go to the pictures now and then'. This remark contrasts strongly with the sordid day of drug deals that she has just had, the deals culminating in the scene where she holds the power and a gun over the yuppie businessman desperate for a fix but demanding to pay by credit card. The melodrama of the night scene with Juáncar is not overtly marked as such – no trademark swelling music, no particular emphasis given to the words spoken: Alex mutters them in her usual monotone. Nonetheless, the desire to move beyond the banality of her surroundings is attempted by means of romantic attachments and family commitment. From an early stage we are aware of the pressures placed upon Alex to conform

5   Alex shares a brief romantic moment with Javi

to feminine expectations. We might not expect it after Alex's striking look that is brought home to use in the first scene: her punky fashions and in particular the haircut. It is an aggressive style that chimes in with the general look of the other, male, gang members, and is far removed from the traditional femininity of melodrama. But when Alex returns home from the shooting of the policeman, her mother comments on how unflattering her appearance is and her need to improve her looks, otherwise she will never attract a man. Shortly afterwards, we see Alex looking at herself in the mirror and experimenting with make-up: clearly her mother's criticism has hit home. When Javi subsequently comments on her appearance she bows her head modestly, pleased at the effects of her efforts to look good.

It is ironic that the two threads of melodramatic attachment will in the end clash with each other to the extent that they serve precisely to immobilise Alex, harking back to the thoughts of Doane quoted previously. Towards the end of the film, after the murder of Juáncar in the street by Esteban, we cut to a backward tracking shot as if we are looking out of the back window of a car, the road receding in the distance. It appears as if Alex is in the back of the car looking behind her as she leaves the Basque Country, finally getting away from the bleak environment that the car is passing through. There is a sense of escape. But in the next scene, Alex is found to be stuck where she

was before, fixated on avenging the death of her brother and ironically paying no attention to Javi's suggestions for starting a new life
elsewhere. Crumbaugh's subsequent comment that, by the end, Alex
and Javi have managed to 'articulate a touching bond' (2001: 46) seems
misplaced, as in fact the couple talk past each other, neither really
responding to what the other says but instead giving a simultaneous
monologue that encapsulates their rather desperate but also disparate
hopes for the future. It is ironic that Javi is finally offering Alex what
she was looking for, a romantic future together outside the Basque
Country, but she is too caught up in her own wish to avenge the death
of Juáncar to hear what he is saying. She has by now become caught
up in the web of violence precisely because of her family commit-
ments. In the end, Alex's commitment to her family will frustrate her
desires for escape and a deeper relationship with Javi.

But Javi, as with some of the tortured men of American melodramas
such as the alcoholic husband of Douglas Sirk's *Written on the Wind*
(1956), does not in any case seem adequate to the emotional burden
Alex places upon him. Javi's inadequacy becomes clear in the ironically climatic scene at the party, where at last it seems as if the relationship between the two of them will be consummated and that Alex will
finally have access to the love she desires. But as they go through the
preliminary stages of lovemaking, Javi confesses that he cannot get
an erection: in the end he does not desire her sufficiently. Elsaesser
(1987: 66–7) talks of a sense of inadequacy pervading melodrama,
which often manifests itself in some form of sexual incapacity such
as impotence or frigidity, and Javi's impotence is a clear symbol of his
inability to fulfil Alex's dreams. (His inability to kill Juáncar's murderer
as Alex wants – because the murderer is their friend Esteban – underscores the impotence still further). Critics of *Salto* have perceived his
impotence not in terms of melodrama but of his status as a Brazilian
immigrant. Isolina Ballesteros links his impotence to his difficulties
with the Spanish language and thus to communication problems
(Ballesteros, 2001: 252). Jaume Martí-Olivella notes that reviews
of the film took little notice of the character (Martí-Olivella, 1999:
211–12), so that Javi is thus 'doubly emasculated: diegetically, that is,
inside the film's narrative, by Calparsoro, and extradiegetically by the
critical reception that has so far obliterated his historical condition
as an immigrant' (212). Javi's status as immigrant also feeds into a
melodramatic reading, however, in that he represents an elsewhere
and thus a form of escape that Alex is frustrated in attaining. The fact

that, as Martí-Olivella observes, Javi as immigrant is neglected both inside and outside the narrative implies that the possibility of escape lies well outside the vision of both characters and critics. This in turn adds a further dimension to Alex's neglect of Javi's invitation to get away: she neglects it because she, like everyone else, is incapable of recognising the opportunity. (Ironically, one of the things he promises her in Brazil is that the sea will make him 'hard', thus by implication no longer impotent.)

## The Basque urban landscape

Having considered Alex's desire to escape, it is time to look in more detail at what it is she is trying to escape from. This chapter will now go on to explore the notion of the void, the emptiness at the heart of both urban youth and Basque society, making particular mention of the squalid urban landscape as representative of a context of urban decay and urban violence.

There has been a tendency in films about the Basque Country to figure debate about Basque national identity through its landscape, particularly when it comes to the militant Basque nationalism of ETA. Barry Jordan and Rikki Morgan-Tamosunas (1998: 184) have commented on the tendency of some filmmakers 'to emphasize the folkloric, traditional, idyllically rural version of Basque life, disconnected from the outside world, a view which was largely out of step with political and social change in the region. Also, more widely, a politically radical Basque nationalism appeared to be somewhat in thrall to an essentialist vision of Basque culture and identity, predicated on just such a version of the Basque Country as an unchanging rural arcadia'. This is not to say, however, that filmmakers could not use the landscape itself as part of a critique of Basque nationalism in particular and Basque society more generally. The clearest instance of this occurs in Julio Medem's debut film *Vacas* (Cows, 1992), where we find romantically wild landscape that nonetheless comes to represent the claustrophobia of rural Basque society, which suggests both violence and inbreeding within the family. In a different vein we find an example of what we might term rural noir, *La voz de su amo* (His Master's Voice, Emilio Martínez Lázaro, 2000), in which the violence, betrayal, disillusionment and intrigue characteristic of the American city in US noir cinema of the 1940s and 1950s is displaced away from the city and into the countryside (Davies, 2003), or a reverse process in the case of films about Basque terrorism, such as *Días contados* (Running Out of Time, Imanol Uribe, 1994) or *El viaje de Arián* (Arián's Journey, Eduard Bosch, 2000), where individual struggles over commitment to ETA's cause create an opposition between

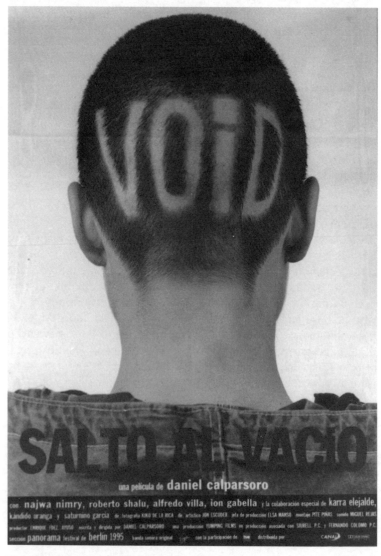

6   Alex as embodiment of the void

the countryside, linked to the ETA collective, and the city, linked to the disenchanted individual terrorist (Davies, 2005). Documentaries on Basque violence, too, have drawn on rural landscape images. *Asesinato en febrero* (Assassination in February, Eterio Ortega Santillana, 2001) explicitly relates the trauma of the victims of terrorist violence to the landscape by moving from shots of the Basque countryside (as the relatives of those lost to violence talk about their loss) to the city where the assassinations took place. Medem's controversial *La pelota vasca*, in which people from various walks of public life offer their often contrasting views on the 'Basque problem', shot against a variety of landscapes, is nonetheless interspersed with sweeping aerial shots of craggy Basque coastlines while Basque music is played.

In all these films there is a posited contrast between the city and the countryside, with the latter coming to represent the Basque Country in contested and problematic ways, while the former comes to stand – equally problematically, but less contested – for an anonymous space that is not so far removed from the void of the Basque urban environment that has graphically etched itself on to Alex's head. The dates of these films – some of them coming after *Salto* – suggest the perpetuation of this trope that has been remarkably resistant to the urbanisation of culture (itself the matter of some debate in the Basque context, as epitomised by the creation of the Guggenheim Museum in Bilbao: see Crumbaugh, 2001) as well as the urbanisation of cinematic *mise-en-scène*. The city, in contrast to the countryside, does not carry markers of national identity or indeed any other form of identity. It is simply a void.

Calparsoro later claimed (when publicising the next film *Pasajes*) that the environment of his films is a character just like the others (Cortijo, 1996). He posits the industrial area of Sestao (where the action was filmed) as the real antagonist of *Salto*, in direct opposition to Alex herself, and refigures this opposition in terms of the natural versus the mechanical, like the grass that grows in a factory (Heredero, 1997: 273). This sense of opposition places Alex in the position of the natural, which points uncomfortably back to the earlier discussion about melodrama, and the female desire to keep family and loved ones together. In this desolate environment Alex struggles to assert what she appears naturally to want, as if her own desires have not themselves been mediated in some way. Since they clearly must have been mediated, it is instructive to ask how this occurred, since nothing in the film appears linked to these desires, which spring up as if from nothing. It can only be because, just as grass will attempt to grow green in an industrial wasteland, Alex must perforce look for romance and family ties: the supposedly natural behaviour of a woman. Alternatively, Justin Crumbaugh (2001) talks of an attempt in *Salto* to find and create beauty out of the urban wasteland in a similar manner to the Guggenheim project, part of an urban regeneration project being planned at the time the film. He talks of Alex's appearance as a result of 'creative sculpting' as well as the appropriate aesthetic response to her surroundings, suggesting that her appearance is both a natural result of her environment and an artistic response to it (Crumbaugh, 2001: 46). It is possible to argue, as Martí-Olivella does (2003: 112), that Calparsoro makes art out of the ruins of the Basque Country just as Alex de la Iglesia did with the Madrid underworld of *El día de la bestia* (and Martí-Olivella quotes Crumbaugh to this effect). But if Calparsoro can make art out of industrial decay it does not mean that Alex can. She is trapped within this work of art, an integral part of it and therefore unable to escape it. She does not have the power of the artistic creator.

Much of the film's setting, both interiors and exteriors, gives a sense of claustrophobia. If, feeling trapped within the tight confines of the car of the opening sequences, we long for an idea of space in which to move outside it, we are subsequently disappointed. At times Calparsoro provides a low-angle travelling shot of buildings that appear to lean oppressively over us. The caravan of the arms deals, the squalid flat of Alex's family, the crowded space of the party, all give the impression of people squashed in together, creating an unbearable but inescapable tension. Ballesteros notes that many sequences are filmed in medium long shot so that we see the whole person cramped by surroundings (2001: 251). Where the vistas do open out they only do so in a mockery of the freedom that space suggests. The rubbish tip, the most overt landscape of the void, simply offers a panorama of rubbish, nothing more. The long path up which Alex climbs in the process of her drug deals feels like an obstacle course, with the obstructions of the people strung out along the path waiting to buy the drugs. The later long shot in which Alex and Javi talk past each other as they stand on an ironically green oasis of grass merely heightens the contrast to Alex's final neglect of an offer to escape the industrial wasteland that sits on the horizon. And the backward tracking shot of this wasteland that appears to suggest flight from it proves illusory, another mockery, since the characters have remained in Sestao. The only time when the vista does reflect a more hopeful outlook is in Alex's discussion with Juáncar of her dreams of romance with Javi, to the backdrop of a night-time skyline with flashes of brilliant light in the darkness. Crumbaugh comments that, at the end of Alex's tirade in response to the yuppie who wants to pay for drugs by credit card, the film 'cuts to an image of melting steel in which bright orange metal swirls and sparks against a black background, evoking a work of abstract painting', this being one of the instances Crumbaugh details of creation and art deriving from chaos (Crumbaugh, 2001: 47), though again we need to observe that Alex is part of the tableau, not the creator of it. Even here, however, the positive note is at best ironic, since Alex's dreams – themselves a notion of beauty amidst the chaos – will never be realised. In addition, Calparsoro observes in his DVD commentary that the sense of filial affection between Alex and Juáncar is deceptive: Juáncar is less interested in Alex's hopes for romance than in scoring drugs. In any case, he himself is the major hindrance to Alex's romantic fulfilment, as his need for drugs and for care ties her to her sordid life and environment, and the wish to avenge his death is what will prevent her from taking up the offer of escape when Javi finally offers it to her.

The sense of claustrophobia and entrapment that pervades the film may seem a contradiction to the notion of the void encompassed in the film's title and etched on to the back of Alex's head. A void suggests emptiness and space rather than being hemmed in by objects, walls, people and circumstances, unable to move. Rob Stone and Helen Jones suggest that the space through which Alex walks is unmappable in terms of Basque nationalism: it is itself a void that goes unseen and unrecognised by the Basque nationalist project or by patriarchal conceptualisations of gender (Stone and Jones, 2004: 52–4).

The landscape, like the characters' lives, has been emptied of meaning and of hope: the void is, in the first instance, the characters' lives, but the landscape also reflects this. What at first appears to be a breathtaking rural valley, reminiscent of the rural arcadias that Basque cinema has liked to use, turns out to be the rubbish tip, with rubbish stretching to the horizon, while the sides of the valley are covered in black plastic. The symbolic use of rubbish here has its precedent: Marti-Olivella demonstrates how the film recycles (as it were) the motif of rubbish that appeared in the earlier film by Ana Diez, *Ander eta Yul*, a film on which Calparsoro worked as part of the crew (Martí-Olivella, 1999: 213–17). Calparsoro, on the DVD commentary for *Salto*, has noted the vertigo we might experience as we watch the gang and their hostage walk around the edge of the deep pit. The disposal of the cop's body into the depths of the pit suggests at an additional level the loss of law and order into the void, a symbolism that could be pushed further to imply the loss of all social cohesion. It is notable that, although Alex warns the others that the cops will be after them now they have killed their victim, they never in fact appear. The void is expressed further in landscape terms in the empty streets such as the one in which Toño (Ion Gabella) crashes the car (in fact a busy road),[1] and the low-angle travelling shots of the street; the empty roads of the backwards tracking shots; the nightscape with only the electricity pylons visible (so that Alex casts her dreams into the void); and the final sequence on the hill behind the backs of the billboards. The final shot of all is a close-up of Alex framed simply by mist; having just ignored Javi's offer of escape to Brazil with him, she is left trapped in the void, her final word being 'fijo' or fixed: this entrapment reconciling the apparent contradiction between claustrophobia and emptiness.

What is Alex's response to the void and to the environment in which she finds herself? She expresses her view pungently in the sequence at the waste tip where the policeman is shot. She makes no comment on the policeman's death, but subsequently we see her wander through the rubbish, muttering, 'What the hell am I doing in the middle of all this shit?' In a fairly obvious way the landscape thematises the emptiness of the characters' lives, the notion that they themselves are no more than the flotsam and jetsam of contemporary society, that they can expect nothing out of life. More significant is the reaction of Alex to the landscape in the fact that she literally inscribes the void on her body – the back of her head to be precise. On one level this might suggest that the void literally marks her: she comes to represent more than any other character the emptiness of the landscape, which is a less positive interpretation than Crumbaugh's claim of creation out of chaos, discussed above. The mere fact that Alex can pose the question at all – why is she here amongst all this shit – suggests a more active engagement with the land; and her shaved scalp suggests at the very least a recognition of the void and an implicit challenge to it. But the challenge remains futile, and the inscription on her head demonstrates the inescapability of the void.

Palacios sees the void in more classic terms. After stating crudely that the marginalised and criminal Bilbao depicted by Calparsoro does not in fact exist (which contradicts Calparsoro himself, who certainly thought it did when he filmed it on location), he goes on more suggestively to compare Alex's environment to Dante's Inferno:

> Parece más bien algún círculo del Infierno que Dante se hubiera olvidado de enumerar, poblado por demonios y condenados que no pueden escapar a su destino. Que cuanto más intentan librarse de él más se ven arrastrados al centro mismo de la miseria y la muerte. (Palacios, 2006: 379)

> (It seems more like a circle of hell that Dante forgot to describe, populated by demons and the damned who could not escape their fate. The more they try to escape, the more they are sucked into the centre of misery and death.)

Palacios's move here suggests a denial of the possibility that Calparsoro's Basque landscape is a real one. Martí-Olivella, as discussed in the opening chapter, claimed Calparsoro himself as guilty of a denial of Basques realities, but it may be that Martí-Olivella himself, like Palacios, prefers to deny a Basque reality out of step with the nationalist mythmaking of Basque cinematic landscape elsewhere. As Kepa Sojo Gil observes of this film and of the next, *Pasajes*, Calparsoro's sort of realism was not that originally envisaged by those who earlier pursued a vision of Basque cinema more in tune with Basque nationalism (Sojo Gil, 1997: 136). At one level, Palacios got his way in that much of the landscape in *Salto* has since been demolished. But with his use of the landscape here, Calparsoro destabilises the fairly constant equation in Spanish cinema of the Basque country with rurality; and the discomfort expressed by Palacios and hinted at by Martí-Olivella indicates the unease that such destabilisation causes. Palacios's mythification distances him from the depiction of a contemporary reality.

## Violence and urban deprivation

*Salto al vacío* placed Calparsoro in the frame of *cine social* and the subgenre of stories about urban youth. Ballesteros links the work of Calparsoro to the so-called Spanish generation X of writers such as Ray Loriga, Lucía Etxebarría, José Angel Mañas and others (Ballesteros, 2001: 244–5) – sharing similar motifs such as the marginalisation and bestialisation of the main characters, their tendency towards gratuitous violence, death as spectacle, a millennial chaos, lack of

solidarity, spiritual vacuum, emphasis on spoken slang and on reference to other forms of media, speed, fragmentation in the representation of images, an inability to distinguish between the real and the
fictitious. In particular, she notes the search for love as the only route
to self-realisation and simultaneously impossible to find.

Central to Calparsoro's concept of the urban youth film is his use
of violence. His avowed purpose for this is to show rather than to tell,
to offer us the emotional impact of violence rather than to explain it
(Heredero, 1997: 261). The film is not designed as a cerebral exercise
by the audience but meant to grab us by the throat (Leyra, 1995b: 357),
suggestive of his belief that cinema-going is itself a violent process
wherein the audience is itself assaulted. There is one indicative shot
in the film that suggests the audience, too, as potential victims of this
violence: our first sight of Alex in a lavatory immediately prior to her
drug-dealing walk is a high-angle shot of her looking straight up and
aiming a gun at us, or so it seems. But Calparsoro does not wish to do
violence to the audience simply for the sake of it but to show to them
the truth of the life that Alex has to lead.

Ballesteros notes (2001: 245) the importance of masculinist ritual
as part of this generation's culture. She goes on to argue that Calparsoro offers a feminine gaze on 'a masculine universe permanently in
conflict with itself, defined exclusively through violence as the only
solution to sexual and social impotence' (248), something from which
male characters suffer both literally and figuratively. While the rest
of the gang seem to struggle for masculine supremacy, it appears to
be Alex who has the real control. Ballesteros points out that the men
act like animals, while the woman holds the reason, a reverse of the
usual patriarchal construct (250). Rodríguez notes that Alex directs
the violence although she does not participate, and suggests a link
between masculinity and violence through the discussion of who has
the balls to kill the policeman, but she does not explicitly state the
irony that, while Javi comments that the one who gives the orders
is the one with the biggest balls, the one who really does give the
orders is Alex, with no balls at all (Rodríguez, 2002a: 204–5). In this
sense, then, we can see patriarchy as not only incapable of realising
a woman's potential – it was ever thus – but also powerless to control
her. It becomes a moot point as to whether there is in fact any law for
the women to break.

In many ways Alex separates herself off from the masculine violence
of the film as testosterone excess, a reaction that Rodríguez perceives

as schizophrenic, underlining the contrast between her inner feelings and the violent world around her (Rodríguez, 2002a: 204). In the opening sequence as the others quarrel with each other, Alex is as tense as they are, but her annoyance is expressed more quietly, often in muttered asides that are hard to hear. She is talking to herself rather than addressing the others. While Alex states that the best cop is a dead cop, she does not participate in the violence towards the cop they capture, nor his eventual death: she merely observes with a sense of distaste and exasperation, taking up a slightly detached stance throughout the scene. This is clearly not to say, however, that Alex is never violent. For her, violence is a reasoned response to the situation in which she finds herself rather than a gratuitous one. Perhaps the nearest she comes to gratuity is her humiliation at gunpoint of the yuppie junkie; but then his insistence on paying by credit card suggests his lack of understanding of the world she moves about in, despite his dependence on her and on it in order to get his supply. Elsewhere, her violence may look excessive to us but 'reasonable' to her, as when she intervenes in the fight between her father and her uncle – itself very violent – and stops it by forcing a gun into her father's mouth. The tactic is effective, and results in the later opportunity to contribute to the family finances by earning money from her uncle at the dogfight.

Her most drastic act of violence comes when she shoots dead two men who are beating and torturing her uncle, who has brought her along to protect him. As Calparsoro observes on the DVD commentary, we do not see her victims die, in contrast to the shooting of the policeman and Juáncar, and the director also works to redeem her by way of the confidential chat she has afterward with Fati (Carla Calparsoro). When Fati asks her how she feels, Alex states confidently 'Bien' (fine) – a masculine-style assertion of being above the shock of killing – but immediately changes her statement to 'Mal' (bad). She *has* been affected, adversely, by the event. These events take place at the dogfight, which Calparsoro describes as a clear comparison with human behaviour (Leyra, 1995c). The lingering shot of the wounded dog dragging itself along might remind us of Alex, constantly hurt, abused and taken advantage of by the people around her, but struggling to get along just the same. But in fact Alex holds herself noticeably aloof from the dogfight. She does not watch it but instead remains alone, head bowed, in another room of the derelict building in which the fight takes place. This could suggest a desire to separate herself from the dog-eat-dog world in which she is living. She may take profit from it but she takes no pleasure.

Such violence as we see in *Salto* is not, however, the violence for which the Basque Country is best known – the terrorism of ETA. The only incident in the film that might have some relation to this form of violence is Esteban's murder of Juáncar while working for a gunrunner whose motivations are unclear. Calparsoro has proved contradictory about this motif. In one interview he denies that the incident has anything to do with ETA (Comas, 1995), but in the DVD commentary says that it is in fact a nod to the reality of terrorist executions of drug dealers (and thus is perhaps another throwback to *Ander eta Yul*, which deals with the conflict between ETA and drug pushers) . The director's comments elsewhere, however, indicate that he may have wished to uncover other forms of violence that the issues of terrorism and nationalism have served to obscure. As Ballesteros states, Calparsoro himself questions the notion that we can determine a Basque nation and a Basque cinema if we do not talk about the social reality that is going on within the Basque Country (Ballesteros, 2001: 247–8).

The insistence on a Basque national identity may have obscured the identity of others: Calparsoro remarks that the film concerns the loss of identity of a generation (Comas, 1995). Both Rodríguez (2002a: 206) and Crumbaugh (2001: 45) observe the use of red, white and green light within the film, though only Crumbaugh adds a footnote to the effect that these are the colours of the Basque flag. This use of filters may perhaps imply that Basque nationalism, too, is an inherent part of the alienation suffered by the characters. Certainly Martí-Olivella believes that, contrary to Calparsoro's claim (on the DVD commentary, for instance) that he is telling a universal story and in support of his own argument (discussed in the introduction), the national body politic is implied by the presence of Javi. 'With the creation of Javi ... Calparsoro (re)inscribes in the national body politic that other one, the still emasculated body of the immigrant subject and, in so doing, he crosses a very local border, that of Basque cinema's own self-repre- sentation' (Martí-Olivella, 1999: 213). But Martí-Olivella's insistence on recuperating the Basque nation through the back door neglects the very real sense of deprivation persistent in the film: this entire underclass is marginalised from the Basque nation as well. If violence is linked to nationalism, the violence of *Salto* can be seen as such only because Basque nationalism has disenfranchised this underclass (and it is well in this context to remember that Basque nationalism arose in the late nineteenth century in part because of the influx of a working class from outside the Basque Country; and to a great extent opposed the supposed pollution of the underclass until ETA began to draw on Marxist and socialist theories in an attempt to draw the working class to their cause).

There is a strong element of class underlying the urban deprivation of *Salto*. Calparsoro notes in the DVD commentary that the film documents an industrial context that is fast disappearing: the factories of the steel firm Los Altos Hornos, seen in the background of the car crash and subsequent argument, have since been demolished. So, too, have the houses in which filming took place – demolished to make way for the sort of bourgeois housing documented later in the film, the *chalet* in which the party takes place and which is still under construction. He also observes in the same commentary the significance of the backs of the billboards in the final scene. The advertisements that would be carried on the front of the billboards suggest the more affluent consumer society to which people like Alex do not have access. The backs of the billboards suggest the reality behind the consumer façade: the billboards literally and figuratively screen us from the downside of contemporary capitalism, something which Calparsoro felt he ought to show.

This aspect of class is posited by María Pilar Rodríguez as a way of distinguishing *Salto* from generation X (in contrast to Ballesteros's comparison cited above). According to Rodríguez, the characteristics of generation X – the crisis in patriarchal authority, a youth consumer market, an international youth culture supported by the mass media, an erosion of traditional morality, the personalisation of values and goals (rather than having community values), and an emphasis on hedonism (Rodríguez, 2002a: 180–1) – characterises the sort of culture of bourgeois youth offered in *Historias del Kronen* (Stories from the Kronen, Montxo Armendáriz, 1995), rather than the working class of *Salto*, where there is no hedonism or indulgence (198). It is worth noting in this context that Alex never indulges in drink or drugs beyond a single joint with Juáncar: the only time we see her put drugs into her mouth is so as to hide them from the police. When the rest of her gang do lines of coke in the car, or pass a bottle around in Esteban's caravan, she refuses. Calparsoro also comments on the character Eva (Noemí Parra) at the party, complete with shaven head that makes her look like a virtual clone of Alex. Eva plays in a bourgeois manner at what for Alex is real and no game. Eva can spout the theory of what is wrong with the world, but Alex must undergo the daily reality of trying to survive in it. I believe it is also worth noting that Eva is more articulate than Alex, who can only express her dissatisfaction with life using variations on the phrase 'I'm fed up with all this shit'; but Eva's more articulate discussion of what is wrong rapidly turns into an exasperating monologue in which she simply ignores whoever she is talking to.

## A claustrophobic *mise-en-scène*

Much of the film's *mise-en-scène* supports Calparsoro's film as visual (and possibly aural) violence, not only through the settings of industrial decay and Alex's hard appearance, but also the sense of claustrophobia and the use of camerawork and colour. The film contains fewer acts of violence than the reviews cited at the beginning of this chapter might suppose, and it offers us tranquil moments in which to take breath, such as the scene where Alex puts on makeup and her conversation with Juáncar. The film, however, offers a more pervasive frantic feeling from the very beginning, where, after the briefest of credits to acknowledge funders, the film cuts to the scene *in media res* of the gang with their victim in the car. Almost immediately they start to quarrel, so that we gain a feeling of tension and aggression with no context with which to explain it. This scene is then cut off abruptly with a cut to the title, and then what will turn out to be a flashback sequence to the attack on the policeman. These opening sequences are thus disorientating, and it is some while before we have enough information to piece together the chain of events (stealing guns from the policeman to sell on to the gunrunners of the caravan sequence). The sense of confusion is exacerbated by the claustrophobia of the cramped scene in the car. Although this set looks clearly fake and tacky (presumably the result of a lack of funds), Calparsoro turns this to his advantage by tinting the car windows green and thus removing any sense of an outside world.

Confusion and claustrophobia are also induced by the camera. In the car sequences it is static, adding to the sense of an inability to escape this confined space. Elsewhere, however, it moves in parallel to the ambience of the scene. Thus in the scene where the policeman is shot, the camera zooms in on the gang from behind as they walk round the edge of the pit, and then cuts and swirls back and forth as the policeman is shot and the recriminations begin (at one point neatly circling round the back of Alex's head to emphasise the word 'void' framed in the middle of this nihilistic scene). Crumbaugh talks of this scene as an example of creative unity emerging out of chaos. While Esteban and Javi fight in the background, Alex and Toño talk in the foreground, forming two distinct spheres of action. But then Toño walks across and unites the composition by, ironically, killing the policeman (Crumbaugh, 2001: 47). The scene in which Esteban loses his finger in the caravan again uses a roving camera in a long take, but this time in a confined space as it weaves round the different characters in the confrontation, underscoring the hysterical nature of the scene – an instance of what Ballesteros calls a hysterical camera to film hysterical action (Ballesteros, 2001: 248). The meeting of Alex, her uncle and the fight organiser is filmed with the camera closely circling round the characters in medium close-up, creating a dizzy sensation. Another notable use of the camera is its tracking shot from Alex's point of view as she embarks on her drug deals: the stream of people coming up to the camera in close-up contributes visually to the idea of the constant demands being made on the protagonist by everybody, and as a chain of obstacles that she has to get round in order to reach the summit, a parallel to her attempt to move beyond the sordidness of her daily existence and her inability to do so. The backward tracking shot of the roads towards the end of the film functions, according to Calparsoro on the DVD commentary, as a way in which to leave Sestao behind and offer us a final note of melancholy to the film, although I would argue that the sense of departure is disturbed by the following and final scene in which it becomes clear that Alex will never leave Sestao.

The camera, then, contributes to a sensation of confused and tense entrapment from which there is little if any relief; it thus attempts to reproduce within us the audience Alex's own feelings towards her predicament and her environment. This effect is enhanced by the predominant note of green to be found repeatedly within the film. At one level the use of green – suggesting nature – within the industrial landscape is ironic: it stems from what Calparsoro perceives as the fight between nature and industry as discussed above (Heredero, 1997: 273). But the use of green has other effects, too. The green tinted windows of the car do more than simply shut out the world beyond: Rodríguez suggests the cold green colour drains the scene of colour and humanity (Rodríguez, 2002a: 202). Green is also used as a colour with which to isolate Alex. The early shot of her alone, poised to participate in the attack on the policeman, is saturated in green (in contrast to the brown tones of the scene outside the policeman's house); a similar green is used in the claustrophobic lavatory where Alex prepares her drug deals; and her bedroom consists of peeling green walls against which her naked body is bathed in a warm gold light, stressing her humanity in this alienating environment. This use of green contrasts ironically with its more usual appearance in terms of a rural Basque landscape in other films.

With his later films Calparsoro makes use of music directly composed for the films; with *Salto*, however, he makes use of pre-recorded music by the Smashing Pumpkins, Stiltskin and El Inquilino Comunista. The use of heavy rock music reinforces the sense of the film as violent, aggressive and iconoclastic. But in fact the music does not cut in for nearly ten minutes, so that the predominant sound of the early scenes is the argumentative dialogue of the gang, within which the quiet voice of Alex is hardly heard; when the music does cut in we start not with the heavy rock but a choral chord. The heavy rock replaces this quickly but functions simply as a very low-volume background to a conversation in the car, suggesting the music to be diegetic (it promptly stops when Toño crashes the car). Calparsoro later intro-duces Billie Holliday singing 'All the Way', a mellow love song that contrasts crudely with the scene of family violence between Alex's father and uncle that the music underscores. As the scene changes to Alex applying make-up, the music changes with the scene to the heavy rock, ironic accompaniment to a peaceful scene where Alex is implicitly addressing her personal desires. The use of the music does not therefore suggest an easy equation of heavy rock with violence and that the music has other functions than a facilely aggressive youth style. Rather, it occurs mostly at moments when Alex has the chance to reflect on her own situation, such as the rock music accompanying the backwards tracking shot of the industrial landscape, or the brief burst of discordant guitar as Alex eats quietly with Javi's family.

An analysis of the music therefore suggests that Calparsoro uses it to do more than simply perpetuate notions of aggressive youth culture. *Salto* is in fact a remarkably quiet film given its content. The loudest use of music comes with the end credits; this, being the last sounds of the film, may have affected critical impressions of it as a loud and brash work. It is this supposed loudness and brashness that garnered the film particular attention, along with a heroine that supposedly embodies these very qualities. The accuracy of such perceptions is questionable for, as we have seen, Calparsoro offers nuances beyond the stereotypes of frustrated youth. A muted style, however, does not fit comfortably with perceptions of a rising young generation, and thus we can surmise that at least some interpretations of the film (particularly in retrospect) derive in part from what critics perceive as to be expected in a body of films from new, young directors.

## Note

1 Calparsoro observes on the DVD commentary that in fact their filming on this street – without permission – caused traffic problems and hold-ups as the workers from the Altos Hornos factory (which is visible in the shot) tried to get to and from their lunch break.

# 4

# *Pasajes*: pathways through nowhere

For his second film, *Pasajes*, Calparsoro immersed himself a little more within the Spanish film industry by drawing on the support of one of the most noted production companies of the contemporary Spanish scene, the El Deseo company formed by Pedro Almodóvar, who had been enthusiastic about *Salto* (Crumbaugh, 2001: 40), and his brother Agustín, and he also drew on the experience of established actress Charo López. This time Calparsoro had access to better resources than before, despite the struggle with funding – for example, a fight instructor, and the music of Alberto Iglesias, who started a regular collaboration with Almodóvar in 1995. This initial brush with the more established Spanish cinema scene was not altogether a happy one. Initially, the intervention of Almodóvar proved a relief, ensuring that the making of the film went ahead after the original producers pulled out. But later there appeared to be a cooling of enthusiasm on Almodóvar's part and a distancing from the finished product. Calparsoro himself suggested that Almodóvar had expected something different, more conventional, from the actual film (Heredero, 1997: 275). Interviews with the director also suggest that working with López was not always easy. Calparsoro observed a generational conflict between López and the other principal actors, all of whom were younger and less experienced (Heredero, 1997: 266). Following the previous method of acting and preparation used in *Salto al vacío*, the actors and director lived together in an attempt to interiorise the plot, action and characters, but López did not participate (Rubio, 1996; Heredero, 1997: 266).

If the director's relationship with more established sectors of the industry was not always comfortable, the reception by the critics also showed a certain amount of impatience. The most damning – and inadvertently, the most informative – comments come from F. M. in the annual *Cine para leer* for 1996, in which the reviewer argues against this being an example of auteurism but acknowledges some signs of a personal style (without saying what this consists of; F. M., 1996: 500–1). It seems premature for a critic to be looking for auteurism at such an early stage of a director's career – certainly Calparsoro thought so at the time, as clear from the title of an interview, 'Dos películas no bastan para juzgarme como director' (Two films are not enough to judge me as a director: Cortijo, 1996) – and it also raises questions as to what F. M. thinks auteurism is, if it does not include personal style. The label of auteur functions here as an accolade which F. M. feels Calparsoro does not merit, while nonetheless crediting him with his own style. Auteurism thus provides a benchmark by which to judge a film and also a director, who only gains the label if the critic feels the director is worthy. Simultaneously, however, the reviewer lumps Calparsoro in together with others of his generation who are fascinated by the visual aspects of film, and contrasts this with the need for a good screenwriter (501). F. M.'s comments suggest how the established industry might perceive the work of Calparsoro as distinct but not in the way preferred of an auteur, and how the generational tag can be applied to subtly denigrate the work in question. The visual element is an integral part of this denigration, as if preferring the visuals to the dialogue is inherently to be disparaged.

Other reviewers judge the film flawed but showing signs of the director's promise (Rodríguez Marchante, 1996; Aldarondo, 1996). They find classical comparisons for the film: Rodríguez Marchante goes as far back as the Greek epic, Trashorras (1996) refers to the *commedia dell'arte* and Aldarondo describes the film more vaguely in terms of a lyricism that contrasts awkwardly with its realist style. These terms of reference suggest, in contrast to F. M.'s review, a desire to elevate appreciation of Calparsoro's work. They also, however, and in line with F. M., indicate that discussion of the film does not occur in terms of the contemporary filmmaking going on around it. It implies an attempt to wrest critique of contemporary film away from contemporary terms of reference to a different set of criteria that are more recognisably 'artistic'. Reviews of the film from abroad were more enthusiastic than Spanish ones (Roldán Larreta, 1999: 358). The film was shown at Cannes, just as *Salto al vacío* was shown in the Berlin Film Festival: this festival continuum formed part of Calparsoro's early strategy to get himself known, and would be pursued further with the next film *A ciegas*, which appeared at Venice.[1]

The Spanish reaction to *Pasajes* thus proved to some extent similar to that of *Salto*, with somewhat less indulgence than that shown to a first-time feature-film director but with some effort to view both film and director as purveyors of some sort of art. At this early stage it would still be hard to consider Calparsoro as auteur but some ingredients for interpretation are already present, in a fairly unified critical reaction. Thematic and stylistic elements are repeated from the first film, implying a consistent vision on specific subject matter. For the second time we have an aggressive female character who nonetheless harbours dreams of fulfilment in a romantic relationship while trying to survive an imprisoning environment. The setting remains the urban Basque Country within which the marginalised struggle to survive. But we also find new elements, specifically lesbian relationships, putative mother–daughter relationships as maternal melodrama, and a more detailed focus on a middle-aged woman as well as young people.

## Creating an object of desire

*Pasajes* presents an instance of a deliberate construction of an identity as the protagonist Gabi (Najwa Nimri) tries to construct not only a new domestic space but an ideal lover/mother figure in Carmina (López), an endeavour doomed to fail. If *Salto al vacío* emphasised the void at the heart of contemporary urban realities, then *Pasajes* suggests a more concerted effort to find passage out of the void through not only romantic love (as Alex attempted in *Salto*) but through a deliberate setting up of a private space. Like Alex, Gabi survives through crime, initially carrying out violent robberies with her partner and lover Gema (Carla Calparsoro), but Gabi tells Gema in the opening robbery sequence that she will leave her, in search of the woman of her dreams; and when Gema dies during one of their robberies Gabi needs a new partner in crime as well. She appears to find both in Carmina, an older woman she sees on the street, who lives a life quite as desperate as Gabi's but who attempts to cloak the reality in elegant dress. It is this specific aspect – above all the shoes that Carmina wears – that attracts Gabi to her, and more on this point will be said below.

As with *Salto* we find that Calparsoro again places the female protagonist into a melodramatic position. Again, too, the context seems unlikely for melodrama, given not only the environment but also the fact that the romantic attachments involved here are now lesbian ones. In addition, on one level Gabi takes over the normally male role of fetishising the woman by means of the green marbled shoes about which she constantly fantasises, and which Carmina eventually wears. So in one sense we are far removed from the bourgeois hetero-sexual relationships of the traditional woman's film, where same-sex desire usually exists as a subtext at best. The relationship between Gabi and Carmina never promises much, given that it seems forced on Carmina, whose life as a drunken cleaner (who loses her job) proves inadequate to sustain the ideal that Gabi has placed upon her. In addition, Gabi does not demonstrate the same ability to nurture selflessly that Alex did in *Salto*: her attitude to people is more exploita-tive. Nevertheless, we can detect Gabi's assumption of responsibility for the relationship – and for her romanticising of it as well – and the caring element she offers to the abject Carmina. She takes care of her, grooms her and tries to better her career prospects and income by initiating her into her own life of crime.

One scene epitomises Gabi's attempts to force this relationship into a familiar bourgeois suburban character where the wife does not apparently work (even though we see her domestic labours, the

7   Carmina: desired object, desiring subject

'husband' is not allowed to see the industry). She invades Carmina's flat uninvited and begins to act the part of a housewife, firstly by putting on an apron and attempting some cooking, cleaning the kitchen floor and then, when Carmina arrives home, hiding away the bustle and activity by sitting at the kitchen table reading a newspaper. When Carmina enters the kitchen Gabi immediately leaps up to make her a drink and ask her how her day was. Calparsoro clearly intends this scene in part as a parody: Gabi proves herself rather inept at domestic tasks (knocking milk to the floor, for instance) and Carmina's angry reaction on finding her home invaded reveals the mismatch between Gabi's desires and the reality. However, the parodic element does not reduce the desire; if anything, it increases the pathos of it and thus makes a more acute impression on us. This reflects Elsaesser's comments referred to previously about the gap between reality and desire in melodrama (Elsaesser, 1987: 67). Melodrama here comes to include not so much the bourgeois as the desire for it; and *Pasajes* offers a grotesque distortion of a bourgeois ideal acted out by the marginalised, who are too far from the ideal to copy it successfully.

Carmina herself reveals a desire for a husband and a child, the latter leading to her dismissal from her job as a hospital cleaner when she attempts to lift up a crying baby. She claims to have a husband in prison but Gabi accuses her of making the whole thing up. The accusation is more than a little ironic given Gabi's own attempt to weave a dream relationship about Carmina, but it explains the jealousy that Gabi experiences when Carmina strikes up a fleeting flirtation with the security guard of the fish factory they rob. Doing this enables the two women to escape detection for the crime, but Gabi is clearly annoyed at the pleasure Carmina seems to take in the episode, while Carmina herself expresses renewed confidence, able to best Gabi in their subsequent argument. Carmina as the object of Gabi's desire is in the traditional feminine position; but the melodrama employed by Calparsoro here as in *Salto* asks the object to become the subject, asks the woman to desire rather than be desired. This may indeed be one of the reasons why melodramatic desire is so often frustrated, due to the impossibility of the desired object desiring in its turn. But as Gabi comes to know Carmina, we become better acquainted with Carmina's own desires: she turns from object to subject. And as the melodramatic subject she must in her turn see the frustration of her hopes. She becomes more dependent on Gabi, only to have her hopes crushed when the latter abandons her. E. Rodríguez Marchante

(1996) perceives Gabi as seeking her identity through a counterposition with Carmina, and Carmina herself as a metaphor. But as Gabi's fantasy becomes concrete with its crystallisation around Carmina, the latter ceases to be a metaphor and comes into relief with her own desires and fantasies. The weight of melodramatic female desire is thus shared between the two women, for while Gabi actively searches for personal fulfilment, Carmina suffers more overtly the frustration of desire.

However, given Gabi's fantasy created around Carmina, it seems initially surprising that in the end she abandons her so swiftly. This is very much a part of her function as what Calparsoro himself has labelled her capitalism in terms of human relations, seeking only her own benefit and not those of others (Rubio, 1996). Ryan Prout (2000: 284) labels Gabi a *femme fatale* in that she is destructive of all those who surround her. Gabi's abandonment of Gema early in the film tells us that she will readily sacrifice real people to her fantasies: as she tells Gema that she is leaving her in search of a woman wearing green marbled shoes there is a rapid cut to Gema's trainers, to indicate that she does not fulfil Gabi's requirements. Almost immediately afterwards Gema dies in a police ambush while Gabi escapes unscathed, a dramatic rendition of the latter's abandonment of her lover. She also shatters the lives and relationships of the other principal characters Manu (Alfredo Villa) and Butano (Ion Gabella): she attempts to persuade Manu to escape with her to America and abandon Butano. Her attempts to seduce Manu delay them sufficiently that the police catch up with them, and Manu as well as the police die in the resulting confrontation. This incident also speaks to Gabi's ability to seduce despite her exploitative nature; it is this capacity, after all, that allows her the opportunity to exploit people. Although Manu is well acquainted with Gabi's character, he is still finally persuaded by her promises of a better life together in America; and, as he lies dying, he vainly calls to her not to walk away and abandon him (to which she reminds him that she told him before that she was a liar).

As for Carmina, Gabi deserts her midway through a robbery in a bar. By now Carmina is apparently an integral part of Gabi's criminal operations, and acts as lookout while Gabi, Manu and Butano swing into action. But once Gabi has seized the money she runs off, leaving Carmina behind in the bar – the last we see of the older woman is a shot of her face with an expression of pained surprise. We never learn more of what happens to her; this forms a part of Calparsoro's tendency towards abrupt endings, leaving loose ends, but it also allows us to see the story develop from Gabi's point of view, in the sense that the film drops Carmina just as Gabi does. It is hard to describe this as identifying with Gabi, as the term implies a measure of sympathy, and sympathy for Gabi is at this point very hard to muster. Although this callousness on Gabi's part seems out of keeping with melodrama, it nonetheless retains the notion that the reality is unequal to the emotions: neither woman can in the end fulfil her desires through the other. In addition it matches the increasing transfer of Carmina from object to subject: as the desiring subject by the end of the film she must perforce be the one to suffer and be abandoned.

*Pasajes* presents us, then, with another strong central female protagonist at odds with the marginal world around her, using romantic fantasy as a way of escape from the misery. But the circumstances do not consequently entail a simple cloning of Alex from *Salto*, as Gabi is a more exploitative and less sympathetic character. In a key speech to Manu, she tells him that she likes to lie and to cheat, that when she wants something she takes it and when she no longer wants it she throws it away. In the same scene she repeats her desire to find the woman of her dreams wearing green marbled shoes, thus hinting at the connection between her romantic desires and her tendency to see people as disposable. Manu makes the connection more explicit by losing his temper with her and mentioning a list of other women who have apparently suffered as a result of Gabi's attitudes. Ego is nevertheless not the only reason for the failure of the relationship to flourish: it also fails because it is unreal, a figment of Gabi's imagination. For this reason Calparsoro did not offer us a more overtly erotic relationship, as he believed it would thus have become more real for Gabi (Heredero, 1997: 276).

It seems strange that critics such as Heredero argue that the three women of the Basque trilogy are in essence the same woman (Heredero, 1999: 99); and it can only be to support such a conflation that Heredero argues that Gabi is on a path of redemption (Heredero, 1999: 96). I cannot find sufficient evidence in the film to support such a reading, particularly given the overwhelming capacity of Gabi to use others that drives the whole narrative. Such a reading can only come about by superimposing the image of Alex over that of Gabi, presumably because of the vital contribution of Najwa Nimri to both roles. It is hard to avoid the assumption that Heredero is really thinking of the waif-like nature of Nimri. A similar reason must lie behind Palacios's insistence that Gabi is simply another reincarnation of Alex (2006: 379). This in turn suggests the fundamental part played by Nimri in the perception (perhaps misperception) of Calparsoro's films.

## Costume and identity construction

The romantic fantasy of *Pasajes*, unlike that of *Salto*, involves a more deliberate attempt to construct a new and better reality. Costume comes to play a role in conveying the idea of melodramatic desire as performance, the hope that you can change reality by changing your clothes in order to act the part (although Alex's efforts with make-up in *Salto* gesture towards this idea); hence Gabi dons an apron when assuming the role of stay-at-home housewife. Carmina's clothes display the contrast between dreams and sordid reality. When we and Gabi first see her she is walking along looking chic (and the camera provides a close-up of her high heels), but she is nonetheless displaying a smart appearance in a rundown area of town, a clear mismatch between her desired reality and what is actually around her. It is her smart appearance, her own attempt to set herself apart from her miserable reality, that draws Gabi's attention to her; thus she comes to offer an illusion of a different reality to the one Gabi experiences. However, it is just an illusion, as Carmina's shapeless overalls and baggy plastic cap in her role as hospital cleaner suggest. Good clothing is clearly a marker of fantasy, which is why Carmina takes such pleasure in it. In the shoes that Gabi gives her, she can literally take a step up to a middle-class veneer. Costume is more problematic as a marker of femininity, however. Gabi appears more feminine than Alex, wearing skirts and heavy eyeliner (as opposed to Alex's hesitant experiments with make-up), and with softer and fluffier hair than Alex with her striking shaven head. This apparent mismatch of feminine look and exploitative behaviour indicates that, for all his imitation of melodramatic storylines, Calparsoro does not necessarily see women reductively in terms of feminine dress.

The clearest marker of costume as an indication of desire is the high-heeled shoe. Gabi refers to green marbled high heels as the marker of the woman of her dreams (with the unkind contrast to Gema's cheap trainers). Gabi's first sight of Carmina stresses both the importance of the shoes in her fantasy and also the specific identity of the woman concerned as irrelevant. As Gabi is bathed in golden light from a passing cleaning truck she sees, silhouetted in the truck's light, a woman slowly walking, with the sound of her heels emphasised on the soundtrack. Gabi is transfixed by the woman's high heels, more so than the woman's face that would signify an individual identity. The golden glow and the mystique of the silhouetted woman walking slowly past suggest the ideal: the next sequence quickly cuts to the reality behind the veneer, as Gabi stalks Carmina, who walks less elegantly now as her high heels are ill suited to the rougher terrain she is crossing. The cold blue light of this scene, along with the backdrop of the miserable block of flats that is Carmina's home, reveals the previous scene for the fantasy that it is. And when Gabi's ideal is finally realised she no longer desires it. After the two women perform a robbery they move through an underpass and then up into a bright light that echoes the golden light of the earlier scene, before finding the green marbled shoes of Gabi's fantasy on display in a shop. Carmina excitedly tries on the shoes and a matching suit: while she does so, Gabi stares at a bare tailor's dummy with another pair of the shoes at its feet – a blank female shape with high heels, the preferred form of her fantasy. When Carmina duly appears in the desired outfit and asks Gabi if she likes it, she simply replies that she will not say anything and abruptly leaves the shop. At the very moment Carmina comes to match the woman of Gabi's dreams, Gabi abandons this dream and shortly afterwards Carmina herself. The robbery preceding this sequence may hint at this outcome, the modus operandi of the crime similar to that of the opening robbery with Gema, as is Gabi's restless attitude throughout the operation in contrast to the more business-like approach of both Gema and Carmina. Carmina will be discarded after the later robbery just as Gema was earlier, leaving us to wonder whether originally Gabi fantasised about a woman in gold trainers before meeting Gema.

The high heel serves as a symbol of both upward mobility and thus the potential for escape but at the same time a femininity that hobbles and immobilises (it is hard to make one's escape in precarious high heels). It is notable that Gabi never aspires to wear high-heeled shoes herself: the heeled shoe is an integral part of the desired object and not the desiring subject. Thus Gabi appears to take on a certain amount of male fetishising in the stress on the green marbled shoe. Buñuel and Almodóvar, arguably the best known names of Spanish cinema, have both, in different ways, encapsulated women as the impossible object of desire in terms of high-heeled shoes. In Buñuel's *Él* (1953, English title *This Strange Passion*) the male protagonist Francisco is first attracted to his future wife when he catches sight of her feet, in elegant high heels, during a church service: this sight of the feet (before the camera pans upwards to show us the woman's face) immediately obsesses Francisco. As in *Pasajes* the shoes rather than the woman's face serve as the real object of desire. In Almodóvar's *Tacones lejanos* (High Heels, 1991), the title refers to the desire for the lost mother – the underlying motivation of the entire plot – but this reference and its connection to high-heeled shoes is only revealed at the end when the dying mother remembers in her turn listening for her own mother and listening to the sound of high heels as they walked along the pavement. Thus again the heels come to represent the unattainable ideal woman; in *Pasajes* Gabi attempts to create the missing woman by supplying the shoes.

Ariadna Gil, on starring in Calparsoro's later film *Ausentes*, observed the effort that was required to be running constantly in high heels, and suggested that Calparsoro rather fetishistically believed all women to wear high heels (Pastor, 2005). Calparsoro's use of the shoe indicates an implicit if not explicit nod to other Spanish auteurs, particularly through his use of the shoe as a form of fetish. Prout (2000: 284–5) reads Gabi's fetishising of the shoes in terms of the male gaze, which certainly coincides with Buñuel's use of the shoe but neglects Almodóvar's use of it as a sign of a close relationship between women (though here, too, the shoe covers a lack or loss). The cinema of the '95 generation demonstrates an intermittent willingness to quote from – or, on the part of audiences, remember – the classic Spanish cinema despite the perception of a turn towards Hollywood discussed in chapter 1, such as the attempt by Amenábar in his first film *Tesis* to quote Víctor's Erice celebrated *El espíritu de la colmena* (The Spirit of the Beehive, 1973, an attempt which ended up on the cutting room floor but which is referred to in subsequent interviews with the director). It implies Spanish cinema as a resource just as much as other film traditions from which directors and audiences can draw; and consequently hints at the need to countenance the possibility of contemporary Spanish cinema as a collage of different elements. A contemporary auteur, then, can use these quotations while maintaining an element of individual interpretation that reminds us of more classic definitions of auteurism. They may also, however, serve to destabilise these references. Buñuel and Almodóvar's shoes appear in the context of comfortable bourgeois living. The way in which Carmina totters in her heels across the waste ground allows Calparsoro to complicate and to challenge the easy fetishisation of the woman by using the shoe to render her an object of desire. Carmina and Gabi's experience of the high-heeled shoes suggests the struggle of women between subject and object – the actual experience of wearing such shoes and the ideal of desirability they supposedly endow. This is capped with the final irony that, when Carmina finally wears the green marbled shoes, Gabi no longer desires her. Calparsoro's use of the shoe, then, gestures at the possibility of new meanings given to old symbols of Spanish cinema when put in new contexts.

Ryan Prout's comparison of *Pasajes* with Luc Besson's *Nikita* (1990) – in terms of the films' use of comic book characters such as the policeman and the boxer (Butano), the occasional use of an underwater perspective, the *femme fatale* as 'androgynous gamin assassin', the retreat into childlike behaviour, the absence of a family (Prout, 2000: 288) – may also be instructive in the sense of reference to European cinema, though there is a Hollywood reference, too, as *Nikita* was remade as the American film *The Assassin* (aka *Point of No Return*, John Badham, 1993). Prout posits that in both *Pasajes* and *Nikita* we find a link between a younger and an older woman that highlights the gulf between femininity past and present. But, unlike *Nikita*, it is now the younger woman who tells the older how to dress and how to act (289). Costume in *Pasajes* stresses a generation gap, but also, perversely, a desire for the older generation to return. The shoes which Gabi perceives as symbolic of her desire are of a style that older women are likely to wear. If Calparsoro's first four films belong to a genre of films about marginalised youth, then *Pasajes* is unusual in finding desirable the symbols of an older generation and seeing these as a retreat from the surrounding urban misery. Carmina becomes the first central older character of Calparsoro's work. Despite the constant emphasis on young characters, however, this desire for the older generation may reflect a more widespread obsession with middle-aged and old characters in films from the '95 generation, as observed by Palacios (2006: 369–70). Through her control over the older woman's clothing, Gabi summons the older generation to return, reminiscent of the desire for reconciliation between parents and children that also exemplifies melodrama.

## Spaces of entrapment

*Pasajes* (1996) as a title offers us a dual meaning. It refers to the Basque town of Pasajes (or Pasaia in its Basque incarnation), but the Spanish name also refers to passages, raising again the possibility of escape which is thwarted as it was previously in *Salto al vacío*. In *Pasajes*, the passages hinted at in the title – the bridges, walkways and corridors which Gabi frequents – do not seem to go anywhere or connect anything: they are marginal places that do not lead to a centre but serve instead to trap the women. The film's structure appears in fact not linear but ultimately circular: Gabi abandons her lover for someone else in the middle of a heist at both the beginning and the end of the film, and on both occasions one of her victims dies in a police shoot-out while she walks away unscathed. The title of the film thus at first sight belies the eventual structure of the film we experience; but the film also suggests that the sense of elsewhere offered by the notion of the passageway is in fact illusory.

Intermittently throughout the film the *mise-en-scène* offers us some form of passageway, a note struck from the very beginning as the film opens on to an inner corridor and the camera begins slowly to track along it, only a foot or so from the floor. We will subsequently discover that this movement suggests the approach of Gabi and Gema to the flat they are about to rob, though this camera cannot be representing this movement realistically (it is unlikely that would-be thieves would move quite this slowly). The proximity of the camera to the floor makes of the corridor a vast space that threatens to engulf the characters: the low angle reduces their power even though they are not in shot. This passageway, then, is not designed to facilitate movement from one place to another but, on the contrary to overpower and entrap. For Gema, killed by the police as she tries to escape, this entrapment rapidly becomes literal, as she never escapes the corridor and passages of the building. Shots of the police as they menacingly approach the camera down the carpeted corridors, or of Gema and Gabi trying to find a way out of the warren of basement passages, ensure that this opening sequence of the film bombards us with the sense of an increasingly frenzied need to escape from the interminable labyrinth, so that it comes as almost a surprise that Gabi manages to get away. This will, of course, prove typical of the character, as she survives while leaving her first victim, Gema, behind. But in fact Gabi merely escapes to more passageways. She is a survivor in her environment but she does not break free of it.

This becomes evident in another pivotal sequence involving a passage, the bridge crossing the harbour away from Carmina's home. The sequence occurs after Carmina and Gabi have quarrelled subsequent to their robbery of the fish warehouse. Carmina is still insisting that she has her own life and plans for a family, while Gabi responds tearfully that she does not understand her. After this scene we cut to Gabi stalking furiously across a bridge of enclosing red struts, hitting the sides rhythmically in a childlike way, while Carmina pursues her in her high heels. The quarrel continues on this bridge, until eventually Carmina knocks Gabi to the ground. The two women are mired in their fantasies, as their argument implies, and their inability to satisfy each other reveals that there is no possibility of escape this way. The point is underscored by the nature of the bridge with its imprisoning girders, and indeed the fact that we never see the women leave the bridge to go elsewhere. A further irony is provided by the vivid colours of the backdrop. The girders of the bridge are a bright red, while the scene takes place against a clear blue sky and the vibrant colours of the docks. These contrast to the prevailing colours of yellow and brown that saturate almost the entire *mise-en-scène* of the film (a change from the greens of *Salto*). The monotony of these two colours means that the occasional intrusion of brighter colours, as here, affords the viewer some relief; but relief proves entirely inappropriate given the ambience of entrapment that these colours decorate. Calparsoro links the browns of the films to stagnation (Heredero, 1997: 277), but the brighter colours ironically make the point, too. An earlier shot of the bridge, as Gabi and Carmina run across it and past green grass, after they flee the hospital where Carmina has just lost her job, suggests escape and freedom. Gabi appears at this point to have rescued Carmina from her dead-end job, with the promise of the upward mobility and fantasy life symbolised by the shoes (a picture of which Gabi drew on a hospital window to get Carmina's attention). The repetition of the motif of the bridge at this point reminds us of these earlier hopes and demonstrates that instead the relationship of the two women has entrapped rather than released them.

Other passageways include the harbour docksides and ladders used by Manu and Butano as they wander aimlessly from place to place, always inevitably returning to the derelict warehouse that is their home. The occasional shot of a boat traversing the harbour simply points up the irony that the sea implies an opportunity to leave this town but that in fact no one is ever seen to leave. In an early scene the two men walk round an old shipyard in which we can see parts such as rusting propellers, which also suggests that any means of escape from life in Pasajes is crumbling away. The passageways also include the narrow path beneath the counter of the bar in the closing robbery, along which Gabi crawls to get to the cash register, and the underpass through which Gabi and Carmina walk and then apparently up into the light, though in fact they are walking towards the pivotal moment of Gabi's disillusionment and their subsequent break-up.

*Pasajes* repeats the sense of industrial decay that we saw previously in *Salto*. Prout talks of *Pasajes* as part of Calparsoro's trio of films of 'geographical disorientation, moral emptiness and urban existentialism', a film that takes the viewer not only into marginal spaces such as corridors and subways but also depressed areas and marginal living arrangements such as the warehouse which Gabi and Gema share with Manu and Butano (Prout, 2000: 283). While *Salto al vacío* induced a sense of claustrophobia, however, *Pasajes* possesses a landscape mostly denuded of people. The few people we do see are dwarfed by their surroundings – the barren terrain with tower blocks as Gabi stalks Carmina, the wharves over which Manu and Butano wander, the solitary quayside where the two couples finally meet. We might see the lack of people as a reflection of Gabi's tendency to use up and destroy those around her so that she is figuratively sucking the land dry of its people. This contrasts to *Salto*, in which the claustrophobic surroundings, rooms crammed with people, parallel the restrictive demands placed on Alex by those around her. Calparsoro's description of Gabi as capitalist takes on a new resonance in a landscape suffering a blight arising from the capitalist industrial project.

Prout quotes critic E. Rodríguez Marchante's observation that the film manifests too much of a 'desire to dress up the film in some kind of make-believe underworld' with no clear location except in Calparsoro's imagination. Prout himself finds this comment odd, since the location of Pasajes seems fairly apparent (Prout, 2000: 285). We may remember Palacios's insistence that Calparsoro's Bilbao of *Salto* did not exist either (Palacios, 2006: 379). As Prout goes on to discuss (286), the void of Pasajes does in fact carry a social, cultural and economic history as a once prosperous port which has since gone into decline by the time of the film. Whereas in previous times Carmina could have found work at the fish factory, now she is reduced simply to stealing the fish. Prout argues that Calparsoro thus reminds his audience of a real and complex Basque history, including its industrialisation and subsequent decay, that is often ignored in favour of pastoral rural landscapes that represent a mythical Basque country (287). It is possible that these denials of the reality of Calparsoro's landscapes by critics such as Rodríguez Marchante stem from an unease at the director's destabilisation of cinematic depictions of the Basque Country. Equally ignored is the lack of opportunity for the people in these urban environments: Carmina finds it hard to get work, Gabi cannot read or write. Butano and Manu hope to make something out of Butano's boxing skills, but Butano never gets the opportunity, and we never see him fighting a real opponent. Manu dubs Butano 'the King of Pasajes', but Pasajes is not a promising territory of which to be king, and in fact Butano only presides over destruction and loss, the closing shot of the film being his desperate weeping over the dead body of Manu.

## Stasis and stagnation

In keeping with the sense of stasis prevalent in the film, *Pasajes* is notably less frenetic than *Salto al vacío* (Heredero, 1997: 277), the roving steadycam of the latter giving way to more conventional framing in medium long shot or medium close-up. The only exceptions to this change are the low-angle travelling shot at the very beginning of the film, already discussed above, and the scene of the police arriving in the first victim's flat, where the camera uses the swirling motion of before, suggesting rapid action. The quick cutting from police to the attempts of Gabi and Gema to escape the block of flats increases the sensation that the latter acts as a labyrinth which is difficult to break out of. (It also serves to mask a potential error: it is in reality hard to believe that the police could be alerted and arrive at the block of flats in the seconds it would take the fugitives to descend in the lift.) The change in approach to the camera reveals that Calparsoro and his cameraman Kiko de la Rica (who also worked on *Salto*) are developing their approach and are not confined to an intent to provide spectacular effects. Given his reputation for crude, fast and violent filmmaking, Calparsoro has slowed his approach at a remarkably early stage, indicating that such a reputation revolves around subject matter rather than style (also that people may well superimpose memories of an earlier film on to another one as they interpret the later offering).

Similarly in terms of music, we have lost the mixture of heavy rock music interspersed with choral chords in favour of mournful string

8   The waif-like Gabi

music composed by Iglesias. This change of musical style coincides with the involvement of the El Deseo production company; in the next film *A ciegas* the soundtrack will revert back to the mixture of chorus and heavy rock of *Salto al vacío*. This change of musical style for *Pasajes* may have come about as a result of production require-ments, or simply because Iglesias was available and willing. The soundtrack otherwise is quite similar to *Salto* in that the predomi-nant sound is that of dialogue. The music here does not have quite the same logic of expressing Gabi's internal feelings as it did Alex's in *Salto*, but nonetheless often ties in with the moments of emotion and melodrama so that, for instance, in a meeting of Gabi with Manu and Butano the music surfaces as she begins to tell Manu about her meeting with Carmina. Yet it is not simply a way of reinforcing these emotions, as the music continues while Gabi and Manu talk about more mundane issues and Butano practises with a punch bag, and it then fades out at an insignificant point. Equally the string music plays briefly during a scene in which Manu and Butano hand over some illegal videos to a contact but disappears before this scene reaches its climax of a violent confrontation. The music thus acquires a sense of randomness that empties it of meaning. This hints at the theme of the void that was more prominent in *Salto* but reappears here (as well as in the empty landscape).

As has already been observed, the prevailing tones of the film are yellow and brown, colours that further underscore the stagnant ambience of the film. This proves particularly appropriate for the interiors, all of which stress the stasis of the characters: even when Gabi and Gema roam around the apartment block of the opening sequence they appear trapped in the labyrinth of beige and then grey passages, going nowhere. The added ironic contrast of the occasional glimpse of a colourful outside world offers only an illusory promise. Very occasionally, Calparsoro changes the colour notes of the interiors, but usually to blue (the hospital, the fish warehouse where Carmina seduces the watchman while Gabi steals fish), the quintessential cold colour that ultimately offers no relief. A rarer touch of colour is the ironic use of red, the colour of the struts of the bridge across the harbour in which Carmina and Gabi have their argument. As previously noted, the cheerful colour of these serves to emphasise the illusory nature of the promise of escape. This motif will be repeated in a very different setting and genre with *Ausentes*, wherein the opening red doors of the maintenance block suggest menace rather than new opportunities.

In the midst of this murk Calparsoro draws attention once more to Nimri and her striking eyes, this time primarily through a heavy use of kohl make-up that contrasts with the more delicate attempts at make-up of Alex in *Salto*. This emphasis is particularly notable in the shots of Gabi with her face under water (which illustrated the film poster), the kohl ensuring that we are aware of her eyes even while they are shut. In other shots in the same scene the eyes are further emphasised by, firstly, the wet hair plastered round Gabi's face, making her eyes appear larger, and the hood of the jacket that she subsequently puts on, which hides her hair and frames her eyes more starkly. Further motifs of the film imply Gabi's childlike nature, such as the way in which she shuffles towards Butano and Manu in this scene in an ungainly manner (with a brief high-angle shot that foreshortens her legs, making her appear more childlike), or the white T-shirt and underwear in which she later wanders around Carmina's flat that suggest infant innocence. At one point she even clutches a teddy bear. Her occasional sulks and pouting lip underscore the childlike image in more negative ways. But if Gabi is wide-eyed and childlike, she is cruel as perhaps only a child can be, with the ruthlessness of ego that has never learnt to think of the needs and views of others. Calparsoro's frequent framing of the character as childlike amidst the gloom is thus deeply ironic, as her personality is as dark as her surroundings.

*Pasajes* appears like *Salto* but – ironically given that this time Calparsoro had more resources – stripped down to the essentials. Both stylistically and thematically Calparsoro shows an individual vision that hints at auteurism despite Calparsoro's own caveat that two films are not enough to establish him as an auteur, as mentioned at the beginning of this chapter. The essential contribution of the central character in each case makes *Pasajes* harder to like as a film given that Gabi is less sympathetic than Alex. This, coupled with the missing elements of aggression in the style that critics earlier detected in *Salto*, may underlie the lack of certainty with which *Pasajes* was received. It helped to establish Nimri as a versatile actress, however, and maintained critical interest in the director's work. The problem of using an auteurist framework that Calparsoro identifies reveals itself in the puzzlement that critics expressed in some reviews; their resort to older critical constructions hints at the difficulties in adjusting to a cinema scene that emphasised newness.

## Note

1 Personal conversation with the author, 17 May 2006.

# 5

# A *ciegas*: the blind side of Basque terrorism

*A ciegas*, the last of the Basque trilogy, again foregrounds a female protagonist against the backdrop of a violent Basque reality with the story of an ETA terrorist who rebels against ETA and flees with her son from the armed struggle. Like its predecessors, the film gained a showing at a film festival, as a contender for the Golden Lion at the Venice Film Festival. Carlos Roldán Larreta (1999: 360) describes the film's presence in the festival as an important triumph for the director; although it got a cool reception there, Roldán Larreta nonetheless felt that the film demonstrated Calparsoro's indubitable talent as a filmmaker. By this time Calparsoro had gathered a core troupe of actors working on his films, most obviously Nimri, but also Alfredo Villa again as the protagonist Marrubi's partner Mikel, and Mariví Bilbao as the housekeeper Paquita, having played Alex's mother in *Salto* and a landlady in *Pasajes*; but there are signs that he is beginning to go further afield to look for actors and to mix his cast.

With *A ciegas* Calparsoro garnered some positive comparison to two of Spain's most renowned established auteurs. Carlos Losilla compares the scenes where Marrubi is held prisoner to 1960s-style Saura (Losilla, 1997b: 14); while Jesús Palacios describes Marrubi's imprisonment as Buñuelesque (Palacios, 2006: 380). These references indicate that Calparsoro's work is viewed in terms of a more traditional style of Spanish filmmaking rooted in both *cine social* and arthouse, rather than commercial terms, again suggesting the use of older rather than contemporary frames of reference. Critique of the film focused around two main issues: the depiction of the Basque conflict and the central section in which Marrubi's employer Clemente (Ramón Barea) holds her hostage. This latter sequence induced harsh criticism from reviewers. Constance Verney, for example, speaks of the gratuitous and disconcerting way in which the story passes from the focus on ETA to Marrubi's imprisonment by her boss (Verney, 1998: 96). Another reviewer, Francisco Marinero (who comments on the laughter that ensued when the film was screened), suggests that the kidnapping by Clemente serves only to make the film the right length (Marinero, 1997). Calparsoro himself viewed Clemente and Paquita as an element of comedy within the film (Fernández-Santos, 1997), indicating that the laughter was deliberately induced rather than inadvertent as Marinero suggests. For Roldán Larreta, this was the low point of the film that sent it deep into ridicule at that point (Roldán Larreta, 1999: 360). The sequence interrupts the flow of the action, although, as Verney acknowledges, there is some connection between this strand of the story and the principal one of Marrubi's efforts to abandon terrorism in that it is only Clemente's knowledge of Marrubi's role as a terrorist that gives him the opportunity to trap and exploit her (Verney, 1998: 96).

The other main issue of critique, that of the depiction of the Basque conflict, taps into questions surrounding a subgenre of Spanish cinema about Basque terrorism. Roldán Larreta argues that *A ciegas* is similar to many other films about the Basque Country in its portrayal of the existential exhaustion induced by the conflict, and provides a list of such films: *La muerte de Mikel* (The Death of Mikel, Imanol Uribe, 1983), *27 horas* (27 Hours, Montxo Armendáriz, 1986), *Ander eta Yul, Alas de mariposa* (Butterfly Wings, Juanma Bajo Ulloa, 1991), *Urte ilunak* (The Dark Years, Arantxa Lazcano, 1992), *Días contados* (Running Out of Time, Imanol Uribe, 1994), *Salto al vacío* (without mentioning that Calparsoro himself directed this) and *Tierra* (Julio Medem, 1995) (Roldán Larreta, 1999: 360). The danger in Roldán Larreta's comments is that it reduces all these films to the same common denominator of one specific conflict; the reality of *Salto al vacío*, to go no further, tells us that social tensions in the Basque Country do not simply operate at the one level of nationalism but at other levels, too, such as the economic. This mixed list might, however, explain why Roldán Larreta goes on to regret that Basque cinema is unable to demonstrate the capacity of British cinema to depict a terrorist conflict (he does not mention Irish cinema: 1999: 361): its approach to conflict must simply be too diffuse. The reductiveness of Roldán Larreta's argument makes it all too obvious why Calparsoro and others have dodged the label of Basque director. Palacios also refers to the conflict as a way of praising *A ciegas*, describing the

film as irregular in quality but refusing to give in to the easy taking
of sides. Its open confusion is an asset (Palacios 2006, 380). This
chapter will discuss *A ciegas* in the context of cinema about Basque
terrorism, but it will also aim to demonstrate that, far from the director's work being subordinate to the moulds of Basque cinema, the
specifically Basque theme of terrorism forms part of his wider view
on female desire and frustration.

## Women and Basque terrorism

*A ciegas* participates in an exploration of the woman in Basque
terrorism that has gone on elsewhere in films such as *Yoyes* (Helena
Taberna, 2000) and *El viaje de Arián* (Arián's Journey, Eduard Bosch,
2000; see Davies, 2005, for a discussion of this film). The use of a
woman as a central character facilitates the study of the emotional
cost of political violence as well as the conflict between the personal
and political and which should take priority. In these three films the
personal comes to take precedence – Marrubi's attempt to make a new
life for herself and her child, Yoyes's attempt to do something similar
with her own family and Arián's effort to escape terrorism after the
end of the romantic relationship that appeared to sustain her political
commitment. It is striking that it is a woman that realises the impact
of violence on people's lives and not men, going back to women's
nurturing role which also has its place in the woman's film. Marrubi's
commitment to ETA seems shaken when she first witnesses the actual
impact of violence as she and Eneko (Vidal Fernández), a fellow ETA
member, raid a house in the film's opening scene. It is significant in
this respect that Marrubi's unease seems to be impelled by watching
the domestic scene within the house, as a woman feeds her baby and
her husband prepares dinner. This scene of nurture, particularly with
the mother and child, allows Marrubi to draw parallels with her own
personal relationships; and thus it disturbs her commitment to the
cause. Instead of shooting the woman's husband Marrubi shoots
her terrorist colleague in the leg, then abandons him as the husband
grabs a gun, shooting at her and shooting Eneko dead. In the middle
of the tense standoff between the terrorists and the inhabitants of the
house the action pauses as the camera focuses in close-up on the face
of Marrubi, covered with a balaclava, and then cuts to her in the same
position but minus the hooding, as if her true individual nature has
come to the surface. This true self is her nurturing self. Perhaps also

9   Marrubi the terrorist

for this reason it has to be another female terrorist, Aitzpea (Elena
Irureta) who, in the film's climactic scene, allows her to leave and
rejoin her child, letting them get away to the new life Marrubi seeks.
Only another woman can see the need to prize the personal above the
political.

María Pilar Rodríguez claims of Taberna's film *Yoyes* that it is 'the first
effort to portray the life and death of a female activist from a feminist
perspective. It questions the sexist environment of the organization
and presents a lucid approach to the private and public life of one of the
most interesting figures of our history' (Rodríguez, 2002b: 157). The
word 'feminist' in Rodríguez's statement is potentially problematic,
and particularly in regard to Calparsoro's film, which preceded *Yoyes*
by three years. Taberna has an overt commitment to films detailing
women's lives, but so does Calparsoro in his Basque trilogy – this is,
as I have already pointed out, one of his distinguishing characteristics. To say he focuses on women is not to make him a feminist, but
his approach to women is not a hostile one. A comparison of the two
films in fact suggests that the stance of the female protagonists is not
so far apart in each case. Taberna commented that her film focused
on Yoyes's emotional life, and organisations such as ETA were merely

background noise from the relevant historical period (quoted in Rodríguez, 2002b: 161). The remarks are close in idea to Calparsoro's own comments that that film is a story of love – or better, a lack of love – than a film about terrorist operations (Fernández-Santos, 1997). Taberna's comments are borne out by her film, wherein Yoyes decides to abandon her commitment to ETA in favour of a quiet domestic life with her partner and child, and accepts an amnesty deal in order to do so. She plans to take up her studies again, but her assassination by ETA in front of her child ends all such hopes. Yoyes is based on an actual historical person, María Dolores González Katarain, one of the first women in ETA to rise to high rank; and Taberna is constrained to some extent by the events of Yoyes's real history. Yoyes (the film character) and Marrubi do not resemble each other in that Marrubi is a mere foot soldier in ETA and does not take the leadership role that Yoyes does. Nor does she have the access to education that Yoyes had: while Yoyes worked in exile for the United Nations and plans to return to her studies in Paris, Marrubi can only occupy a dead-end job in a laundry. Yet it is remarkable how Taberna's story dovetails with that of Marrubi: in both cases we are privy primarily to the character's emotional life and the renunciation of the causes for personal reasons. Rodríguez qualifies this identification of such renunciation with traditional femininity by pointing out that other ETA members have also followed this trajectory (2002b: 163), though I do not feel that this caveat is sufficient explanation.

If, as Rodríguez suggests, Taberna offers us 'a new way of understanding a female subjectivity by placing the protagonist in an environment that, previous to this film, had been occupied exclusively by male members of the organization' (Rodríguez, 2002b: 161), then it becomes arguable to what extent Calparsoro's version is not new. The most crucial difference, it would seem, would be the gender of the director, which brings back to the fore not only the question of auteurism but also that of a male gaze. Is a female director inevitably more feminist than a male one? Calparsoro and Taberna come remarkably close to each other in favouring the personal over the political, and allowing the woman's emotional and familial needs and desires to be prioritised over political commitment. This is in one sense hardly a feminist position for either director, recycling as it does once more the notion that women's concerns are those of the private and not the public sphere (though the equation of ETA with the public sphere is itself deeply problematic). On the other hand, the focus on the close emotional ties of Marrubi and Yoyes facilitates the blurring of boundaries between the public and the private, and the addressing of women's concerns as they fight for their nationalist cause.

To some extent, following the trajectory of women and Basque nationalism set out by Carrie Hamilton, the conservative nature of the woman in melodrama chimes in neatly with the conservatism of Basque nationalism. Hamilton comments that women were largely invisible in representations of ETA in the 1970s and 1980s, and remarks that this invisibility 'must be seen in the context of the general tone of nostalgia in ETA's writings ... a harking back to a "golden age" of stable social relations, epitomized by the mother at home. Thus, ETA's gender discourse of the 1960s and even much of the 1970s did not so much reflect women's realities as react against them, masking the important material changes in woman's social, economic and political roles' (Hamilton, 2000: 160). By the time of *A ciegas* women have become more high-profile, in films at least, taking a more decisive role (see, for instance, the character Maite in *El viaje de Arián*); yet this is not to deny the continuing glance backwards of some nationalist movements that implies the return of the woman to the home. While women's participation in nationalist movements has often been marginalised and rendered invisible, they have often functioned in symbolic terms as representative of the nation (Marianne for France, Britannia for the UK); in the Basque case, there has been a tendency to assume an authentic Basque society as matriarchal (although, as Hamilton observes, not unproblematically; Hamilton, 2000: 156–7). It is striking, then, that *A ciegas* indicates an underlying contradiction in this: it is Marrubi's return to the 'home' – that is to say, a valorising of her maternal role above that of her nationalist commitment – that jeopardises the operation in which she participates.

There is, however, a distinction between Marrubi's ability to renounce terrorism and survive, and the death meted out to other female terrorists for abandoning the struggle and betraying the cause. While we can argue that Marrubi escapes because another woman allows her to – Aitzpea, who not coincidentally is the one responsible for the child's care while Marrubi is on the run – such a reaction is not inevitable for women. We can contrast Marrubi's fate with *El viaje de Arián* where Arián's female colleague Maite executes her for her transgression. Marrubi and Aitzpea share in traditional womanly emotions, care for a child, while Maite and Arián do not. Thus it takes the collusion of another terrorist in valorisation of the personal above the political to facilitate an escape from terrorism. But, in terms of the trilogy as a whole, Marrubi may be also able to escape precisely because she renounces violence as a form of expression. Alex and Gabi before her do not perceive violence as something that can be taken up or dropped at will. Violence for them is simply an integral part of survival in the milieus in which they find themselves. It is not that Calparsoro himself wishes to move away from violence: as we shall see with his next two films, violence remains an integral part of his style. The sense of entrapment in the trilogy is nonetheless intricately entwined with a violent environment, and the renunciation of violence therefore signals the possibility of escape.

Calparsoro's habit in his first three films of grounding his story through one dominant character coincides with the usual procedure in films on Basque terrorism to individualise the story. This is already implied with the emphasis on women in the films discussed above, but it occurs with male terrorists, too (such as *El lobo* (The Wolf), Miguel Courtois, 2004; *Días contados*). ETA as a collective is rarely dealt with, and then usually in positive terms – for instance, *La fuga de Segovia* (The Flight from Segovia, Imanol Uribe, 1981). Thus any critique of violence is usually displaced on to the individual, and ETA as a collective is barely touched (see Davies, 2005). Weaknesses become individual weaknesses rather than problems of the collective position. This might be simply a move of safety on the part of directors since critique of ETA carries very real dangers: interviews with Calparsoro and Nimri hint at threats made concerning the release of *A ciegas* (see, for example, Fernández-Santos, 1997). In this way opting out of ETA becomes a personal affair that fudges over issues of political principle. Calparsoro claimed that the film was not a study of violence, commenting:

> He construido personajes que parecen sólidos, pero que son débiles, que no valen nada. Se trata de desmitificar a supuestos héroes que en realidad sólo son asesinos. Esa desmitificación era uno de mis propósitos y para ello me he tomado las licencias que he querido. (Fernández-Santos, 1997)

> (I have created characters who seem solid but who are weak and worthless. It's a case of demythifying so-called heroes who are really only murderers. This demythification was one of my aims and that is why I have taken the licence I have.)

Thus it is not just Marrubi, for all her centrality, who demonstrates dilemmas with commitment to ETA but all the terrorists who come in contact with her: they all reveal moments of vacillation. The weaknesses and dilemmas, however, are depicted in personal rather than political terms. In this, Calparsoro takes a similar line to most other directors who treat the Basque conflict in their films, but this line also coincides with his avowed purpose of showing the emotions rather than the rationality of a situation.

## The retreat from the political to the personal

The impulse towards melodrama in *A ciegas* is not so pronounced as in the previous two films – a sign perhaps that Calparsoro was about to move on – but Marrubi's emphasis on the personal echoes the woman's film once more. It also expresses the alienation from the nationalist enterprise: this alienation being another element of melodrama mentioned by Elsaesser (1987: 62). Calparsoro himself commented that the use of terrorism as a motif allowed him to develop extreme situations, uncontrollable passion, confusion and hidden desires. He defines a terrorist as a fascist disguised as a romantic or idealist who claims to fight against oppression ('A ciegas', 1997: 108). This functions as an effective description not only of radical nationalism but of melodrama. One could arguably find a melodramatic impulse in fact within nationalism itself – with its own links to Romanticism and the rise of the bourgeoisie – in which case it is hardly surprising that it frustrates women's desires, since much of melodrama functions both to make female desires apparent and to obstruct them. There is more generally a sense that the stagnation and frustration of life in the Basque country requires an exaggerated idealism and dream in order to look beyond the trap of life in Euskadi. Both nationalism and melodrama imply a conservative look back to a traditional order that has apparently been lost. Yet there is a movement away from the melodramatic impulse in the trilogy, as finally we have a character who does manage to escape the trap of frustrated dreams. Calparsoro comments on the fact that Marrubi finally escapes in the light of his whole trilogy within which *Salto* represents infancy, *Pasajes* puberty and *A ciegas* a maturity that facilitates Marrubi's escape (Heredero, 1997: 277). Heredero posits the idea of escape from the very beginning of the film, when in a small flash during the raid we see Marrubi without her hood. Calparsoro agrees, arguing that it demonstrates her division between being a terrorist and being a person. The director perceives terrorism as a form of trap within which people must struggle to find their own identity within a situation that they cannot escape (Heredero, 1997: 279).

Although Marrubi seeks to retreat from the armed struggle in favour of a new life with her partner and her son, she spends most of the film separated from them. Because of her initial transgression against the Basque cause, committed, as we have seen, precisely because of her maternal impulse, this impulse is denied as her son is taken away from her and put in the charge of a substitute mother, while a rift develops between her and her partner Mikel that will never be fully bridged. Calparsoro reinforces this element by a classic melodramatic example of people who appear fated not to meet. Mikel comes to Clemente's flat looking for Marrubi and leaves a message for her with the housekeeper Paquita. He tells Paquita that Marrubi should escape to France, that he loves her and that she should not worry about her son. As this conversation proceeds, Marrubi herself is hidden, watching and listening. Her fear that he had come to kill her in retribution has proved to be unfounded. She therefore tries to leave her hiding place, but the door is stuck; once she finally emerges from there, the front door also sticks. By the time she gets out, Mikel is at the bottom of a long staircase and can no longer hear her calling to him. She has missed him through what can only seem like fate.

10   The fragile and fearful Mikel

The putative nuclear family of this film is ultimately unsustain-able; and not only because of Marrubi's troubles. Calparsoro describes Mikel as embodying fragility and fear, scared to betray his ideology because that very ideology sustains his own identity; but, as Mikel cannot survive without Marrubi either, so his only solution is suicide (Demicheli, 1997). The suggestion of suicide comes from Mikel leaving behind his gun clip at his last meeting with Marrubi. She finds it and chases after him to give it back, but they are separated by the tracks running through the railway station where they have met, and she cannot hand Mikel back his ammunition before he is gunned down by police. In fact I believe the possibility of suicide is more tentative than Calparsoro's comment would imply, as it is unclear whether Mikel deliberately abandons his ammunition; and certainly Marrubi blames herself for his lack, calling to him across the rails that she did not spot the clip lying separately when she gave him his gun. Perhaps in the end the ambiguity does not matter. Whatever his intentions, the loss of ammunition signifies Mikel's unmanning in which Marrubi plays some sort of part, this emasculation reminiscent of Javi's impotence in *Salto al vacío*, which again prevents the realisa-tion of desire. It is ironic, then, that in *A ciegas* that we finally witness a successful sexual encounter, in contrast to the impotence of Javi with Alex and Gabi's impossible relationship with Carmina (in which we see no sexual encounter beyond a kiss). The emphasis here is less on the sexuality and more on the desperate nature of the encounter: Calparsoro himself argued that he wanted to stress emotion rather than eroticism at this point (Heredero, 1997: 282); and the encounter serves as an end of the relationship rather than the opening out of romantic possibilities. The irony of this finality is reinforced by the soft golden light which bathes the couple as they make love and the golden mist into which Mikel walks to meet his death.

As if these levels of irony were not enough, the setting of the station serves to emphasise still further the unbridgeable gap between melodramatic romance and despair. As Mikel falls to the ground under the impact of the bullets his head drapes over the platform and points to the railway tracks below. The tracks serve as a sign of escape, of elsewhere, of moving on; but in the end their symbolism proves illusory. The rails serve instead as a sign of separation: at this place of transition and movement Marrubi and Mikel are about to go their separate ways. And not only that but, since they are on opposite sides of the tracks, the couple are going to go in opposite directions, Mikel towards death and Marrubi towards a new life. The love scene runs parallel to the conversation between Aitzpea and a character known simply as the taxista or taxi driver (Javier Nogueiras) in the station café, so that after the love scene Calparsoro gives the film a chronological twitch to move the film back in time, this slight rupture occurring so that, according to Calparsoro, the love scene between Marrubi and Mikel becomes seamless, without intercutting a parallel sequence that breaks up the mood of the moment. This enables Marrubi to understand the significance of the two sequences once Mikel is shot dead (Heredero, 1997: 281). The result is that we perceive Mikel's death twice, from different viewpoints. This filmic device indicates that Mikel's death has different meanings for different people: to the other members of ETA this is the death in action of a colleague, while to Marrubi this underscores the end of her relationship with him and simultaneously the chance of a new life. These different meanings hint at a response to the critiques of Martí-Olivella and Gabilondo discussed in the introduction: not everything can be reduced to one nationalist meaning.

## Violence as female empowerment

Inserted into the terrorist plot is the incident where Marrubi is kidnapped by her employer. Marrubi works by day at a dry-cleaner's, and from the beginning we are aware of the interest she holds for Clemente, the head of the business. When she turns to him for help after the debacle of the failed mission, he responds by holding her prisoner and forcing her to dress up like a maid in a short dress and apron, wearing the traditional terrorist hood which normally acts as a disguise and mask but here serves merely to mark her out in the role of the terrorist she is ironically trying to abandon. A similar image of Marrubi was used as the poster image for the film and forms the background for the opening credit sequence. This use of the image complicates the film's negotiation of sex and violence. Palacios observes that Marrubi has felt suffocated by a masculine environment rendered perverse by its obsession with sex and violence, as exemplified by Mikel's refusal to renounce the armed struggle and Clemente's sexual desire. She flees the world of masculine violence for a more tranquil one (Palacios, 2006: 380). Yet the same image in publicity and in the credits draws attention precisely to Marrubi as perceived through this prism of masculine sex and violence, offering up the

perverse attraction of a *femme fatale* (and in this image, never repli-
cated exactly within the film's action and separated from its proper
place in the sequence in Clemente's home, Marrubi is pictured armed
with a gun that offers the hint of masculine power). This image,
used to attract us to the film, leads us astray, suggesting from the
outset that Marrubi will be empowered through these masculine
obsessions rather than rendered powerless as actually happens. On
the contrary, Marrubi takes power back not so much by seizing the
weapons symbolic of masculinity but by a gesture towards emasculation. Clemente requires her to fellate him, and she takes the opportunity to bite his penis and then take advantage of his consequent pain
to overpower him (and only then does she seize the gun). If Clemente
humiliated her, she proves equally sadistic in her turn; and the film
dwells for some minutes on two duplicate sequences when she forces
the housekeeper Paquita to imprison her employer in bubble wrap
and sticky tape, before then imprisoning Paquita likewise. The image
of Marrubi entrapping the couple offers another hint at the notion
that she and Calparsoro are ready to move on from the stagnation that
frustrated Alex and Gabi. If they are imprisoned in their own situations, Marrubi now imprisons others.

The interrelation of personal relationships with violence clearly
relates to the emphasis on violence in the previous two films,
suggesting Calparsoro's rather bleak outlook that there is always the
potential for violence in relations with other people, and that female
sexuality invites the possibility of abuse and exploitation. The potential
for violence is not confined to terrorism but appears at every level of
Basque society, so that – in contrast to the impression given in the
previous two films – violence is not ghettoised in lower-class areas
and situations but permeates the entire class structure. Indeed, the
unequal relations indicated by structures of class and gender always
imply violence. Terrorism encompasses the potential to destabilise the
prevailing order of power (though this does not guarantee that in turn
any new order brought about by such terrorism will be any better);
by renouncing terrorism Marrubi finds herself immersed back into
the old power structures in which she is abused by her employer. The
pervasiveness of violence thus provides some unity between this plot
strand and the main one of Marrubi's renunciation of terrorism. In his
discussion with Heredero Calparsoro describes Clemente as typical of
the bourgeois Basque unaffected by terrorism but basing his fantasies
upon it. When Heredero suggests that this section and the rest appear

to come from two different films, repeating the note of criticism mentioned at the beginning of the chapter, the director replies that he hopes this is not the case, as he argues that this sequence and the main terrorist theme is all part of the same world, two sides of the same coin (Heredero, 1997: 281). The incident with Clemente and Paquita serves also to destabilise a simplistic equation of Marrubi's renunciation of terrorism with a renunciation of violence per se. And thus this may suggest another element of movement away from the stagnation and despair of the previous two films: Marrubi overcomes the powerlessness that Alex and Gabi experience as part of an underclass.

## The absence of landscape

Of all the films in Calparsoro's oeuvre, *A ciegas* is the one that least insists on the landscape as a central element of the film. As we have seen, *Salto al vacío* and *Pasajes* utilise the industrial landscape to underscore the entrapment of Alex and Gabi. As we will also see in later chapters, Madrid forms a central and complex part of the themes of *Asfalto*, the landscape of Kosovo throws into relief the alienation of the Spanish soldiers of *Guerreros* and the idyllic setting of a suburb contributes to the horror of *Ausentes*. In *A ciegas* setting works rather differently. We do encounter outside landscape shots, but the central character Marrubi finds herself for the most part in gloomy and claustrophobic interiors. She has less opportunity than Alex or Gabi to roam around outside, trapped as she is for much of the film in the (almost literally) suffocating atmosphere of the laundry or imprisoned within Clemente's home. This contrast proves ironic, since in the end she is better able to escape her surroundings and her situation. Another interior in which Marrubi spends a fair length of time in the film is the safe house to which she and Mikel go after she has shot Eneko, and where we first encounter Aitzpea. Almost immediately this interior setting will prove to be threatening to Marrubi and her care for her son; as she goes to talk to the child as he settles down to sleep, Mikel reveals to Aitzpea what Marrubi has done, and Aitzpea responds by seizing a gun from Mikel, telling him he cannot stay there and that 'it's got to be done', hinting at execution of Marrubi for her transgression. Mikel's own response is to take the child away. This interior is a setting for a threat of death and the separation of mother and son; and thus in the first instance for Marrubi's oppression and the frustration of her desire. Yet Marrubi proves equal to any threat to her own life by wresting the gun from Aitzpea and later escaping through the window as explosives go off and the police raid the place.

When Marrubi does venture outside she continues to appear trapped, enclosed by the streets outside the laundry as she talks tensely to Mikel, psyching herself up for the raid with Eneko that is about to take place; or later in the confined street in which the protest against Eneko's death takes place. By ensuring Eneko's death Marrubi has indirectly caused the chaos of this scene, as she seems to realise, lifting her hand to her mouth in horror and then staring at the posters of Eneko on the walls, as firebombs are thrown and the scene mounts to a new level of claustrophobia as smoke begins to envelop everything. The posters of Eneko reinforce the symbolic nature of the way in which the walls enclose her, as if the nationalist process has done the same. But nonetheless Marrubi weaves her way through the crowd, often going significantly in the opposite direction to them. The scene closes with an ironic juxtaposition of the glow of the fires caused by the riots with the Christmas lights hanging above the streets, which could be interpreted in a variety of ways. The juxtaposition might suggest a loss of Christmas spirit, of reconciliation and peace; but they might also suggest the faint but visible hope for Marrubi amidst the murk of nationalist violence. The Christmas lights have their counterpart in the Christmas tree that formed a part of the background of the nursing mother, the sight of which impelled Marrubi to resist such violence.

One place Marrubi rarely ventures is the countryside and, on the one occasion she does so when raiding the house with Eneko, her incursion is marked by her decisive renunciation of fighting for the Basque cause. As I discussed earlier, rural landscape provides a routine backdrop for film plots related to issues of Basque nationalism. In *A ciegas* Calparsoro ventures for the first time into the countryside, but he does not let Marrubi linger there for long. The fact that her transgression takes place in the countryside underscores her rejection of nationalism, and we never see her there again. But we do find Mikel and Aitzpea in the country, suggesting their continued immersion in nationalism. Their hideout is here, where they quarrel over Marrubi's fate. Aitzpea accuses Mikel of lacking the balls to see to Marrubi and says that she will take care of her, implying she is more determined and committed than he is. Ironically, of course, she will allow Marrubi and her son to leave together peacefully; but here in the country it is easier to talk the tough terms of the armed struggle. The scene suggests the intransigence of the conflict within this rural Arcadia, though it may also imply a Basque nation divided against itself. But the rural Arcadia can also be faked. Marrubi attempts to call another member of her group, but the call is picked up by the police, who attempt to trick her into giving information away. She is not fooled, gives a false name and hangs up. But meanwhile the police have taped the sounds of Clemente and his housekeeper Paquita, muffled by gags. When the police hear the sound they assume the noise is of cows (which we could hear in the background in the earlier scene), and this leads them directly to Mikel and Aitzpea's (now empty) hideout. In contrast to earlier comments by critics that deny the reality of Calparsoro's urban Basque environment, it is the countryside that proves most easily faked. The fakery does, however, put the police on Mikel's trail; thus the countryside contributes to the death of a nationalist, whilst Marrubi, who stays in the town, escapes.

The countryside is also the breathtaking backdrop to what turns out to be a scene of dilemma and indecision, as the taxista has a rendez-vous with another man on the bridge of an isolated river valley. The other man refuses to be involved in whatever the taxista has planned, since he knows him to be part of an ETA operations team. The taxista denies this, but since we have previously seen him with Marrubi and Aitzpea, and will later see him talking to the latter in the station café, his denial rings hollow. The scene ends with the taxista standing alone on the bridge looking out unseeing at the rural scenery before him while the camera pans across it. The equation of the rural with the nationalist struggle thus becomes further entangled with deception and indecision. If the taxista is aware of the symbolism of the Arcadia at which he looks, it is one already lost to him, as he is already on the path that will lead to his death at the café. He will in fact be shot by his own side: Aitzpea shoots him in order to make good her own escape. This use of the Basque landscape brings a contemporary edge to the saying *et in arcadia ego*: this beautiful landscape is redolent of death. If Marrubi is to survive, then, she must avoid the rural. By lacking the country landscape with which the other characters have a link, she manages to survive and transcend the nationalist struggle.

## Coordination of colour and camera

For the most part, *A ciegas* employs the same drab colours that were found previously in *Pasajes*, with a strong emphasis on beiges and browns. Much of this colour is carried by Marrubi herself, dressed in the opening scenes in a dull beige that matches the dull brown of Clemente's clothing. Sometimes, however, the browns give way to warm golden glows that usually serve to highlight melodramatic moments for Marrubi. The house she and Eneko raid is suffused with a warm golden glow that idealises the domestic scene and contrasts strongly with the dark, wet night through which Marrubi creeps to get to the house. Similarly, as we have already noted, the station in which she and Mikel make love for the last time is bathed in a golden mist. Other occasional notes of colour are detectable, such as the greeny glass of Mikel's car, which is a throwback to the car of *Salto al vacío*, or the sickly green of Clemente's home. The colour scheme of the entire film therefore contrasts strongly with the opening credits of stark red and yellow pixels, which first form an eye that is recognisably Nimri's trademark (the balaclava she is wearing serves to frame the eye more distinctly). Across the pixels flash images suggesting violence such as guns and bullets, and then images of Mikel and Marrubi in cold blue-black and white. The opening credits hint at the potential colour and violence behind Marrubi's beige façade, repeating the contrast in bright and dull colours found in *Pasajes*, but to different ends. The browns and beiges in which Marrubi dresses inevitably distance her from the aggressive look of Alex and the childlike clothing of Gabi, and reinforces the notion of Marrubi as a woman with family responsibilities. There is an ironically implied contrast with Marrubi's name ('marrubi' is the Basque word for strawberry, with its connotations of redness: as I commented in relation to *Pasajes*, red is a colour hardly used by Calparsoro). Since in the previous films, and particularly with *Salto*, critics responded strongly to Nimri's embodiment of the protagonists, the drabness of Nimri's character now may have had something to do with the cooler reception given to *A ciegas*.

The soundtrack on the whole bypasses the slow, mournful strings that provided the soundtrack to *Pasajes*. The opening credit music, however, begins with fairly rapid, menacing string music which in turn gives way to a mixture of the chorus and rapid rock music, providing virtually a music bridge from *Pasajes*. The string motif reappears at intervals to suggest the tension between Marrubi and the other characters; and often as a bridge from one scene to another (including a slower use of strings as the scenes to the countryside from a Marrubi imprisoned by Clemente). For the first time Calparsoro makes a more conventional use of the strings, too, as they underscore Mikel's speech to Paquita that expresses his love for Marrubi, and lead up to the shoot-out at the station and as Mikel dies. An early use of rock music comes as Marrubi and Mikel get into the car to set out for the initial ETA assignment, suggesting Marrubi's transformation from downtrodden employee to a woman of action. It is used similarly for a shot of terrorists preparing for action as they watch television, during the street riot in response to Eneko's death, and as people flee from the station shoot-out, offering a common equation of rock music with violent action. Billie Holliday is heard once more, singing 'All of Me' as Clemente humiliates Marrubi at gunpoint. The soundtrack of *A ciegas* thus has strong similarities to that of *Salto* but the use of strings is new; and they differ from the use made of them in *Pasajes*, suggesting a more conventional link between music and emotion than Iglesias's score for *Pasajes* offered. This might imply that the soundtrack of *Pasajes* was highly influenced by the involvement of the El Deseo production company and Almodóvar's musical collaborator.

In terms of camera and editing, the swirling camera of *Salto* has by now been left far behind in favour of editing from various angles, such as in the raid on the house, where the characters involved are shot from different vantage points. A device that Calparsoro uses here and nowhere else is the thematic linking of scenes by way of the reporter who speaks live from the hospital where Eneko lies dying. The reporter connects up the disparate groups of characters – Marrubi, Clemente, a terrorist cell – who all watch his reports. In the first instance of this, we cut from the separatists watching the television back to the reporter, then to Clemente who watches the same report as the separatists while looking in the same direction as them, equating him with them. It underlines the suggestion that he carries the potential for oppression of Marrubi just as they do; and that the different sectors of Basque society are not as distinct as they might like to think. *A ciegas* also unusually offers small comic touches such as the eyeline match of Clemente, now watching the television while bound and gagged, with a shot of a pig in a pen (as part of a programme on traditional Basque culture): the match equates the two. A more contrasting match of camera movements links the film proper to the opening credits, which end with the camera panning down a pixellated pair of legs, reaching the shoes, and then cutting to Marrubi's feet and a slow pan up to her face. This is the first time Calparsoro used such matching shots and this, along with the loss of the swooping steadycam of the two previous films, makes for a more staid, but also more deliberate use of the camera that fits with the suffocation of the film's slower pace. Calparsoro also breaks slightly from the straightforward chronological pattern of *cine social* with the time overlap of scenes at the railway station (so that we see Mikel die twice), and the insertion of the shot of Marrubi beneath her mask, which could not have happened in reality. Another device which contradicts the apparent realism of the film is the framing of Marrubi's face in the central diamond-shaped window pane of the door to the room in which Clemente imprisons her. She broke this pane to make contact with Paquita and yell abuse at Clemente, but in reality she would surely have broken a lower pane of glass (she has to stand on tiptoe to reach the central pane). The lower panes of glass do not, however, provide the same opportunities for good framing.

The camera and editing suggest a more concerted design to *A ciegas* than some critics were willing to recognise, yet it is nonetheless true that the film is more loosely structured than the previous films, and possibly with some redundancies: the kidnapping section in particular could easily have been shorter. More than any other of Calparsoro's films, *A ciegas* confronts the demands of critics for a good screenplay and good plot. Plot can be problematic in terms of social realism, since reality is more episodic than narrative, so that the high value placed on plot by many Spanish critics may be counter-productive with this genre. However, *Salto* and *Pasajes* possess firmer narrative structures than does this film which, given its subject matter, probably needed it more than they did. *A ciegas* therefore lacks some of the richness of the previous two films – another sign, perhaps, that Calparsoro was ready to move on from his Basque settings. Nonetheless, the film demonstrates a level of complexity missed by some of the critics, which challenges some of the tenets and clichés of Basque cinema; it also demonstrates the development of Calparsoro's craft in terms of theme and technique. To take his craft still further, it had become time to stretch it beyond the confines of the claustrophobic Basque settings to new scenes and new scenarios.

# 6

# *Asfalto*: violence *à trois*

Just as Marrubi abandoned the armed struggle for Basque nationalism in *A ciegas*, so Calparsoro himself left behind a decaying Basque
landscape for new settings: central Madrid in *Asfalto* and its suburbs
in *Ausentes*, and the countryside of Kosovo for *Guerreros*. For his next
two films he also diluted the emphasis on a central female protagonist
in preference to a more ensemble cast (though the emphasis on the
female protagonist would return with Julia in *Ausentes*). Nonetheless
the change in approach with *Asfalto*, the film immediately following
the Basque trilogy, did not mean the rejection of all the elements that
previously characterised Calparsoro's work. Prior to his making of
*Asfalto* Calparsoro was asked what he intended to do next after the
trilogy; he replies that he would continue to emphasise both action
and feeling and to place characters in extreme situations, with a new
focus on the couple (Heredero, 1997: 283). And to a great extent that
is what *Asfalto* offers. The characters of the film live lives at a frenetic
pace on the criminal fringes of Madrid, surviving through drug deals
and robberies, at odds with their elders and occasionally with each
other and not averse to using violence to express their emotions.

Critics as usual offered a mixed reaction to the film, but it garnered
a fair amount of praise, getting a better reception than *A ciegas*, and
with some justice as it is a better film. Alfonso Santos Gargallo hails
*Asfalto* as the best so far of Calparsoro's work (Santos Gargallo, 2000:
52), with subtle and complex characterisation: 'Calparsoro tiene las
ideas muy claras sobre el origen de los conflictos humanos, que
sitúa en los márgenes de libertad de cada individuo que se acaban
donde empiezan los del prójimo' (Calparsoro has clear ideas about the
origin of human conflict, situated in the margins where one person's
freedom ends and another's begins; 53). He does, however, argue

that life lived constantly at the extreme edge means that the most climatic moments of the film lose their intensity, such as when Chino destroys the florist's window with a baseball bat (53–4). Jesús Palacios is positively rapturous about the film, arguing that *Asfalto* demanded not so much film critique but an act of love in the private projection room of our dreams (Palacios, 2000: 14). This remark reminds us of Calparsoro's own belief that cinema was there to assault us and inspire our emotions in the dark of the projection room: he and Palacios concur here that cinema is an emotional rather than intellectual exercise. The gap of a few years did not cool Palacios's response; he would later observe that *Asfalto* was the summit of Calparsoro's film noir of youth (Palacios, 2006: 380), reminding him of the French *polars* of the 1970s with figures such as Alain Delon and Jean-Paul Belmondo (381). Discussing the film primarily in terms of film noir, Palacios argued that *Asfalto* was the closest the Spanish film industry had even approached to a masterwork in the genre, and it was a pity that he had not matched his achievement since then (381). Since Palacios is talking primarily about film noir, and Calparsoro has since gone on to make films in other genres, this criticism is not as cutting as it might seem. Rubén Jardín also argues that *Asfalto* surpasses the Basque trilogy (Jardín, 2006: 398). C. L. claims that the thriller aspect of the film is absurd and inconsistent, and recycles the usual complaint about Calparsoro's screenplays, even though this time the director collaborated on the script with Santiago Tabernero (with the added input of Frank Palacios). Nevertheless, he believes that Calparsoro knows how to film (C. L. particularly liked the shots of legs and cars), and summarises Calparsoro in the following terms:

> Guste o no, Daniel Calparsoro es un cineasta atrevido en el panorama español. Como un toro y con una voluntad admirable, hace todo lo que se propone y, contra crítica, consejos y resultados de taquilla, en menos de cinco años ha estrenado cuatro largometrajes. (C. L., 2000: 80)

> (Like it or not, Daniel Calparsoro is a daring director in the Spanish landscape. Like a bull, with admirable willpower, he achieves all he sets out to do and, against all criticism, advice and box-office results, he has released four feature films in less than five years.)

This is a fine example of backhanded criticism, in which C. L. admires Calparsoro for his sheer perverseness in going his own way against all advice and all evidence to the contrary. He has, however, noticed that for all his perverseness Calparsoro has managed to direct four feature-length films in a context that is not propitious to him. C. L. puts this down to sheer force of will but, as many directors know to their cost, this does not get films made by itself. Calparsoro has achieved *something* beyond simple wilfulness, though this review does not specify what it might be; C. L. concludes by acknowledging *Asfalto* as a must-see film for no other reason than to induce polemic, which harks back to Corrigan's comments discussed in the introduction and the idea that auteurism serves to destabilise. Polemic will do this, but so does not only Calparsoro's insistence on going his own way against the grain of the Spanish film scene but also his success in doing so, with four feature-length films.

Although critical reception of *Asfalto* was not, then, unanimously positive, it still had good things to say about Calparsoro's achievements. Reasons why this might be so are speculative. It is not enough, I believe, to say that *Asfalto* simply is a better film, since it stands accused of the fault of a poor screenplay similar to the previous films. *Asfalto* certainly is a better film in terms of a more polished technique, suggesting that Calparsoro was continuing to learn his craft, but the following two films, *Guerreros* and *Ausentes*, are equally polished if not better and yet, as we shall see in subsequent chapters, *Guerreros* got heavier press coverage but a more equivocal response, while *Ausentes* gained a fair amount of negative criticism. Still, the fact that Calparsoro's film techniques move away from the grungier end of the spectrum imply a new level of attainment in the eyes of some critics. Another factor that might contribute to the distinction between this film and the later ones is that now we are in 2000 when the positive perception of Spanish cinema after its resurgence in 1995 still lingers. By the time of *Guerreros* we are in 2002 and writers on Spanish cinema are beginning to perceive a new crisis in the industry, which might in turn impact on reviews (see, for instance, Huerta, 2006; as I discuss in the chapter on *Ausentes*, the later film is held up as an example of the low state to which Spanish cinema has been reduced). A further factor in the more positive evaluation of *Asfalto* could be the setting. We have moved away from the Basque Country, a country or region that many Spaniards identify with a nagging and intermittently violent conflict and a claim to independence which some Spaniards at least would refute. And we have moved to Madrid, the capital, where many of these film critics work. It might even be because, after three films told unremittingly from the point of view of an angry and marginalised young woman, the point of view has now become more diffuse. The critique of *Asfalto* comes at a time when there is still a sense of confidence in a youthful industry that has now consolidated itself. Calparsoro appears to have moved closer to this sense, coinciding with the mood in the industry.

## The central trio

One clear reason for the film's comparative success with the critics was the central trio of Lucía (Najwa Nimri), Chino (Gustavo Salmerón) and Charly (Juan Diego Botto). Palacios describes them lyrically as spirits made flesh, perfect images of perfect bodies; intertwined in a triangular relationship that is epic, homoerotic and pansexual (Palacios, 2000: 14). Calparsoro himself describes the film as his most sensual and romantic so far, although he implicitly contradicts Palacios in saying that the story is not an epic but rather is about how sensuality can be found anywhere – including, presumably, the back streets of Madrid (Casanova, 2000: 46). One could perhaps take a midway stance between the two to say that the triangle of love between the three characters offers them an extra dimension that prevents them being simply mired down in marginality as the women of the Basque trilogy were. This would be in keeping with Calparsoro's plan that *Asfalto* would be a film in which people enjoyed themselves rather than suffered along with the characters; a film in which he provides more light, more love and more happiness (Trasobares, 1999). Nonetheless, this extra dimension offered through the triangular love relationship is ultimately unsustainable and it is not available to all as a channel of escape. While at the end of the film Lucía and Charly eventually escape Madrid together, Chino abruptly abandons them and heads back to the city.

The fact that Calparsoro and the critics combine in their enjoyment of the triangular relationship should not blind us to the fact that from the beginning it is steeped in tension. Initially, Charly finds Lucía an intrusion on the partnership he has with Chino; Charly and she quarrel when she wants more money from the planned drug raid on a Frenchman's flat. That there may be an element of homoeroticism in the relationship between Charly and Chino is offered as a possibility early on. As Chino and Lucía make love, the camera cuts back frequently to Charly in the next room nervously drinking beer, then spying on the lovers until he can bear it no longer and bursts in on them. Charly's thoughts are opaque here, although his voyeurism implies envy and a desire either to join the lovers or replace one of them. The hostility of his interaction with Lucía in the sequences before and immediately after the lovemaking scene suggests that she is in the way, thus in turn implying a homoerotic desire for Chino. These early scenes posit Chino as an object of desire over which Charly and Lucía will fight each other. It does not prepare us for the final outcome in which Chino himself slips out of the equation and Charly and Lucía desire each other; unless perhaps we are familiar with René Girard's concept of the mimetic triangle in his book *Deceit, Desire and the Novel* (1972) in which the rivalry of two men for the same woman forges a strong bond between the two of them that eventually can bypass the woman entirely. This version of the triangular structure has been turned on one side in *Asfalto*, so that Chino comes to occupy the position of the woman.

Girard's mimetic triangle tells us of the men but leaves the woman as a cipher rather than a person intricately involved in the three-way relationship: we hear nothing of how she might react to the growing bond between the men. In *Asfalto* we do, however, witness Chino's growing unease as Charly and Lucía grow closer. Charly starts to make moves on Lucía surprisingly quickly given the hostility he demonstrates in the early sequences; his abrupt change is slightly jarring. It might come about because of the heist at the Frenchman's flat that precedes his new attitude; Chino shoots the Frenchman, panics and leaves, thinking he has killed him. Lucía stays and helps Charly to find the drugs they were looking for, making the robbery a successful operation. When the three agree to meet up later at a café, Charly and Lucía make the rendezvous but Chino does not. Charly's transference of interest to Lucía might therefore come about because she demonstrates that she has the 'balls' where Chino does not, and thus she rather than he is Charly's partner.

The later sexual scene *à trois* in Charly's home, for all the beauty of expression of love between the three characters, demonstrates Chino's increasing unhappiness both at being made to share Lucía with Charly and his own increasing marginalisation in the relationship. Chino suspects (quite accurately) that something was going on between the other two when he arrived at Charly's place and accuses Charly of this, but Lucía immediately walks in and initiates the sexual threesome, saying that she refuses to choose between the two men. Calparsoro does not show the sex scene in full: instead we cut from its early stages to the aftermath, as Chino lies awake and unhappy.

Although Lucía then tells him that they make a good threesome, afterwards she and Charly sit outside together to look at the stars while Chino stays inside to ring his brother for help and comfort. When he later joins the other two they are sitting inside a large abandoned tyre, in which there is no room for Chino as well. Further tension appears when, after Charly goes to prison following a drugs bust, Lucía and Chino plan to set up home in their own flat but Lucía sees Charly in secret. Yet Charly and Lucía are at odds once he leaves prison and she tells him to leave her and Chino alone. Chino, learning about the secret meetings between the other two, spies on Charly at his home. The suggestion of a close bond that verges on the homoerotic does not disappear, however, with the increasing convergence of Charly and Lucía. During the drug deal in Charly's home, the police arrive and Chino is shot in the confusion. Charly grabs hold of Chino in a stance almost as if the two were lovers, as he drags him to safety. Nonetheless, the underlying tension emerges here, too, as Chino blames him for the mess and they start to quarrel and fight in the midst of all the mayhem. (In fact Chino rather than Charly is more directly to blame, as his earlier phone call to his brother brought about the latter's intervention and the consequent gunfight). These elements, taken together, suggest the triangle as an unhappy and unsatisfying combination, if not devoid of its moments of affection and potential for erotic pleasure.

On the other hand, the three characters demonstrate loyalty to each other in preference to apparently closer ties such as family. Chino is furious to find that his own brother Antonio (Alfredo Villa) bears the responsibility for setting up both Charly (twice) and Lucía, and this brings him to join the other two once more for the final scenes of the car crash and the flight from Madrid. The coming together again of the trio combines with Lucía's final rejection of her mother Clarita (Antonia San Juan): Clarita's angry reaction at this rejection suggests that she, too, was in competition for Lucía's love and has lost. But the new formulation does not last. As the three protagonists drive away from Madrid, the car stops suddenly and Chino gets out, says an affectionate but wordless goodbye to the other two and starts to walk back while Charly and Lucía carry on in their original direction. This sudden breaking of the trio, after their reconciliation, can surprise us. Calparsoro explained the ending by saying that Chino is a more traditional character than the other two and is thus unable to share; he does not possess the same free spirit that they do.[1] Earlier he remarked that in *Asfalto* he assumes that his characters will find a way out of their situation (Casanova, 2000; 46) – thus contrasting with Alex and Gabi, who remain trapped in their situations. The ability to escape forms a crucial part of the director's more upbeat approach to urban youth in *Asfalto*. But if the characters escape they do not do it together. Love may or may not therefore be shown to exist on an epic scale, but *Asfalto* does reveal it to be also competitive, not only between the central trio itself but also between that trio and those that surround them, the families of Lucía and Chino.

Tensions between characters are of course an integral part of ensemble playing (and will prove very obvious in the next film *Guerreros*). If we are talking of an ensemble, however, the character of Lucía stands out a little more prominently than the other two. Those familiar with Calparsoro's work would already be inclined to give Lucía more attention because she is played by Nimri, who also played the dominating protagonists of the three previous films. One might also argue that we notice Lucía more because she functions more overtly as an object to be looked at. Javier Ángulo observes that while we are used to seeing her as introverted and disturbing, in *Asfalto* she has an expressive role that allows us to appreciate her physical attractiveness, which her previous films did not (Ángulo, 2000: 33). Lucía's high heels and short skirts make her more overtly sexy than the punk look of Alex, Gabi's childlike demeanour and the generally drab clothing of Marrubi, whose one excursion into overtly sexual clothing, the maid's outfit, suggests exploitation and abuse far more than sensuousness. Lucía as a desirable sexual object features strongly in an early sequence in a nightclub, where the camera introduces us to her in a low-angle shot with her legs centre frame, ending in short shorts. As she walks slowly and seductively the camera follows behind her offering virtually a fetish of her legs to match the shoe fetish of *Pasajes*. Calparsoro thus presents Lucía as an object of desire, emphasised further by the cut to the next sequence as Chino and Charly wait for her. Nimri herself said she wanted a role that stressed her body and liked the short skirts and high heels, though she also expressed concern that the provocative look might distract from the emotions she was trying to express. She wanted to be seen as more than an attractive body (Ángulo, 2000: 33). The focus on Lucía distracts from the Girardian structure of the trio outlined above, since it appears that she must function as the object over which men will compete. But such an assumption also disregards Lucía as an active agent, which

11    Lucía and Charly say goodbye to Chino

was one of the reasons why Nimri said she liked the role so much. She comments that Lucía is not simply a survivor but someone who loves life and who does exactly what she wants to do (Ángulo, 2000: 33).

The prominence of Nimri/Lucía, then, coupled with the characterisation, comes across as a development of the earlier focus on three active female subjects in the trilogy, rather than a radical break with it. The male characters become more dominant than they were previously, and the female character functions more overtly as sexual object as well as subject; but Calparsoro finds a new way of figuring female subjectivity, now involved in equal and reciprocal relations rather than remaining ultimately alone as in *Salto al vacío* and *Pasajes* and, to a lesser extent, *A ciegas* (since Marrubi does at least have her son, though we barely see any developed bond between them). The melodramatic halo around the women of the trilogy has, however, diminished if not vanished altogether. Since *Asfalto* deals with reciprocal if tense relationships the possibility for fulfilment and romance, as we shall see in the discussion of setting below, counteracts the frustration of desire we saw in the trilogy. The satisfaction of desire in the melodramatic sense requires at least one other person to achieve it, and hence this move away from melodramatic frustration is marked by Calparsoro with the move to an ensemble.

## The institutionalisation of violence

Although Calparsoro previously gained a reputation for an excessive use of violence, the actual acts of violence of the films are graphic but few. What is more pervasive is an atmosphere of such desperation that it becomes saturated with an ever-present potential for violence. In this respect *Asfalto* demonstrates a change in approach. Calparsoro himself observes that the characters do not suffer the consequences of violence, and while in *Salto* the violence was not pleasurable – you did not desire to see it – in *Asfalto* there is more pleasure to be found in the violence, which is thus more superficial and more American. While in the earlier films he was as much interested in the aftermath of the violence as violence in itself, here there is no aftermath: the characters commit violent acts and simply move on.[2] Certainly it is hard not to take pleasure in some aspects of the film's violence. Chino's brutal destruction of the florist's shop may seem excessive, but it is also cathartic for both him and for us as he takes revenge on all the double-crosses that have emanated from the criminals (including his own brother) who lurk literally behind the shop's façade. The car crash offers other pleasures. The film opens with flash forward shots of the crash but no explanation for how the crash has come about, thus presenting it as a mystery which is later solved as the crash repeats itself in the chronological course of events; and we take pleasure in the resolution of the mystery. Calparsoro shares this device with the better known car crash of *Amores perros* (Alejandro González Iñárritu, 2000), although the two films appeared too close together in time for one to have influenced the other. We can find also a perverse pleasure in car crashes (an excessive example is the multiple pile-up of police cars in *The Blues Brothers* (John Landis, 1980)), so the re-run of the crash in *Asfalto* heightens the pleasure. The use of violence in the Frenchman's flat, however, reminds us more of the desperate forms of violence that occurred in the Basque trilogy; Calparsoro has not left this entirely behind. Nonetheless, we can perceive a shift from the violence typical of *cine social* to that which provides more evident spectacle, and therefore provides a step towards violence as both social critique *and* as spectacle that typifies some contemporary war films, of which Calparsoro's next film *Guerreros* will be an example.

Another notable shift is the increasing emphasis on violence as not simply part of a marginalised culture but as institutionalised at all levels. This will persist in the depiction of the Spanish army in

*Guerreros* and is already hinted at in *A ciegas*, where the violence of marginalisation is linked to the violence traced through the Basque nationalist project. Basque nationalist violence forms part of a spectrum of institutionalised Basque politics. In a similar way, the violence of the trio in *Asfalto* blends seamlessly between criminality and institutionalisation in that Chino commits violent crime along with his friends, but he also joins the police. His brother Antonio, also a policeman, typifies this blurring of boundaries between law, criminality and violence. He conspires with the drug dealers in the florist shop to frame Lucía (the man who robs her of her drug money is later to be found in the back of the shop talking to Antonio). Likewise, when Chino and Antonio chase a drug dealer through the Retiro park, Antonio catches the dealer but then removes something from him and lets him go, also suggesting complicity.

Chino straddles this border between crime, the law and violence. Of the three characters he might arguably be considered the most violent, with the shooting of the Frenchman, the destruction of the florist's and the car crash all immediately due to him. His relationship with his brother is also confrontational and occasionally gives way to violence. One reason for this might be that Chino is also the tensest of the trio as he is gradually sidelined within it. Another reason might be that he takes after his brother. At one point as Chino and Lucía move boxes into their proposed new home, Antonio grabs her round the throat when Chino is not in the room, and tells her he will not let her ruin Chino's life. Later in the sequence Chino and Lucía quarrel: he hits her, and she tells him he is becoming more like his brother. But the violence may also arise from Chino's role in the police (to which both brothers belong, indicating that the violence may come just as much from there as from blood affinity). Chino acts as the convergence of individual, rebellious violence and violence as patriarchal and institutional in his dual function as both young delinquent and as the policeman supposedly tracking down such delinquency. Once Chino becomes a cop his new career acts as a marker of the increasing gap opening up between him and Lucía. They can no longer share in the same escapades; he expresses to her his worry that if she keeps on with her drug deals sooner or later their paths will cross. She reminds him that her drug deals paid the deposit on their new flat which will aid their escape from their respective families. This contradictory position, reinforced by his presence at drug deals simultaneously with his desire to go into the narcotics division of the force, creates another level of tension within the character. When Chino first goes home after the shooting of the Frenchman we see him hide his gun, and as he does so the camera dwells momentarily on his bandaged wrist in close-up. Calparsoro never explains the bandage but it offers us the possibility that Chino's expressions of violence include self-harm or attempted suicide, a small but telling indication of the pressures he lives under.

Chino's role in the police is marked by the desire for excessive control on the part of Antonio, who sees Chino's career as utterly opposed to his life with Charly and Lucía. He is right in one sense, as the job of policeman functions as one of the elements that eventually separate Chino from his friends. But the criminality of the trio might look all the more attractive for its potential for liberation from patri-archal control. Although Antonio is Chino's brother he sees himself very much as the latter's substitute father. He not only lectures Chino about the company he keeps – the main reason for his set-up of Charly and Lucía is to separate them from his brother – but also nags him to do his studying. Antonio is keen to see Chino enter the force as a reinforcement of family ties and also a sort of new brotherhood; once Chino has become a cop Antonio complains that he does not spend enough time getting to know his colleagues. He also helps to smooth Chino's path towards the narcotics division through his connections in the force. But underlying Antonio's concern is a well of violence that occasionally spills over into his interactions with his brother, such as when he finds Chino's hidden gun and holds it to Chino's face, which prompts a physically violent quarrel, or when he threatens Chino at gunpoint as the latter attempts to drive away with his friends. The fight between the brothers eventually impels Antonio to put his foot on the accelerator and propel the car at suicidal speed into its crash. In the relationship between the two brothers, then, the institutions of family, patriarchy and the law combine to produce virtual fratricide.

*Asfalto* thus suggests that violent degradation is not the monopoly of urban youth but endemic of a society that is rotten to the very core of its institutional structures. The violence comes primarily as a result of the interaction of urban youth with these structures: outside of them the violence is less frequent. As Nimri said of her own character, Lucía can make her own way through life without needing a gun; this was an essential part of her character on which Nimri insisted (Ángulo, 2000: 33). Charly resorts to vicious kicking of the Frenchman once the latter starts to regain consciousness, but otherwise uses violence very little: certainly not once we have learnt that Chino plans to join the police, when the tension between the law and criminality come into play. From that point on, violence emanates from the ambiguous relationship between Chino, crime and the law. If tension was the principal outcome of the erotic triangle posited in the previous section, then violence is the outcome of this second triangular structure.

The notion of crime as endemic in society is of course hardly a new perspective. We can find it in the veiled critique of Francoism of the *nuevo cine español*, in European social-realist cinema, and also in Hollywood blockbusters (though in the latter there is often a hero to clean house). One might perceive a danger with *Asfalto* that Calparsoro is gradually running out of steam with the vein of violence, suggesting that this element of his style acts as a constraint rather than a basis for innovative cinema. On the other hand it might also suggest a retention of auteurist style while converging with other forms of cinema, and in particular the genre cinema that would encapsulate Calparsoro's next offerings: the war film and horror. Both Palacios (2000 and 2006) and Jardín (2006) discuss *Asfalto* in terms of the thriller and contemporary noir. I do not myself consider the film as an example of noir, and do not include it in my own overview of the genre in contemporary Spain (see Davies, 2007), though the boundaries of this particular genre are notoriously hard to define. There is a better case for seeing the film as a thriller, but to see it in these terms does not mean we have left the *cine social* of the trilogy behind completely. We can also make connections between the characters of *Asfalto* and the heroines of the trilogy who seek to escape the marginality in which they find themselves, and the tensions of urban living in all four films. This goes against Kinder's proposed divide between the violence in Spanish cinema and that in Hollywood cinema discussed in the introduction: as I observed there, the use of violence has become more diffuse since then. But it also serves to mark Calparsoro as auteur even though the use of violence has subtly changed in *Asfalto*, and Kinder noted this use of violence as an element in defining the Spanish auteur historically. So Calparsoro's work by this stage may resist previous perceptions that might define and pigeonhole it, and in doing so it participates in the blurring of boundaries between Spain and Hollywood carried out by other directors at this time (see Allinson, 1997). And yet the trademark of social-realist violence that characterised the trilogy can still be used at this point as a prism through which to view his films. Thus through his use of violence he both challenges older notions of the Spanish auteur and simultaneously reinforces them.

## Madrid as setting

*Salto al vacío* and *Pasajes* made significant play with the industrial landscape of the Basque Country: *A ciegas*, however, drew on the Basque landscape far less. Much of the action of that film takes place in dark interiors with few identifying features, suggesting both claustrophobia and anonymity. If such settings suggest that the notion of entrapment in the Basque trilogy has become unbearable, then the landscape of *Asfalto* suggests a release, a freedom in keeping with the more upbeat tone of the film. *Asfalto* is set in Madrid. Calparsoro said on commencing shooting that he wanted the whole city of Madrid to form part of his film (Trasobares, 1999), and at the end he dedicated the film to the city itself. He likes Madrid, finding it welcoming, sensual and full of an unusual light. Its open nature, free from self-absorption, reflects the open nature of the film (Casanova, 2000: 46). This openness may characterise the city itself, but less so contemporary Spanish cinema's obsession with it. Much cinema of the Franco era preferred countryside settings, or contrasted the corruptness of the city with the purity of the countryside (most famously in José Antonio Nieves Conde's film *Surcos* (Furrows) of 1951). Madrid might feature as a backdrop to comedies (mostly), but without its specificity impinging on the film's action or meaning. This changed with the return to democracy. Madrid became more prominent above all in the first decade and a half of Almodóvar's career: his work in this period revolutionised the concept of Madrid to one of a hedonistic or frenetic playground although, as Ewa Mazierska and Laura Rascaroli observe, this does not mean that Madrid is simply a postmodern paradise (Mazierska and Rascaroli, 2003: 30). It also, however, formed an appropriate setting for new forms of filmmaking that now emerged, such as a thriller and neo-noir, genres that tend to thrive on cityscapes. The generation of '95, with its perceived taste for the contemporary and for youth, also proved drawn to the city. Madrid has been used as an integral part of de la Iglesia's black horror comedy *El día de la bestia*, with an unusual comic use of the landmark Kio Towers as a mark of the devil. It has functioned as an example of globalised bourgeois living in Amenábar's *Abre los ojos*, although key shots and sequences that offer a more specific identity include Madrid's major thoroughfare the Gran Vía and the top of the Torre Picasso (with the Kio towers visible in the background). *Cine social* is not forgotten, however; in films such as Fernando León de Aranoa's

*Barrio* Madrid becomes a landscape of poverty with further identifying marks such as the Madrid metro.

Calparsoro's use of Madrid as an environment with which the characters interact and are at odds differs from the smoother Madrid of films such as *Abre los ojos* in which the city operates as a generic rather than specifically national reflection of a protagonist's search for identity. Alfonso Santos Gargallo describes Madrid as Calparsoro's fourth protagonist (Santos Gargallo, 2000: 54), which suggests a more active engagement of and with the city. Madrid assists in reinforcing the perfect images of perfect bodies observed by Palacios (2000: 14). Calparsoro inserts brief sequences in which the trio are seen walking through the crowded streets of the city, usually to musical accompaniment (and sometimes wearing sunglasses): these shots in particular emphasise Lucía's long legs and swaying hips as she walks. The sequences serve no useful narrative purpose but are included to show the trio not only as cool young people but also at one with the vibrant city in which they live and operate. Their interaction with the city does not, however, function only in this way. For instance, when Lucía is robbed of her drug money and she runs after the thief, the film cuts to an overhead crane shot that reduces her size and thus by implication her power, appropriate after her significant loss. The camera movement finishes with an aerial shot of part of the city, implying that Lucía's individual concerns are engulfed by the sheer size of it. Madrid, too, participates in the tensions of youth trying to realise their dreams. Santos Gargallo perceives a contrast between Lucía's character, which he describes as a submerged iceberg, and the sticky asphalt of Madrid (Santos Gargallo, 2000: 53), and this image underscores not only the notion of Lucía as 'cool', contrasting to the heat of the city, but also that of the city as clinging and imprisoning, from which she struggles to free herself. This image is at odds with the suggestion that the trio are at one with Madrid, but we can reconcile this as another example of the dual nature, positive and negative, of many key motifs of the film and above all the trio itself, a source of love but also of tension. Madrid's embrace is both warm and dangerous.

Of all the films so far *Asfalto* offers the most light and sunshine (though later *Ausentes* will go much further in its use of both). Calparsoro wanted to portray Madrid in the light of summer, depicting it as not simply hot but warm and friendly.[3] This might provide another reason why the critics took more favourably to the film than they had to the preceding trilogy. Whereas the latter stressed darkness, dull colours and claustrophobic interiors, Madrid by contrast offers a more attractive level of light. If Nimri was keen to appear as a sexier character (as cited above), then Calparsoro provides a sexier setting. A clear use of this is the night-time skyline of Madrid that forms a backdrop to Charly and Lucía as they kiss, bathed in a warm golden light. The camera then cuts to a reverse shot in which we see dawn coming up behind them over Madrid, casting a pinkish light on the scene. This depicts Madrid as virtually a fairytale setting in which the prince and princess inevitably come together (and the film does offer up such a romantic interpretation, if at Chino's expense: he appears uncomfortable against this backdrop). Here, too, however, we find mitigation of this positive relation between the characters and the city. We can see the Madrid skyline only because Charly does not live in central Madrid as the others do but on its margins, in an isolated small house amidst wasteland, a throwback to that of the Basque Country in *Salto* and *Pasajes*. Madrid may offer promise but it is a promise that is not close at hand, and the love between Lucía and Charly thrives best on its outskirts, prefiguring their abandonment of the city altogether.

We observed in discussion of the Basque settings of *Salto* and *Pasajes* that in the case of each film a charge was levelled against the settings as real. This is a charge that is also hard to level at *Asfalto*, which uses well-known settings such as the Gran Vía as well as the Retiro park through which Chino and Antonio chase a drug dealer, and identifiable locations such as the Antón Martín metro station passed by Antonio in his pursuit of his brother. Nonetheless, Santos Gargallo comes close to this charge when he argues that Calparsoro mythifies his characters to the extent that they become unreal rather than rooted in a nearby Madrid (2000: 54). This notion of mythification chimes in with Palacios's description of the film in terms of epic (Palacios, 2000: 14): epic and myth remove the story from the here and now, which conflicts with Calparsoro's emphasis on a specific contemporary location. Jardín observes this conflict and awards victor's honours to the characters and their emotions at the expense of the setting:

> pero el buen hacer técnico y el cándido sentido de la transcendencia que Calparsoro aplica a las relaciones entre sus personajes terminan por resolver el filme como un funcional drama de pasiones tardoadolescentes, que se las arregla incluso para vadear la impostura de la marginalidad que retrata, más bien impropia del Madrid de fin de siglo y cercana a una realidad referencial. (Jardín, 2006: 398)

(but the good technique and the clear sense of transcendence that Calparsoro applies to the relations between his characters end up by resolving the film like a functional drama of late adolescent passion, which manages even to surmount the imposture of the marginality it depicts, inappropriate for Madrid at the turn of the century and close to a referential reality.)

While much of this difficulty lies more with the conceptualisation of the film in epic or mythical terms than with the use of setting, it does nevertheless suggest that the characters are not completely at one with their environment and must therefore rise above it. But this does not reduce the problem of the refusal of some critics to recognise the characters as living in a certain tension with their environment. While it was easy to dismiss the settings of a possibly less well-known Basque Country as unreal, conceived primarily in the mind of the director, it proves more difficult to dismiss a very recognisable Madrid, and so the characters must be rendered as mythical and thus not to be perceived on the same level as the contemporary reality of the city.

The tensions of the film that imbue the cityscape come together in the final sequences of the car crash in the Gran Vía and the subsequent flight from Madrid. The crash looks like a re-run of the opening sequence of the film, although in fact the action is shot from a slightly different angle. As Calparsoro confirmed,[4] the Gran Vía has been shot so as to make it appear wider than it actually is. Thus, when the trio clamber out of the car and begin to stagger along the street, they seem to be walking in an unusually large arena, with a gaping crowd set some way back. Accompanied by a sudden silence after the frenetic noise of the car, the fight and the crash itself, the distorted setting gives the impression that the characters are moving in some vast space rather than the more claustrophobic thoroughfare that the Gran Vía actually is. They are in their own private bubble of space, separate from the surrounding population, bound together in their own personal pain (which brought them to such a pass) but nonetheless an interrelated unit. The first sounds to intrude on this scene are those of Antonio, who disturbs the scene just as he has disturbed the trio. If the crash acts as a microcosm of the trio's ambiguous relationship, then Madrid and its landmark is inextricable from this. And indeed we can go further and argue that Madrid is inextricable from the functioning of the triangular relationship, for as they drive off into the country Chino stops the car, bids his companions a sad but silent farewell and starts to walk back towards Madrid. Charly and Lucía, however, continue

12    The car crash in the Gran Vía

on their way through the beauty of the woods either side of the road. I like to think of this as their continuation into a fairytale landscape (since woods are redolent of fairy tales) that was hinted at earlier as they kissed in the dawn light, away from Madrid's central core. The trio can thus only function as such within the confines of Madrid, but ultimately Chino is more in tune with its tensions and violence than the others, and thus he returns to where he belongs.

## The colour, sound and look of optimism

Much of the change we have already discussed above can be considered as changes of style: the more upbeat approach to the film, the use of violence for its own sake, the use of a new setting that takes us away from the grunge of the Basque industrial wastelands, and the emphasis on light and warmth. In addition Calparsoro provides a faster pace suggesting a move away from the stasis of the trilogy. This fast pace may be one reason why some critics have perceived the film as a thriller. The resemblance to the thriller prefigures Calparsoro's more overt move to genre-based cinema with his next film, facilitating a transition from *cine social* to a convergence with styles and genres more closely linked to US cinema. The move from the Basque Country to Madrid – from a decaying industrial landscape to a lively urban environment more readily associated with fashion, youth culture and affluence – facilitates this move away from *cine social*.

The soundtrack includes music by Mastretta and by the group Najwajean, consisting of Nimri and Carlos Jean, the start of the most hailed collaboration of Calparsoro since his discovery of Nimri. Najwajean would later provide the music for *Guerreros* while Jean on his own would provide it for *Ausentes*, and in each case the music would be greeted with pleasure by critics. The music contributes to the thriller atmosphere; again, it is often more fast-paced and buoyant than the heavier rock music used in *Salto* and *A ciegas* or the mournful strings of *Pasajes*, and we have lost the choral accompaniment to some of the more static shots of the trilogy. The opening musical sequence is slower, but its hint of James Bond immediately introduces us to the notion of a thriller. It thus contributes overall to the sense of movement, pleasure and hope in the film. The soundtrack provides more variety of instrumentalisation, with saxophones, clarinets and accordion as well as synthesised beat: Chino's destruction of the florist's shop occurs to the sound of classical guitar with orchestral accompaniment. This change in musical provision also coincides with the move towards genre cinema. While the alternation of rock and choral chords of the earlier films suggest the combination of aggression and stasis, the later films use music appropriate to the relevant genre; thus faster-paced music for a thriller-like film.

The notion of the thriller is further enhanced by the use of the flash-forward opening credit sequence, which makes an impact that immediately engages the viewer and supplies a mystery that offers a modicum of suspense. Unlike the thriller, however, suspense is not the key element of *Asfalto*, which prefers to follow the twists and turns of the triangular relationship rather than the crimes committed. The opening sequence equally coincides with Calparsoro's taste for opening his films *in media res*, and is particular reminiscent of *Salto* in which we see the policeman taken hostage before the scenes that lead up to this event. And if we find the initial crash a violent opening to the film, Calparsoro immediately breaks the speed of the action with close-ups of the crashed car as the music starts and the credits pan leisurely over the top of the images (and no sign of any people). This allows the audience time to dwell on the mystery of the crash. The film continues this fairly conventional pacing of the action, with the violent scenes interspersed by scenes of dialogue, sex and romance before the return of the climactic scene of the crash. The pace is supported by more conventional camerawork and framing, the swirling steadycam of *Salto al vacío* now missing, although the camera does occasionally pan round, the central trio characters are framed for the most part in medium close-up, stressing both the tension and passion between them but also suggesting a more claustrophobic atmosphere that contradicts to some extent the sense of Madrid as a warm and open city. But when the camera does open out to offer a wider panorama, that panorama is nearly always of Madrid. The camera is now in the charge of Josep María Civit, with whom Calparsoro would also make *Guerreros* and *Ausentes*, the move towards genre thus echoed in a change in camera style with a new cinematographer.

Claudia Larraguibel describes *Asfalto* as a film of pastel tones (Larraguibel, 1999: 107). We have already noted the pink light of the dawn over Madrid, to which we can add the soft greens in the florist's and the Retiro park, the dappled sunlight of the closing country sequence, or the gentle contrast of yellow and pale blue as Chino emerges on the horizon in search of Charly and Lucía in the tyre. We have lost the cold and dull colours of the Basque trilogy. The pastel tones are repeated in the colours of Lucía's clothes (although the unusual use of red for her shorts at the beginning of the film, and her bright orange shirt later, are noticeably anachronistic). The warmer colours of the film still leave room for Calparsoro's trademark use of more acid or sickly greens as he has done in the trilogy, such as the yellowy greens of the walls of Lucía's flat that reflect the tension of the relationship between Lucía and her mother to which the colour provides a backdrop. The frequent movement between the warm and soft colours to some harsher ones is reminiscent of the oscillation between tenderness and tension among the trio.

*Asfalto* functions overall as a pivot in Calparsoro's filmmaking from *cine social* to genre cinema, the focus on urban youth carried over from the Basque trilogy but with touches of a thriller mode that points at a change of direction. Simultaneously, Calparsoro begins to make changes in his collaboration team: this is the first film in which he uses co-writers, a new director of photography and the musical collaboration of Carlos Jean, and the last in which Nimri stars. This indicates the pattern that will also pertain to the next two films, that in terms of theme we find a consistent emphasis on violence and aliena-tion figured through the landscape as well as the characters, but in terms of style and (more overtly in the following films) genre signs of change are noticeable. Where *Asfalto* differs from all the other films is in its generally warm, upbeat tone and bittersweet ending. This appears to coincide with the mood of the critics, who gave the film a positive reception overall. Calparsoro demonstrates more prominent signs of development with *Asfalto* (though this is not to say that he did not develop his approach over the previous films), signs which indicated a move away from the Basque despair that caused unease in some earlier reviews. From the point of view of the critics it would seem that at last Calparsoro is maturing as they wish him to do (though this then raises the question as to why such maturity is necessary). They have not as yet moved to the more pessimistic frame of reference beyond 2002 that allows them to use Calparsoro as a scapegoat for the problems they perceive within Spanish cinema.

## Notes

1 In conversation with the author, 17 May 2006.
2 In conversation with the author, 17 May 2006.
3 In conversation with the author, 17 May 2006.
4 In conversation with the author, 17 May 2006.

# 7

# *Guerreros*: Spanish alienation in a foreign landscape

Calparsoro's next film, *Guerreros*, makes a more overt move towards genre films more typical of Hollywood than European fare, the war film having been dominated by Hollywood. *Guerreros* tells us of a troop of Spanish soldiers acting as a peacekeeping force in Kosovo, who undertake a mission to repair an electricity generator in the exclusion zone. A confrontation with rebel forces embroils the young soldiers directly in the war, and for the rest of the film they simply try to survive in hostile territory. Calparsoro has not, however, left behind some of his earlier themes and styles: the sense of gritty realism remains with us in *Guerreros*, as does the theme of young people trying to come to terms with an alien environment, and of complex and tense relations with their peers and those apparently in authority around them. He also extends the ensemble playing introduced in *Asfalto*; ensemble playing is in any case a common characteristic of the contemporary war film. The war film facilitates the consideration of how disparate people, at odds with each other, might nonetheless come together to form a unit. Vietnam War film platoons, in particular, are often composed of disparate characters, sometimes crudely divided into idealists and cynics, who nonetheless function as a unit to some extent when under enemy fire.

For *Guerreros* Calparsoro had a budget of 600 million pesetas, double the amount he had for *Asfalto*. The screenplay was written by Calparsoro and Juan Cavestany, who was also responsible for the script of *Los lobos de Washington* (The Washington Wolves, Mariano Barroso, 1999). It was shown to representatives of the United Nations, the Spanish army, the Serbs and the Kosovans, none of whom raised any difficulties. Although some sections of the film were shot in Kosovo itself, most of the exterior shots were filmed in Pirineu de Lleida in

Spain; throughout shooting the Spanish army gave advice and assistance, to the extent that the actors spent some time in an army barracks
learning to act and move automatically as soldiers would. As with
*Asfalto* the film used the music of Calparsoro's now ex-wife Nimri
and her collaborator Carlos Jean, music that the director felt softened
the story and provided emotion. Calparsoro himself commented that
he enjoyed the shooting, and compared the support that he got this
time from the scriptwriter Cavestany, the team, the resources and the
producer to his previous films where he was accustomed to get each
picture out any way he could (Casanova, 2002: 90).

Critical reception was mixed and raises questions as to how Calparsoro was perceived on the Spanish scene now that he was more established. Jesús Palacios (2002: 18) hails the moral ambiguity of the film
and the good cast, particular Eloy Azorín as the central character Vidal,
and lauds the film as evidence that Calparsoro is the most mature
and coherent director of his generation. J. L. Sánchez Noriega (2002:
179–80) comments on the possible debt to Oliver Stone and suggests
that there is a touch of audiovisual grandiloquence and aggressive-
ness which impedes unbridled enthusiasm for the film's critique.
He acknowledges the newness of what Calparsoro has achieved by
venturing into the territory of the contemporary war film (2002: 180)
but he criticises him for poor characterisation and dialogue. Rubén
Corral (s.d.) had originally found *Salto* boring, while *Guerreros*, on the
other hand, provided an indication of 'tolerable cinema'. With this
film Corral takes hope that Calparsoro, like Almodóvar before him,
will curb his excesses. Such a comment again raises the question
as to why excess needs to be curbed. It seems to be taken as read
that a good director must mature and a sign of that maturity is a
more sober approach in terms of both style and theme. Carlos Rosal
(2002), however, argues that the film demonstrates the sad truth that
all Spanish directors who gain any amount of prestige end up making
vacuous films – a contrast to the hope that Calparsoro earlier held out
with his first films. He acknowledges Calparsoro's unity of vision,
though he does not feel that this is automatically to be praised. But for
him the narrative does not progress, and the characters do not develop
or mature (though Carla Pérez's role as Balbuena is an exception).
Francisco Marinero (2002) praises the film as a good spectacle but
feels it does not work as well when it comes to narrative and drama;
he finds a lack of logic and clarity, which to some extent repeats the
earlier critique he made of *A ciegas* despite his warmer reception of

*Guerreros.* The desire to make Eduardo Noriega's character complex results in him being merely vague, while Vidal's transformation seems too forced. This sample of reviews reveals a recognition of Calparso-ro's emphasis on the visual experience, his consistency of theme and style; and simultaneously an irritation with the script and the charac-ters, and – not always implicitly – a desire that Calparsoro would settle down and learn his place in the scheme of Spanish cinema. Sánchez Noriega's critique of grandiloquence and Corral's wish for the director to curb his excesses indicate a compulsion to make Calparsoro 'grow up', reach a new maturity. While young exuberance was all very well in 1995, the climate was different in 2002, the period in which Spanish critics were later to see Spanish cinema as in crisis once more, as discussed in the introduction.

## The war genre, the Spanish situation and auteurism

The 1990s and the early years of the twenty-first century saw a new flourishing of the war film in the USA, and also its rise in European cinema. European film revisited World War II, but this arose as much from the impulse to make historical costume dramas as it did from depicting war on film. The dominance of Hollywood cinema in terms of the contemporary war film arises not only from the power of its film industry but also the USA's active military engagement through the latter half of the twentieth century and into the twenty-first – Vietnam above all. However, the Balkans conflict, and Europe's participation in it as part of the United Nations peacekeeping forces, formed the basis for a small cluster of European war films such as *No Man's Land* (*Nikogarsnja zemlja,* Danis Tanovich, 2001), *Welcome to Sarajevo* (Michael Winterbottom, 1997) and *Pretty Village Pretty Flame* (*Lepa sela lepo gore,* Sdrjan Dragojevich, 1996). Even Jean-Luc Godard drew on the conflict for his film *Notre musique* (Our Music, 2004). *Guerreros* also belongs to this group of films.

This development coincided with a renewed interest in the war film from Hollywood. Despite the appearance of contemporary European war films, such a genre is nonetheless heavily associated with the USA, as a result of Vietnam war films such as *Apocalypse Now* (Francis Ford Coppola, 1979), *The Deer Hunter* (Michael Cimino, 1978), *Platoon* (Oliver Stone, 1986), *Full Metal Jacket* (Stanley Kubrick, 1987) and *Hamburger Hill* (John Irvin, 1987) that our perception of any war film must inevitably be coloured by our awareness of these films. The Vietnam films of the 1980s and 1990s stressed not only graphic realism but a sense of nihilism, a confusion as to why the soldiers were fighting at all and a depiction of warfare as reducing men to the level of animals, as opposed to the emphasis on heroism that characterised films during and immediately after World War II. However, during the 1990s a new surge of US patriotism in the government and in American society more generally was out of step with the angst of the earlier Vietnam films. As the turn of the century approached, films began to appear that offered a more positive picture of US military action: *Saving Private Ryan* (Steven Spielberg, 1998), *Black Hawk Down* (Ridley Scott, 2001), *Pearl Harbor* (Michael Bay, 2001), *Behind Enemy Lines* (John Moore, 2001) and *We Were Soldiers* (Randall Wallace, 2002). Philippa Gates describes this latter wave of Hollywood war films as more idealised (Gates, 2005: 302, 303). She goes on to note that such films tend to 'offer a relatively uniform glorification of American patriotism and heroism, not unlike the pre-Vietnam World War II film', and points out that the questions of why America is at war in the first place, and its justification for doing so, are never posed (306). Barry Langford (2005: 126) notes that films that emphasised humanitarian actions in Kosovo, Beirut and Somalia were not attractive – though he quotes no examples other than an exception to this rule, *Black Hawk Down*, which, he implies, was successful because it adopted the motif of the embattled platoon of World War II and Vietnam films rather than the new emphasis on humanitarian intervention. Gates sees these contemporary films as using an increased emphasis on realistic special effects to claim a sense of greater authenticity to such films, but argues that the use of strong and violent realism disguises the moralism of such films: 'they do not necessarily offer a more *accurate* portrayal of war and most often merely mask increasingly idealistic moral assertions' (2005: 298).

Europe has not experienced the same need for military vindication nor the upsurge in patriotic ideology that the USA has. The European war film thus does not demonstrate the moralistic tendencies of the US war film: there is not the same compulsion to prove the heroism of one's own armed forces, nor the justness of their cause. Instead, it perpetuates the sense of confusion prevalent in the earlier Vietnam films, where nobody was entirely clear as to what was going on (this confusion counters the charge of a lack of clarity proposed by critics such as Marinero above: such confusion is not necessarily a fault). The complexities of history and politics that led to the different wars in the Balkans in the 1990s are better suited in any case to this earlier sort of war film than those such as *Saving Private Ryan* and *We Were Soldiers*. The overwhelming effect of Balkans war films such as *Guerreros*, *No Man's Land* and *Welcome to Sarajevo* is the terrible human cost of the war to both soldiers and civilians. The peacekeeping film draws on notions of futility and confusion from the earlier Vietnam war films, but complicates the sense of guilt by the fact that often the protagonists – the peacekeeping forces – are supposed to be no more than bystanders.

Langford (2005: 108) argues that:

> different national experiences of conflict and of victory or defeat ensure a remarkable dissimilarity in the generic conventions by which wars are rendered in different national cinemas – sometimes even curtailing direct representation altogether (for instance the 'unavailability' of Second World War combat as a direct topic in postwar German cinema).

Langford's statement is contradicted by his later comment (111) that (at least in terms of World War II films) 'what is true for Hollywood is true as well for the national cinema of every other major combatant'.[1] Yet it hard to avoid the question of American influence on the making of European war films, whether the American war film is taken as a model or as a target against which to react.

If, as Langford tells us, the situations between the USA and other nations are quite distinct, the situations of the USA and Spain seem particularly incompatible. Hollywood cinema has a relatively long history of (a.) its country at war in the twentieth century and (b.) making films about the country's conflicts. The only major conflict of the twentieth century in which Spain has been a protagonist is the Spanish Civil War: it did not participate in the World Wars. As a consequence, war in Spanish films is confined either to earlier conflicts that verge on the costume drama rather than the contemporary war film (such as *Agustina de Aragón* (Agustina of Aragon, Juan de Orduña, 1950)) or, perhaps more notoriously, the clutch of films in the earlier years of the Franco era that glorified the Spanish army to coincide with Franco's ideological perception of it as fighting to recuperate Spain's lost noble character: *Raza* (Race, José Luis Sáenz de Heredia, 1942), *Los últimos de Filipinas* (The Last in the Philippines, Antonio Román, 1945), *Sin novedad en el Alcázar* (The Siege of the Alcazar, Augusto Genina, 1940). Thus the lack of subject matter and a possible Francoist taint has rendered the Spanish contemporary war film virtually non-existent. Even with the recuperation of the 'lost' history of the losers under Franco that is still ongoing within Spanish cinema, the fighting of the Civil War itself is not dwelt on with the concentrated effort at realism that characterises the recent Hollywood offerings (exceptions might be made of Vicente Aranda's *Libertarias* (Freedom Fighters, 1996) and Ken Loach's *Tierra y Libertad/Land and Freedom* (1995)). Warfare itself becomes part of a soft memorialisation of the conflict which stresses the poignancy of loss without dwelling on how bloody the loss might have been, as in, for example, *Soldados de Salamina* (Soldiers of Salamina, David Trueba, 2003). And Spain's lack of participation in international conflict (until the controversial involvement in the invasion of Iraq in 2003) means that there is little material to support a specifically Spanish war genre. The only previous attempt at a contemporary war film in Spain was *Territorio Comanche* (Comanche Territory, Gerardo Herrero, 1997), about Spanish TV reporters in Bosnia.

It is thus in this vacuum that Calparsoro made *Guerreros*. He comments on the DVD version of the film that since there has never been a Spanish contemporary war film before, he lacked referents. In terms of Hollywood this is uncertain: Calparsoro comes close to the Vietnam films of the 1980s in his characters, plot and *mise-en-scène*; but referents in Spanish film he certainly lacked. And even when compared with Hollywood output (particularly as regards the moral motivation of contemporary films that Gates analyses) the motivation is not the same. There is at this point no need to justify becoming involved in military conflict – indeed, the Spanish soldiers in the film are supposedly there to prevent rather than participate in conflict. Spain was not responsible as such for the outbreak or the continuation of the war, which was not about issues of any interest to Spain. There is little sense of a need for justification or idealisation.

The Spanish military has historically stood for the unity of Spain. In *Guerreros* the Spanish army represents Spanish disunity and fragmentation, to say nothing of a diminished reputation in international eyes. While the Spanish forces of the film grouse about the unwillingness of their Italian allies to back them up as far as the frontier, the French soldiers are themselves disparaging the Spanish as worthless. In the confrontation with Kosovan soldiers, Lieutenant Alonso (Eduardo Noriega) is forced to back down in front of the adamant French officer who insists that the Kosovans hand over their weapons and in addition reproves Alonso like a child for showing him up in front of his men. Ironically, the French officer is right in his reading of the situation: the Kosovans have set up an ambush and will later be seen taking away the tanks and vans for their own use. Alonso's more peaceable reading would seem more reasonable if it were not for the fact that Calparsoro allows the audience to see the Kosovan snipers camouflaged in the bushes. In a shoot-out that rapidly descends into chaos the camera emphasises the Spanish in full retreat – altogether a very different notion of the Spanish army from that promoted during the Franco era.

Calparsoro wished to vindicate the work of the Spanish army in Kosovo (Asúa, 2002: 24), something that Eduardo Noriega also stresses:

quiero destacar la labor de los militares españoles allí, porque he visto una iglesia serbia rodeada de militares, 24 horas sin moverse de su puesto para que no la quemen, les he visto llevar a niños al colegio y les he visto trabajar con pico y pala para ayudar al pueblo. Así que yo sólo puedo estar agradecidísimo a ellos y muy sorprendido. Y me gusta decirlo porque hacen una labor humanitaria importantísima, digna de alabar y de agradecer. (Asúa, 2002: 24)

(I want to emphasise the work the Spanish military are doing there, because I have seen a Serbian church surrounded by soldiers for 24 hours without moving from their post so as to ensure it wasn't burnt down. I've seen them escort children to school, and I've seen them work with picks and shovels to help the people. So I can only be very grateful to them, and very surprised. And I'm pleased to say it, because they are doing very important humanitarian work, worthy of praise and thanks.)

And the film does serve to indicate that the mission of the contemporary Spanish army is now very different from its historical one; the stress Noriega places here on discipline is revealed as precisely humanitarian. Although Noriega's experiences are not directly reflected in *Guerreros* (although we do see the soldiers work to restore a church), there is offered nonetheless not only a picture of innocents abroad but the desire of the central character Vidal to help the people he has come to Kosovo to watch over (before events radically change his attitude). The film demonstrates how experience of warfare, less glorious than the military actions envisaged by Franco, rapidly undermines these noble ideals. Altogether, it is very remote from the earlier glorification of warfare in Spanish film under Franco. If any films can come close to Calparsoro's in terms of initial premise, at least, they might be *Black Hawk Down* and *Behind Enemy Lines* which also start from a premise of peacekeeping, though in both the American films the US troops are glorified, looking out for each other, working as a team, and morally in the right, as Gates suggested. Palacios (2002: 18) takes a comparison with *Black Hawk Down* as a point of departure, and argues that where in the American film there was a divide between the soldiers and the soulless zombie-like creatures they were fighting, in the Spanish film the soldiers becomes the soulless zombies.

## Realism

From 1980s' Vietnam films in particular the war genre has insisted on blood-spattered realism. Calparsoro makes strong efforts to ensure authenticity – the assistance of the Spanish army attests to this, as does the physical training undergone by the actors, something commented on in interviews with Noriega, who suffered an eye injury during production, leading to temporary loss of vision. Interviews and commentaries on the DVD version of the film stress the physical endurance needed to make the film; for example, the sequence in which the soldiers escape down a (very cold) river. Some sequences were in addition filmed on location in Kosovo, so that the cast and crew experienced at first hand the life of the Spanish forces in Kosovo. This process echoes the immersion of the cast in the ambience of the urban Basque Country for *Salto al vacío* and *Pasajes*. Thus the performance of the actors draws very close to reality in that they virtually became soldiers for the duration of shooting, and Calparsoro acknowledges the need for actors who could handle the demands of shooting in very demanding conditions. Noriega remarks in an interview on the DVD that that was one of his hardest films in terms of interpretation, direction and production. (Calparsoro would himself participate in some of the required activities to give his weary cast some measure of encouragement and empathy.)

The location scenes in Kosovo include at least one place where fighting had gone on only six months before. The scene in which refugees throw stones at the passing peacekeeping convoy threatened to impinge on real life: the staged confrontation was monitored by Serb forces in helicopters, who thought that something really was happening in Kosovo. Moreover, the early sequence with the refugee camp and the church had to be constructed and filmed in Spain, because if in Kosovo they had appeared to be reconstructing a church of one religion, then the other side would have had nothing to do with the cast and crew. Although these incidents were clearly unintentional, they nonetheless contribute to Calparsoro's sense that cinema itself is a violent process: certainly it began to play an active role in the conflict. Furthermore, many of the characters in the film are drawn from life. In his DVD interview the director notes that, apart from Vidal, all the characters are taken from soldiers he got to know in Kosovo. He drew on testimonies from soldiers for the scenes where the characters are separated and imprisoned in the Serbian camp. In the latter he is supported by director of photography Josep María Civit, who comments that news footage of Kosovo is very recent in people's minds, and for this reason everything had to be pretty much true to life. Moreover, Calparsoro's style oddly enhances the realism in that the story, like war itself, is confused and messy: the abrupt, confused and claustrophobic sequences of *Guerreros*, with its switches from frenetic and violent activity to aggressive conversations that reveal pent-up frustration, are all reminiscent of the earlier trilogy and particularly *Salto al vacío* and *Pasajes*.

The stress on realism did not avoid criticism on precisely that point in the review of Eduardo-Martín Larequi García (2003), who argues that the title proves to be overblown as the soldiers are nothing like warriors (a comment that appears to miss the irony latent in the title). He argues that, while it may be true to life to depict soldiers anxious only to protect their own skins and to make as little effort as possible, there are serious objections to the way in which Calparsoro shows the characters to be virtually autistic with severe communication problems, rather than comrades in arms. To him this is the result not of realism but of a poor script. Larequi García, as not only a fan of war films but as an ex-soldier, finds an odd combination of vacuous solemnity and barrack-room crudeness, plausible in real conversation but not in the cinema.This comment undermines the criticism here, as while the critic berates the director for a lack of authenticity, he now admits the possibility of authentic dialogue in reality but not in terms of cinema, thus presuming that the latter must be clear and polished in order to qualify as authentic. Larequi García's review is more concerned with authenticity than other reviews considered here, but what he really desires is a film closer to the US fare being released at the turn of the century in contrast to the earlier, messier Vietnam films of the 1980s. His desire for unity in the troop and his feeling that the lack of communication is unrealistic suggest that he is faulting Calparsoro for not introducing the element of morality, a sense of common purpose and of loyalty, which the critics quoted above find in films such as *Saving Private Ryan* and *We Were Soldiers*. This is also apparent from his comment that actor Eloy Azorín is still too green to be adequate in the dramatic role of Vidal, neglecting the possibility that this is precisely the point: the earlier Vietnam films considered the effect of combat on raw recruits as well. Larequi García's review hints at not only the importance of the US war genre in attempting to assess Calparsoro's achievement but also the sensitivity of the Spanish film scene to developments in contemporary Hollywood cinema, so that Spanish films might be judged by the very latest trends in the USA, even though the war experiences of the two countries are quite dissimilar.

It would be valuable to know how far Spanish audiences might share a desire for overt morality in war films; certainly the overwhelming opposition within Spain to the country's subsequent involvement in the second Iraq war (which began in the year following *Guerreros*'s release) indicates that they did not feel the same need as American filmmakers to recuperate a sense of patriotic mission to the war film. Such an observation concerning Spanish audiences is not conclusive: one cannot assume an automatic correlation between opposition to a particular war and unwillingness to watch certain war films. Nonetheless, it suggests a certain validity of Langford's comment (2005: 108) quoted above concerning the need to distinguish between different national experiences of warfare, although his comment that this entails 'dissimilarity in the generic conventions' needs some modification when we consider *Guerreros*. Calparsoro's plot and characterisation are very close to the Vietnam films of the 1980s in terms of graphic bloodshed and an ambience of animalisation and nihilistic despair. He is, however, not in step with the ethos of more recent US war films. This indicates that, while Calparsoro has drawn either implicitly or explicitly on the US genre, he is not concerned to place his films on a par with the latest American releases. The film is more comprehensible within Spanish sensitivities – the cultural awareness in a democratic Spain of the military associations of their past, the need to recuperate a more positive image of the Spanish military, fears of what military involvement can do to people. Calparsoro effectively marries the American genre with the Spanish situation.

## Vidal as perpetrator and victim of violence

What of the implications of a war film for Calparsoro's consistency as
auteur? We could argue that in fact the contemporary war film is the
perfect vehicle for Calparsoro given his previous work that stresses
alienation through violence: it extends his earlier emphasis on the
world as an inherently violent place and develops it in new ways. As
with the police force in *Asfalto*, the film maintains the motif of institutionalisation, since war is perhaps the ultimate form of institutionalised violence. Even though these Spanish soldiers are in Kosovo on
a peacekeeping mission, the end product still appears to be the alienation of youth from both the environment they work in (and therefore
their mission) and from each other, which the violence expresses.

Thus the location of Kosovo is on one level incidental. Calparsoro
claimed that Kosovo merely acted as a backdrop, the specificities
of the situation not mattering so much: it happened to be conven-
iently close, as Eloy Azorín took pains to point out (Casado, 2002).
Nonetheless, Calparsoro does give a nod to the specific conflict in play
through his use in the opening credits of religious images intercut
with and superimposed on the images of the soldiers, to indicate that
although this is a contemporary war the roots date back many centu-
ries and can be found in religion among other things. The religious
link is repeated as the young Spanish soldiers work on the repairs to
a church. Beyond this, however, we learn little of the historical roots
of the conflict. More particularly, we never learn about the Kosovans
and the Serbs: we see those who cross the soldiers' path only from
the soldiers' point of view. This repeats a commonplace of US war
films both in the heyday of films about Vietnam and the more recent
offerings such as *Black Hawk Down*: the story is only told from one
side. This alienation from the local inhabitants is of a piece with the
alienation the characters experience as they wander lost through the
Kosovan countryside, as I will discuss below.

A central element of *Guerreros* is the corruption of innocence and
idealism as young soldiers descend into a hell in which, in terms
of violence, they become indistinguishable from the local inhabitants. This is distinct from the Hollywood approach to humanitarian
missions, as in *Black Hawk Down* and *Behind Enemy Lines*, in which the
US troops keep to their ideals. In *Guerreros*, innocence and idealism
are in fact contributory factors to violence. When Vidal is determined
to intervene to prevent the torture and death of a refugee in the camp,

against orders not to interfere, he not only forces the rest of his troop to come to his rescue and thus immerse themselves in the tortuous labyrinth of the camp but also precipitates fighting and squabbling amongst themselves. This is underscored further with what seems at first glance to be a rather crude contrast of activities in the barracks. We hear in voiceover Vidal writing a letter to his father, telling him that he wants to help these people who are Spain's neighbours but that the people seem to be living in another century. As we hear this we see a sequence of shots of the soldiers killing time – doing paperwork, press-ups, reading, washing up – which opens and closes with a solider playing a violent video game with tanks. The sequence ends with a close-up of the video game as a tank is blown up. What seems to be at first a blunt opposition of Vidal's idealism and the violence of the video game that simulates warfare is made more complex by Caparsoro's notion of the soldiers as little more than children in a holiday camp, as he commented on the DVD: the game-playing, for all the simulated violence, still suggest a childlike mind. And thus it also suggests how easy is the transition from the innocence of childhood to the hell of warfare. This is confirmed by Calparsoro's comparison of the film to William Golding's *The Lord of the Flies* where children become savages ('"Guerreros", retrato de unos soldados españoles en la guerra de Kosovo', 2002). We are reminded, too, of the innocent, fairytale dreams of Alex in *Salto al vacío* and Gabi in *Pasajes*: *Guerreros* resembles these films in demonstrating that idealism and violence can co-exist in the same person.

The film contains some notably violent set pieces, above all that of the death of Mónica the interpreter (Sandra Wahlbeck) blown up by a landmine as the troop, fleeing a second encounter with rebel forces after an earlier ambush, run into a field. Her very audible agony as she lies dying is excruciating not only for us the audience but also the soldiers holed up nearby. This is the moment in which the protagonist Vidal also begins to assert himself and demonstrate his ability to think and act under pressure. The validity of his ideas are confirmed by the support of sergeant Rubio (Rubén Ochandiano), who earlier had despised Vidal. But Vidal's new confidence is accompanied by the ability to kill (in contrast to his hesitation when confronted by the torturers in the refugee camp). When Alonso sends him out in the field to Mónica, he suffocates her and thus puts her out of her misery – a brutal solution to the problem of what to do with her.

Vidal's assertiveness accompanies a degeneration into further

violence. Having later escaped with some of the others from their
Serbian captors, he and they attack a local soldier for their safety and
also for the soldier's food. Vidal has by now become more violent
than the others, for all their desperation, as we can observe from his
frenzied stabbing of the enemy soldier and the parallel murder of
a farmer who catches them eating. But his degeneration is marked
above all by the final scene of the film. As the desperate band start to
walk through the village, lights come on (as Alonso has repaired the
electricity generator that was the original object of the mission). Shots
are fired to celebrate the return of light; and the Spanish soldiers
panic and start shooting. They are quickly surrounded. Calparsoro
dwells comparatively long on this scene, in contrast to the frenetic and
violent action of the previous scenes. The slow 360° pan round the
surrounding villagers as from the Spanish soldiers' pov, and then the
reverse shot dwelling for several seconds on the soldiers themselves,
dirty, wounded, uncertain and jumpy, underscores the latter as trapped
animals. At this point Alonso arrives with Ballesteros (Jordi Vilche) to
tell them the mission is over and they are going home. While the
others lower their weapons, Vidal continues to keep his raised, almost
frozen in this hostile position. As Alonso reassures him once more
that he has fulfilled his mission, Vidal slowly lowers his gun. At this
point Calparsoro introduces a parallel to the first exchange we see
between Alonso and Vidal, when the former reprimands the latter
for acting against orders in the refugee camp. At that time, Alonso
tells Vidal to look him in the eyes. He does so again here, and we too
look into Vidal's red eyes and scarred face – the final, climactic shot
of the film. The initial assumption here might be that Calparsoro is
stressing the distinction between the earlier innocent Vidal and the
violent animal to which he has been reduced. While this contrast has
a certain amount of validity, the distinction is not as clear-cut as this.
For the original scene arose as a result of Vidal's desire to get involved
in the war rather than passively watch events unfold: the readiness
to take aggressive action rather than simply keep the peace is there
throughout.

The capacity to which Vidal is able to absorb the violence around
him extends as far as the violence that is also done to him, most particularly when he is buried alive in a mass grave beneath a pile of dead
bodies. It is also apparent in the hallucination of torture he experiences while imprisoned: he imagines he is smothered with a plastic
bag in the same manner as the man he tried to help in the refugee

camp. After a quick cut to the corridor outside and the Serb soldiers idling, we cut back to see Vidal sitting alone. There is no plastic bag but he is struggling to breathe as if there were one, panicking, hitting out at the air. He begins to fling himself at his prison walls until one gives way in an unlikely fashion and sets him free. By immersing himself in the Kosovan continuum of violence, then, Vidal becomes victim as well as perpetrator, and hard to distinguish from the people he is there to protect. Vidal comes to represent the convergence of different forms of violence – individual and institutional – in the same person, rather as Chino did in *Asfalto*. Throughout his work Calparsoro has used violence as the preferred form of expression of an individual trying to resist her environment. As he increases the focus on male storylines, so he brings into the mix the institutional strand of violence: institutional violence is inherently patriarchal and thus implicit in the increasing focus on male attempts to come to terms with the surrounding violence. The ensemble playing, however, suggests that violence is an essential element of an intricate network of human relations. And in this network we the audience are also impli-cated: again the director demonstrates his wish to make the viewer experience the violence as directly as possible. Calparsoro makes it clear that he wanted the audience to experience the same sensation as the characters of entering into a war they did not understand or know, and undergoing the same experiences (Casado, 2002).

13   Vidal as perpetrator and victim of violence

## Beauty and alienation in the Kosovan landscape

Calparsoro's own expressed attitude towards the Kosovo setting
mentioned above – that in fact it is nearer to Spain than we might
at first think – also suggests a continuum in the alienating effect of
the landscape, linking back to the alienating landscapes of earlier
films. The landscape of most of the film differs greatly from the
urban settings of Madrid and the Basque Country we have previously
considered, with a strong emphasis in the central section of the film
on the countryside and mountains of Kosovo. Nonetheless – aside
from the fact that some of these backdrops were actually filmed within
Spain anyway, so that in practice if not in presentation we are still
talking about Spanish landscape – we have not lost complete touch
with the notion of urban living as squalid and marginal. Although
the Kosovan towns and villages visited by the Spanish peacekeeping
force are not on the scale of Bilbao or Madrid, these are nonetheless
wasted places, reduced to ruin but where people still go about their
daily business, trying to survive in a deprived environment. A crucial
difference, however, is that this time the central characters do not
move seamlessly through the landscape as Alex does in Bilbao and
Lucía in Madrid. The soldiers of *Guerreros* simply do not understand
the landscape within which they are moving. It is alien as well as
foreign; and they cannot interpret it.

Indeed at times the landscape overwhelms them, as in the scene
where their tank rolls backwards into the river, threatening to drown
them. Their escape downriver emphasises their struggles in this
environment: the river is fast and swirling and the soldiers fight hard
to keep their heads above water – emphasised by the occasional shot
of the water from their pov. The wounded driver Gómez (Iñaki Font)
does not in fact survive the river journey and is last seen floating face
down in the water. As they move deeper into the scenic countryside,
they discover too late that the green fields are mined: the mines cost
the interpreter Mónica her life. The calm shade of the woods in which
they subsequently take shelter to rest, and the panoramic mountain
vista that Vidal pauses to contemplate as he does a perimeter sweep,
form the backdrop to the constant bickering of the soldiers, and the
indecisiveness of their leader, as they try to decide what to do next.
The ground later appears to swallow them whole as they take refuge
in a large pit in the ground, which will turn out to be a mass grave.
(The fact that the soldiers – admittedly stressed and confused by this

point of the film – do not recognise the hole for what it is until too late suggests not only their naivety and inexperience but their total aliena-tion from the conflict, and the landscape in which it takes place).

War is, course, an experience that tends to alienate many who partic-ipate in it, willingly or otherwise; and such alienation is a staple of the war film. This motif is further extended in *Guerreros* by the interna-tional nature of the peacekeeping forces as well as the fact that the warring factions also speak a variety of languages. We hear not only Spanish but Albanian, Kosovan, French and English. The Spanish soldiers do not cope with this Babel of languages as well as the French and Serb forces do: only Alonso and Mónica can communicate in a language other than Spanish, while Marceau (Olivier Sitruck), the French soldier who retreats with the Spanish troop, communicates comfortably in English. But the Spanish soldiers do not understand each other very well, either; and this element of alienation from within clearly stems from 1980s Vietnam war films such as *Hamburger Hill* in which the soldiers are at odds with each other. Bickering amongst themselves is commonplace in the Spanish troop despite Alonso's gospel of unity reiterated on various occasions. National identity disintegrates into a welter of confused mutual incomprehension. By the end of the film the group has been reduced to a small number that do indeed act as one, but their actions are both brutal and wordless (very different from the way in which the trio of *Asfalto* operates as a unit, through love for each other as well as a need to survive). This smaller group includes Marceau, who was only previously able to talk to Alonso because of the language barrier. Alonso is no longer in the group but by now it does not matter: the soldiers' need to survive is so basic that it no longer requires verbal communication; and the French soldier is no longer clearly distinguishable from the Spanish. The Babel of languages begins to assert itself as the Spanish move into the heart of the country, and as the terrain becomes more treach-erous: their increasing struggle to communicate reflects their struggle to negotiate the terrain. They can survive in this landscape only by letting go of culture, nation and language altogether.

## The war film and gender

*Guerreros* is the film in which Calparsoro concentrates most keenly on male characters as opposed to his earlier emphasis on female charac-ters. To some extent this is hard to avoid, given that – as noted above

– the army is a form of patriarchal and institutionalised violence: it is also one particularly associated with men attempting to prove their masculinity on the battlefield. A good deal of this problematisation of masculinity is bound up with the persona of Eduardo Noriega, who plays the part of Alonso. By the time of *Guerreros* Noriega had established himself as part of the new stable of stars that had come into prominence in the latter half of the 1990s in Spain. Chris Perriam (2003: 176) posits Noriega's performance in *Abre los ojos* as an example of 'critiques of modes of masculinity'. Similarly, in discussing Noriega's performance in the film *Nadie conoce a nadie* (Nobody Knows Anybody, Mateo Gil, 1999), Perriam observes that

> Noriega invites stronger and more various identifications: socially with the young man in crisis; sympathetically and erotically with the beautiful body threatened by imprisonment, coercion and exhaustion; intellectually and dramatically with the man who becomes the unwilling witness to violence [...]. (Perriam, 2003: 176–7)

Similar elements can be found in *Guerreros*, by which time Noriega has a nuanced star persona of virile masculinity that can nonetheless be potentially damaged. Calparsoro's film contributes to these nuances, with a role that allows Noriega's masculine persona to seem hesitant and lacking in confidence, suggesting the insecurity at the heart of the masculine enterprise that has occurred previously in his roles. His insistence in the first half of the film on unity among the troop seems naïve, and he has little rapport with his soldiers. The undermining of Alonso's authority comes, however, at the road block,

14   Lieutenant Alonso hesitates

where the French officer dismisses Alonso's suggestions of how to handle the problem. As the situation disintegrates and the soldiers retreat, they become less responsive to his commands, until eventually Ballesteros suggests to sergeant Rubio that he take command as the lieutenant does not know what he is doing. Only at the end does Alonso regain any authority, when he defuses the tense stand-off at the end of the film; and he does this by gently soothing and reassuring the soldiers rather than by any overt action. Even in this film, however, it seems that Noriega's role as *galán* has not entirely deserted him, at least according to Agustín Gómez Cascales, who in interview with the actor asked him about the pleasure of the fans in seeing him wear khaki underwear. The actor replied that he was surprised by this, but he felt that his role contained a certain amount of seduction, not at a sexual level as such but as a way to bedazzle his troops (Gómez Cascales, 2002: 22). The link between both the vulnerability and the seductiveness implied by his state of undress while held captive, and his feminine indecisiveness, suggests a masochistic position for both the role and the star occupying the role. Noriega contradicts this statement elsewhere, arguing that Alonso is a terrified young lad like the others, but with the burden of command (Asúa, 2002: 24). This suggests a reduction of Alonso's/Noriega's personality down to a level shared by all, where what makes him stand out from the rest is the mismatch between his responsibility and his ability to cope.

If Alonso's indecisiveness, coupled with Noriega's status as an object to be looked at, serves to feminise this character, then other elements also serve to problematise the link between military action and overt masculinity. Far from the military in *Guerreros* functioning as a monolithic patriarchal entity, it shows masculinity as fragmented and isolating. None of the male soldiers (apart from Vidal) reveal any bonds with each other. Their leisure activities in the barracks are solitary (in contrast to Balbuena's sharing of a glance with Mónica while they are in the washroom): their communication with each other does not advance beyond verbal sniping. None of them seem to be friends. Vidal is not, however, totally isolated; and it is typical of Calparsoro's oeuvre that the soldier he seems closest to is the troop's sole female soldier, Balbuena. Calparsoro integrates Balbuena fairly effectively into the troop in an egalitarian way: Ballesteros snipes verbally at her just as he does Vidal but he does not use her gender as a tool with which to denigrate her. And Balbuena is as capable as the others of indulging in the childlike side of war, making clear, if higher pitched, warlike howls as she directs the machine gun during their retreat. But her gender is not incidental. In the sequence where the soldiers kill time in mundane activities, she is seen brushing her teeth alongside the interpreter Mónica – the only time in this sequence that any soldier seems to be sharing an activity: the other soldiers are enclosed in their own private bubbles, oblivious to the others around them. The fatal wounding of the interpreter in the minefield affects Balbuena very badly: she is determined to go and rescue her friend and is prevented only by Vidal wrestling her to the ground. The other soldiers, meanwhile, dither about what to do next: Alonso in particular is unsure as to how to act, eventually deciding to rescue Mónica because that is what the regulations demand. Balbuena's decisive and violent act echoes the chopped finger scene in *Salto*, in which Alex acts swiftly in confronting the dealers and ensuring that Esteban gets to hospital (along with his finger), while her male companions respond with far greater uncertainty. More particularly, when the soldiers are captured in Ruica and pushed into cells, Balbuena is separated from them and dragged into a soldiers' dormitory. We next see her alone and shaking: she has been raped.

Her gender allows her to experience a certain amount of solidarity with Vidal. After the latter has been dressed down by Alonso, he returns to his unit; and Ballesteros picks a fight. When Rubio arrives to break up the fight, Calparsoro divides the soldiers up in an intriguing two-shot, from the sergeant and most of the unit to Vidal and Balbuena by his side, alone together in shot, thus separated from the rest of the unit. The positioning of the two actors and the camera, and their framing in a large archway, seems to both shrink them and distance them from their unit. It is subsequently Vidal who finds and rescues Balbuena after the rape, comforting her and wrapping her in a blanket; Vidal who acts to prevent her rushing heedlessly out to Mónica under sniper fire; and Vidal who serves to put Mónica out of her misery by suffocating her and ending her pain. These threads of connection are comparatively small: in contrast to his previous films Calparsoro does not put the woman centre stage and thus the links between Balbuena and Vidal are not that prominent. Nonetheless, his empathy serves to feminise Vidal to some extent. This empathy inevitably brings back traces of the actor Eloy Azorín's landmark performance as Esteban in *Todo sobre mi madre* (All About My Mother, Pedro Almodóvar, 1999), a film in which Esteban shows a comfortable, reciprocal, warm relationship with his mother: masculinity in Almodóvar's film becomes a hollow signifier that cannot but be imbued with the overwhelming sense of the feminine and the maternal.

*Guerreros* thus arguably feminises its principal soldiers, reminiscent of Yvonne Tasker's argument against a simple equation of the feminine with women and the masculine with men in the war film, as the two ideas of gender may be expressed across a range of characters regardless of biological sex (Tasker, 2005: 180). It does, however, counter Tasker's claims on images of women in the military in films such as *Courage Under Fire* (Edward Zwick, 1996) and *G.I. Jane* (Ridley Scott, 1997). Tasker believes that

> these images of military women are normalized precisely through, and not despite or against, discourses of masculinity. Is it too much to wish for a film criticism that is alive to such images, rather than discounting them as exceptions that once more prove the rule of gendered hierarchies? (180)

Balbuena's status is to some extent normalised in this way, and yet her presence also serves precisely to disrupt the usual discourses of military masculinity in *Guerreros* in the way that Tasker might hope for.

## Cold colours and synthesisers

In terms of *mise-en-scène* and camera *Guerreros* coincides closely with the war genre more generally, thus fitting easily into the genre and signalling Calparsoro's move to embrace genre filmmaking (although, as we will see in the next chapter, he can innovate as well as follow generic dictates). The camera style must almost inevitably change from *Asfalto*, given the nature of the action being filmed. We find fewer medium close-ups and more long shots and medium long shots that allow the camera to take in the troop as a whole and their manoeuvres (though close-up shots within the tank reflect the claustrophobia of the latter). There is more rapid cutting to shots from different angles (notably the death of the French army officer, seen rapidly from different perspectives). The director also includes motifs from his earlier work, such as the claustrophobia of the tank, a confined space that becomes still more claustrophobic when the tank falls backwards into a nearby river and starts to fill with water. The panic that this induces is heightened by the use of the underwater camera inside the tank, and the fact that there are so many people trying simultaneously to escape this small space with its shrinking pocket of air. This scene harks back to the claustrophobia and confusion of the caravan scene in *Salto al vacío*. On the other hand the sweeping camera of the latter film is now left far behind, and the more conventional camerawork reflects Calparsoro's greater access to funds, with more cameras to shoot from different angles. A different use of the camera occurs in the scene where Alonso is dressing down Vidal towards the beginning: Calparsoro comments on the DVD that although there is hardly any movement in this scene, nonetheless the camera moves almost imperceptibly, suggesting the tensions quivering in the air.

In terms of colour, we are back to the cold hues that character-ised the Basque trilogy. The use of green is inevitable, given the rural sequences, but, although this time it derives from nature rather than the oxidised industrial landscape, it equally reflects the alienation of the characters. Green and khaki tones also derive inevitably from the costume of soldiers' uniforms: they are ostensibly designed to blend in with the countryside, adding a subtle irony to the soldiers' aliena-tion from the landscape. But the first colour to strike us is the blue of the opening credit sequences, which washes the opening images of all other colour and warmth, appropriate to the images of warfare, although red (a colour that appears rarely in Calparsoro's work) might be more readily associated with war. The cold blue reappears intermit-tently throughout the film to maintain this chilly tone. We have lost the pastel tones of *Asfalto* as well as its warm light (the mission of the troop is simply to restore light): the light will return in *Ausentes* but not the warmth.

For the first time, the music (from Najwajean once again) is prima-rily synthesised, providing a haunting accompaniment to the action from the very beginning, with the use of string sounds over the cold blue of the opening credits (accompanied by the only instance of voice-over in Calparsoro's work to date, explaining the context) that fades out as the initial battle gets under way. The film also employs a motif of notes reminiscent of Latin American pipes, a slow synthesised theme with light drum pulse (as the tanks move slowly and gracefully across the dawn horizon) or the very occasional use of voice. Only rarely does the music speed up to suggest action, and ironically one example of this is precisely over the sequence of the soldiers killing time with games, chores and letters. Alternatively, slower music is used to accompany the soldiers as they retreat under attack and float downriver, or the escape of Vidal and other soldiers from their impris-onment. This counterintuitive use of music nuances further the contradictions between the ideals of warfare (particularly in the more gung-ho patriotism of recent Hollywood offerings) and the reality, thus aligning *Guerreros* with the ironic tone of other European films about the Balkans conflict.

By now Calparsoro has acquired a more sophisticated technique enhanced by the greater resources at his disposal, and aided by his more recent collaborators such as Carlos Jean and Josep María Civit. If Calparsoro can be classed as an auteur this clearly does not preclude him from experimenting stylistically and adapting his thematic concerns to the constraints and challenges of a genre as specific as the war film. Thematically, however, the continuity with the earlier work remains, as does the negative critique of the screenplay. Reviewers nonetheless acknowledged Calparsoro's achievement in a genre generally neglected in contemporary Spanish cinema, and still perceived ability in the director's work. The positive tone of reception thus continues from that of *Asfalto*, suggesting that Calparsoro has successfully crossed over into genre work.

## Note

1 This specific point is arguable; it is hard for instance to see how Germany's experiences can simply reflect those of Hollywood – and Germany was after all, a major combatant.

# 8

# *Ausentes*: shining a light on horror

For *Ausentes*, his most recent film to date, Calparsoro turned from the war film to another genre, horror. In interviews at the time of the film's release he confirmed that he wants to try out different genres: 'Desde "Asfalto" siempre intento tocar varios géneros, no centrarme en una línea para ver si soy capaz de manejarme' (I have wanted to try out different genres ever since *Asfalto*, rather than concentrate on one form, to see if I can handle it; 'Daniel Calparsoro: "Ya se me han pasado las ansias de ser protagonista"', 2005). This is in keeping with his belief that a director must test himself or herself through the boundaries and limitations of the genre film, which ironically allows him or her more latitude to offer a specific vision of the world than less precise film forms.[1] If Calparsoro's work is always violent then there is a certain logic to making a horror film, as horror always implies violence whether it explicitly shows it or not. The violence of horror indicates the fearful disruption of the prevailing order, and the menace to human life itself. In addition, Calparsoro's preference for female protagonists both coincides with and develops female subjectivity that is characteristic of horror, as established in the work of Carol Clover (1992) and Barbara Creed (1993); while horror also coincides with remote and marginalised landscapes, though here again Calparsoro provides a new twist.

The horror film has had a fairly large input from the United States but, unlike the war film, Hollywood does not possess a virtual monopoly on the horror genre. Other national cinemas have also produced horror, including both Japan and Europe. Spain itself has produced its own body of horror films, although until recently this corpus of films was barely recognised by the establishment and was usually dismissed as cheap fare designed to make a quick profit and without artistic intentions. With the rise of the '95 generation, however, horror became more mainstream and so did the place of horror in the Spanish canon. It is now an acceptable genre for study by academics of Spanish cinema. Andrew Willis (2004: 239–40) identifies two distinct strands in contemporary Spanish horror production; the ironic hybrid of horror, which parodies the genre, and horror that avoids the parody in favour of a more pure and sincere appreciation of the genre.[2] The ironic parodies include the early work of directors Alex de la Iglesia and Santiago Segura, while the sincere strand encompasses more recent films, notably the output of Jaume Balagueró – *Los sin nombre* (The Nameless, 1999), *Darkness* (2002) and *Frágiles* (Fragile, 2005). Some of Amenábar's films, in particular *The Others* (2001), might come in under this category. Other films use horror as a vehicle for films about the young (usually middle-class): *Tuno negro* (Black Serenade, Pedro L. Barbero and Vicente J. Martín, 2001), *El arte de morir* (The Art of Dying, Álvaro Fernández Armero, 2000), *Utopía* (Utopia, María Ripoll, 2003). As Willis argues, the sincere version of the genre has had good success in the Spanish film industry, acceptable to mainstream critics as well as cult audiences (2004: 247–9). This version of horror has now become more prominent than the parody of directors such as de la Iglesia and Segura, as the demands of audiences and critics here coincide. As Willis comments: 'Critically, then, Spanish horror seems, increasingly, to be becoming assimilated into the world of serious cinema, or rather, one strand of Spanish horror cinema, the one that maintains the values of the critics who write about them' (249). He concludes his discussion by claiming the parodies to be more subversive (249). Willis highlights here the role of the critic in making some versions of horror more acceptable than others although other factors also come into play in their critique, such as the perennial longing on the part of some Spanish critics for an elusive form of 'good cinema' that attracts audiences while being an artistic product. Willis further observes the role of the crossover to international audiences (248), including productions such as Balagueró's, which are shot in English and use American and British actors (such as Calista Flockhart and Richard Roxburgh in *Frágiles*). This may be another reason why the parodies have been sidelined, as they often tap into more specifically Spanish cultural genres such as the overtones of black humour in de la Iglesia's *El día de la bestia*, which recycles the Spanish style of the grotesque as well as references to don Quijote, and also a joke about the Kio Towers in Madrid which would bypass an international audience.

These points are all germane to a discussion of *Ausentes*, a film that clearly fits into Willis's second category of Spanish horror, the new sincere. Calparsoro's reputation for hyperrealism has entailed an avoidance of parody, and coincides more with the realism Willis perceives in Balagueró's *Los sin nombre*. Willis describes the world of the latter as 'offered to the audience through accepted cinematic codes of realism' (246) and further observes: 'the overwhelming choices in terms of the film's form focus on the creation of an overriding sense of realism' (247). This emphasis resolves the potential contradiction between a supernatural element of horror and Calparsoro's hitherto manifest stress on realism in his work. The potential for crossover also comes into play within the film: it is absent of specifically Spanish markers that characterise the Spanish parody version of horror and thus easily transferable to non-Spanish audiences. Calparsoro has mentioned the interest in America of a remake of the film.[3] And the critical reaction also informs us about the critics' approach to Spanish horror as well as to Calparsoro himself.

Much of the critical reaction to the film focused on what was perceived as too close a homage to earlier horror film, and above all *The Shining* (Stanley Kubrick, 1980). J.O. (2005: 110) is typical in arguing that there are too many references to other horror films, mentioning not only *The Shining* but also Roman Polanski's *Repulsion* (1965) and the stylised sequences of some contemporary Asian horror. Freixas (2005: 24) offers particularly harsh criticism of *Ausentes*'s quotation of other films. The criticism of Calparsoro as slavishly copying horror classics on the part of the Spanish critics neglects the fact that horror is a particularly self-referential genre in which earlier horror films are knowingly quoted. This became apparent in the USA with the *Scream* trilogy in particular (Wes Craven, 1996, 1997, 2000), which artfully and explicitly played on genre expectations derived from earlier horror films while nonetheless ultimately fulfilling them. Calparsoro himself lays proud claim to the recycling of horror elements, arguing that such recycling is positive, and refutes the idea that everything must be original ('Daniel Calparsoro se pasa al suspense con "Ausentes"', 2005). As we shall see, Calparsoro has in fact provided some original touches in his film, in particular his suggestion of horror in the full light of day rather than in darkness, a point also noted by reviewers and interviewers.

Once more Calparsoro's film received a mixed reception from the critics, including the usual complaint about a poor screenplay (for example Montero Plata, 2005). An interesting moment of critical schizophrenia occurs on this point. Javier Ocaña in *Cinemanía* writes a feature article on the film in which he refers to the scriptwriters as 'un triángulo de guionistas de lujo' (a deluxe trio of scriptwriters), including Calparsoro himself as well as renowned Spanish writer Ray Loriga and experienced director Elio Quiroga (Ocaña, 2005: 94). However, the review of *Ausentes* in the same issue complains that the screenplay ends in a series of magic tricks in which little is comprehensible (J.O., 2005: 110). These opposing evaluations of the script point up the difference between the feature article, often used to puff a film, and the review, which has more scope for negative criticism. Although the magazine does not make it clear, it is very likely that Ocaña and the reviewer J.O. are the same person. One would then assume from the function of the two different forms of critique that Ocaña's negative review is closer to his true opinion, but the confusion suggests the complexity of the relations between the Spanish film industry and the critical apparatus which both depends on the industry and simultaneously needs to hold it at a critical distance. By now Calparsoro has worked with different scriptwriters, yet receives the same criticisms every time, suggesting, if not proving conclusively, that Calparsoro's rough and ready approach to the screenplay is what prevails.

Some critiques of the film can be read as backhanded compliments to it. Vicente Sánchez M. (2005) argues that the film is quite simply empty, if nonetheless well made. The emptiness is surely precisely the point of the film: the central character Julia has lost her job and thus meaning to her life, so that the perceived emptiness of her surroundings reflects her state of mind. Thus a sensation of emptiness derived from the film would appear to be an effective transmission of its meaning. The same point is praised by J.O. (2005: 110) as a metaphor of solitude. Both Sánchez M. and Laura Montero Plata (2005) accuse the film of a certain degree of incoherence, but that, too, works in its favour, since the incoherence can be thought to express the gap in perception between Julia and the other characters. *Ausentes* also garnered some more overtly positive critique, such as the good use of visuals complemented by the music of Carlos Jean (Montero Plata, 2005), the atmosphere (Sánchez M., 2005), and the strength in direction that has always characterised Calparsoro's films (J.O., 2005:

110). Of the actors, Ariadna Gil as Julia came in for the most praise, while her counterpart Jordi Mollà as Samuel received more negative critique. Miguel Ángel Huerta disliked Mollà's excessive and baroque performance, which Huerta felt to be both unbearable and unbelievable (Huerta, 2006: 102).

Huerta's review makes Calparsoro a convenient scapegoat for all that he perceives to be wrong with Spanish cinema:

> Con todo, *Ausentes* es, en mi opinión, la mejor película de Calparsoro. No es mucho decir a favor de su filmografía, claro, que un film que solo tiene una premisa dramática clara y un desenlace efectista sea lo más sobresaliente de su trabajo. Pero es, me temo, lo más a lo que puede aspirar buena parte del cine español actual, un cine por lo general acomodaticio, falso y cansino. (Huerta, 2006: 102)

> (Still, *Ausentes* is in my opinion Calparsoro's best film. This is not saying much in favour of his work, of course, that a film with only a clear dramatic premise and a sensational denouement is the most outstanding thing in his work. But I fear this is the most that a large part of Spanish cinema can aspire to, a cinema that is generally acquiescent, false and lifeless.)

Huerta thus does not mark Calparsoro out as individually mediocre but as part of a general malaise that he perceives at the heart of the Spanish film industry, a malaise so bad that a good dramatic idea is an achievement in itself. It is beyond the scope of this book to make an exhaustive survey of how many other directors supposedly represent this sorry state of affairs in the eyes of the critics, but Huerta's comments do at least suggest the possibility that Calparsoro comes in for criticism simply because he does not fit in with an undefined ideal, so that reviews of *Ausentes* in the end tell us little as to how to evaluate it. While critique at the time of the trilogy indicates a more active engagement with Calparsoro's developing style of filmmaking, by now (and in keeping with the new sense of crisis that scholars and critics began to perceive from 2002) Calparsoro seems to be judged more in terms of the state of the industry. This is further indicated by the point noted above that the reviewers, while recognising references to other horror films, seem unable to assess *Ausentes* either in terms of contemporary horror generally (since they neglect the reverent homage and quotation that forms part of the seriousness of Willis's new sincere horror) or Spanish horror specifically. The critics do, however, appear to treat Calparsoro as an auteur to the extent that he is also judged in terms of his own work: Huerta, for instance, compares

*Ausentes* to Calparsoro's previous work (2006: 101) rather than to other horror filmmakers such as Balagueró or Amenábar. Arguably a mark of an auteur might include the fact that he or she is only ever judged in terms of his or her own filmography even when the demands of genre imply a different set of criteria by which to judge; while with *Guerreros* Calparsoro was treading virtually virgin soil in terms of the Spanish contemporary war film, Spanish horror is well established – and yet the criteria of this genre are barely used. This can also be seen in the perennial criticism of the screenplay, which again neglects the horror criteria; the confusion detected in the screenplay can be very easily ascribed to the mystery and suspense demanded by horror, as we shall see. Despite Willis's argument that critics have accepted the genre in its serious guise, it appears that they do not like its ambiguities – how else can we explain Freixas's irritation at the film's open ending (Freixas, 2005: 24)?

## Horror in the full light of day

What sort of horror does Calparsoro offer us? This is horror of the more subtle kind, with nothing approaching a monster except the apparently ghostly María (Mar Sodupe) who wanders intermittently about the house. The nearest entity that approaches the concept of the monstrous is precisely the concept of nothingness: this is what scares Julia the most. Some of the most effective scenes of the film reveal nothingness as terrible in itself, such as the sequence in which Julia wanders around an apparently empty supermarket until, panicked by the absence of people, she abandons her shopping trolley and flees. More generally, the absence of anybody in the idyllic suburb contrives to make the bright and sunny landscape rather creepy. That Julia is marked and haunted by emptiness, however, is suggested even before she arrives at the suburb, since in the film's opening sequence she walks through an unpopulated landscape of office blocks until she collapses, mostly obviously overwhelmed by the fact that she cannot find work but also because she has been abandoned to emptiness.

What is unusual about this emptiness is the bright light of day with which it is exposed. Comparatively few scenes take place at night and those that do see Julia inside the house. Emptiness is outside, it is sunny and it looks pleasant. Calparsoro points out that at night you can hide – as Julia indeed attempts to do initially – but there is nowhere to hide in the daytime (Pastor, 2005). The light of day exposes the horror of Julia's nothingness. To underscore this, the most ordinary of objects take on overtones of horror, such as the washing machine that starts up by itself, the milk carton that reappears on the kitchen table, the empty supermarket and the cats that invade the garden and laundry room. In his director's commentary on the DVD of *Ausentes* Calparsoro emphasises the light and the rarity of horror films that are made in the summer sunshine, seeing this as a way to transform the everyday world into a nightmare, so that we see these ordinary things in a new way. In the dark the shadows help this transformation, but it is more of a feat to make this transformation in daylight. He argues that he is attempting to turn normality into something like a lunar landscape. The emphasis on light is what gives a twist to Calparsoro's quotation of *The Shining*. While the pursuit of the wife by a husband who has turned crazy as a result of the isolation, protecting her son and helping him escape through a window are plot elements of both films, in *The Shining* the isolation is real rather than in the mind of the woman as in *Ausentes*, and the landscape of *The Shining* is cold, inhospitable and in the main chase scene nocturnal, as opposed to the bright sunshine that prevails as Samuel chases Julia. The comparison of the two films points up the fact that much of the horror in *Ausentes* stems precisely from the sunny idyll of the backdrop.

A further contrast between the two films lies in the fact that in the end it is the woman rather than the man who appears crazed and dangerous, lashing out in a frenzy with her knife, while (it is suddenly revealed to us) a group of bathers attempt to restrain her. The semi-naked bodies of the bathers, rendering them more vulnerable to her knife, reinforce Julia as dangerous and violent. One particular way in which Calparsoro's filmography coincides with horror is his preference for a female protagonist, a feature that has also characterised many horror films, as observed by Carol Clover (1992). Clover's concept of the Final Girl, the androgynous and asexual woman who survives the monster or killer, has become a cornerstone of academic writing on the horror genre: it emphasises woman as subject and as point of identification for the audience. The horror monster in turn is almost invariably male. For much of the film, Julia resembles the Final Girl of Clover's formulation. She is androgynous, despite her mothering role: Ariadna Gil, who plays the role, has a slim, boyish appearance and – although she has played *femmes fatales* in Spanish retro noir films – is well known for her role as a woman who acts the part of a man in the Oscar-winning *Belle Epoque* (Fernando Trueba, 1992). She is also asexual for most of the film. *Ausentes* includes a shot of Julia and Samuel making love but this occurs early on in the film and any sexual element to their relationship subsequently appears to wither. She is exposed to the terror of monsters, above all the sheer emptiness discussed above, but also the mysterious María, the malevolence of her elder son Félix (Nacho Pérez) and in particular the threat of Samuel, who doses her with drugs, locks her up and later chases after her with a hammer. Since for most of the film we see events from her point of view we are encouraged to identify with her, trusting that her perception of events is correct. Calparsoro encourages this explicitly through the opening sequence in which flashbacks to her rejection for a new job are juxtaposed with shots that draw closer and closer into Julia's eye, ending with an extreme close-up. In this sense we share in her subjectivity. This familiar path through horror came in for savage criticism from Huerta (we can only hope that the potential sexism of his comment was inadvertent):

> Con haber visto más de media docena de *thrillers* con atención, cualquier espectador puede anticiparse a la pobre meta a la que llegará una narración exclusivamente sustentada en el punto de vista de la protagonista femenina. (Huerta, 2006: 102)

> (Having watched more than half a dozen thrillers attentively, any audience member can predict the weak ending at which a story sustained only by the point of view of the feminine protagonist will arrive.)

While spectators may be all too familiar with the Final Girl, their expectations are thwarted as it turns out that Julia herself is the monster; Huerta appears here to miss the twist. (Huerta's comment may also inform us of a dislike for female-centred narratives that might explain his general distaste for Calparsoro's work.)

Barbara Creed's approach to horror (1993) considers the maternal as monstrous, a framework that can also be considered to fit Julia, though Creed's theory implies the woman as object for the most part, rather than subject as Calparsoro does here. Creed draws in turn on Julia Kristeva's *Powers of Horror* (1982) where Kristeva equates horror with processes of abjection. Kristeva's theory incorporates the maternal role: she states that 'devotees of the abject ... do not cease looking, within what flows from the other's "innermost being", for the desirable and terrifying, nourishing and murderous, fascinating and abject inside of the maternal body' (Kristeva, 1982: 54). These flows include urine, blood, sperm and excrement. Barbara Creed has in turn used these ideas to propose that horror texts tend to render the maternal in terms of the abject, linking the mother and bodily waste together in a relationship that signifies the possibility of regression to a point prior to our incorporation into the symbolic order (Creed, 1993: 8–15). This concept of horror appears to have little to do with *Ausentes* at first blush; although, as she gradually turns into a monstrous being, Julia becomes smeared with substances that suggest the abject – blood, earth from garden pots that she knocks over, water from the swimming pool – it is striking how clean for the most part everything is (thus in harmony with the bright light of the film). This film noticeably lacks the ooze, slime and deformity of many horror films. Julia's grubbiness suggests that the maternal threatens the paternal symbolic order represented by this spotless suburb. Another formulation of the abject by Kristeva helps us rather more. Kristeva argues:

> Narcissism ... appears as a regression to a position set back from the other, a return to a self-contemplative, conservative, self-sufficient haven. Actually, such narcissism never is the wrinkleless image of the Greek youth in a quiet fountain. The conflicts of drives ... cloud its water, and bring forth everything that, by not becoming integrated with a given system of signs, is abjection for it.
> Abjection is therefore a kind of *narcissistic crisis*, it is witness to the ephemeral aspect of the state called 'narcissism' with reproachful jealousy. (Kristeva, 1982: 14)

It might at first glance be problematic to square the term 'narcissism' with the crisis that Julia undergoes, but she nonetheless experiences a crisis of self, of the ego, after her inability to find work and her loss of purpose. If Calparsoro insists on female subjectivity, such subjectivity is what is ultimately at stake in his version of horror. This crisis becomes subsequently linked with her retreat to the suburbs, and while Kristeva's description of the 'self-contemplative, conservative, self-sufficient haven' does not necessarily apply to a specific place, this description encapsulates neatly the suburb to which she moves. And the crisis over the conflict of Julia's aims – her desire to make the bourgeois idyll work out and her desire to rediscover her sense of self through her career – comes to trouble the clear waters of life in the suburbs, at one point literally as her final mad frenzy pushes her into the neighbourhood pool. The abjection, then, is the manifestation of Julia's fears through the transformation of half her family into threats to her own sense of self (with another small marker in terms of the

15   Julia: monster and victim

flows and fluids of Samuel's injections), and the erasure of other people from the landscape, other people being an essential part of the process whereby we can recognise ourselves as individuals. Abjection consists of the disintegration of Julia's sense of self.

Therefore, Calparsoro turns the role of the woman in horror inside out, splitting both the divide between subject and object and between monster and victim within horror, and also the way in which these divisions follow along the lines of gender binaries. We see monstrosity from the inside, and that there is no clear distinction between monster and victim – the monster *is* the victim. Calparsoro liked Gil in the part of Julia for her ambiguous mixture of vulnerability, coldness and power, presenting both sides of the story (Galindo Frías, 2005), and in turn suggesting this split. We may detect here a link to the Basque trilogy and to *Asfalto* not simply in the position of woman as subject rather than object but in the complexity of that positioning. The female protagonists of the first four films are for the most part sympathetic (though Gabi of *Pasajes* is more problematic), but they participate in violence and aggression that (particularly, if reductively and stereotypically, for women) render them not far from the monstrous. Julia shares with Alex, Gabi, Marrubi and Lucía the need to have her own desires recognised, and like Alex and Gabi she remains trapped within her environment with no hope of escape. Like the women of the Basque trilogy she lives life on the margins. Unlike the other women, however, she is imprisoned not within an ambience of poverty but in a world to which many aspire as an ideal.

## The bourgeois nuclear family

The ideal apparently embodied by Julia's world functions on two levels: the ideal of the bourgeois nuclear family and the tranquil green suburb. These ideals are a new departure for Calparsoro, better known for his more obviously unpleasant and demanding environments (the industrial Basque wasteland, the underside of Madrid, Kosovan battlefields). The delving under the surface of middle-class life is perhaps the most surprising development, less in keeping with Calparsoro's track record in *cine social*. It is, however, quite typical of horror where principal victims, particularly if they take the form of a family, are often middle-class. While the primary target of some cinematic monsters and killers is young women (although any men that get in the killer's way will also be struck down), the nuclear family provides an alternative target. While this use of the family in horror suggests a fear that the family is under threat (a conservative reading), horror may also expose the contradictions and conflicts embedded within the nuclear family. Jordi Mollà makes this connection on the DVD commentary when he says that what he finds frightening about the film is the very fact that the fear comes from within the family rather than from without. In this enclosed world of the suburb there is nothing outside on to which the characters can project their fears: thus, argues Mollà, they project them on to each other.

Gil and Mollà previously played a troubled married couple in *Segunda piel* (Second Skin, Gerardo Vera, 1999), in which Gil's character tries to determine why her husband is acting strangely. It turns out he is having a gay affair and is struggling to come to terms with his homosexual desires. The trace of Gil's performance there crosses her performance in *Ausentes* where again Gil's character must try to figure out why her husband is behaving so oddly. Viewers who previously saw *Segunda piel* might be more inclined to see Samuel as the place in which the answers to the questions posed by *Ausentes* must be found. In fact, Julia herself holds the key and appears to be the source of the problem. In both films, however, conflicts arise because the family cannot satisfy all desires. The family is still something to which the protagonists wish to continue their commitment, yet it also suffocates the expression of self. If Julia becomes monstrous, this is in great part because she has no future except that of housewife and mother, roles which cannot satisfy her desires for individual recognition. This may explain why the only people she can perceive are her family, since she has no identity except within it. It may also explain why she reads their reactions to her as hostile, particularly Félix, though the final revelation of his bewilderment by the pool suggests she has misread him. Samuel and Félix prevent her from realising herself: Félix malevolently dismisses her on more than one occasion as incompetent, saying that it is not surprising she could not find another job, while Samuel suggests to her early on that she should set her sights lower. Both characters soon come to act without any reference to her. The younger son Luis (Omar Muñoz) depends on her more to the extent that he shares her point of view, confirming her in her belief that something in the family setup is wrong. The reasons why he believes her are obscure, though it may be linked to the fact that he is younger and thus closer to the maternal, not yet inducted into the patriarchal symbolic: it is notable that he has more problems than his brother in adjusting to life in the suburb. On her part, however, she has found the only character who will affirm her, and this motivates her to rescue him at the end while making no similar attempt for Félix.

In this nuclear family setup Julia's problems are perceived in terms of her inability to function as mother and housewife. Félix aggressively claims that her inability to perform the functions of a housewife – going shopping at the supermarket and providing adequate meals – is a sign that she is losing her mind. On one occasion when Samuel accuses Julia of hitting Luis, she denies doing so and then adds that the children need a mother and she cannot be that. Ocaña's feature article states that Julia is in fact not the children's natural mother, the children deriving from Samuel's previous marriage (Ocaña, 2005: 95). *Ausentes* in fact leaves this question ambiguous, though there are clues that support such a reading, such as Félix's bald and angry statement that she is not his mother, a statement which nobody contradicts. There is also the framed family photo which keeps reappearing in the living room despite Julia's repeated attempts to hide it. In this photo Julia has been replaced by another woman, who might be the phantom figure María who haunts the house, though it is hard to tell exactly. This might mean that Julia is haunted by the idea of the previous wife, or simply that her confusion over her sense of self means that in her own mind's eye she erases herself from her family and finds a replacement. María comes to function as this replacement: Julia's fear of her stems from a fear of being replaced, as she has been in the job market, but also an inadmissible desire to escape. The fear may eventually be realised since, at the end of the film as

Julia is led away to an ambulance, we glimpse a flesh-and-blood María comforting Samuel and his sons, thus positioning herself as Julia's substitute. Nonetheless, the final shot of the film is a zoom on to the family photo, but now Julia has taken the other woman's place. While the preceding shot might suggest Julia alone and free as she surveys the empty suburb, this closing shot suggests the family as a trap she could not ultimately escape. But Julia's earlier erasing of herself from the photo may also stem from a desire to escape the nuclear family. During the interview for the job she does not get, her interviewer asks her if she is married with children and she replies that she is not. At the point in the film at which she says this we know no different, but soon it transpires that she was lying. The inability to get a job is also linked with youth and with children. Julia is not hired because the firm in question prefers candidates with less experience who can be subsequently shaped and moulded. Very soon afterwards, as Samuel and Julia pack up ready for their move, he tells her not to move a box and she responds that he shouldn't treat her like a child. Then she comments that if she were a child she would have a job. The young and children, then, are also marked as threats to her identity.

These elements taken together present Julia as the bad and inadequate mother, perhaps the wicked stepmother, but since we are positioned from the start to see events from her point of view, we cannot objectify her as simply monstrous. The pain of the opening sequence in which she fails to get a job further inclines us to sympathise and take her part. Wicked stepmothers, too, have their subjectivity. The indication that the bourgeois nuclear family bears some responsibility for Julia's malaise also traces itself through Julia's relationship with Samuel. Ironically, Samuel finds satisfaction in the family environment: he works from home as a designer of video games, and strengthens his relationship with his sons, who test out his games for him. Unlike Julia he claims to fit in well in the new home: he attends neighbourhood meetings and has made friends in a short space of time (because, as his sons say, he is nice). Calparsoro liked Mollà for the part of Samuel because of his appearance of a pleasant young man but nonetheless with hidden depths (Galindo Frías, 2005). María Casanova also notes that Samuel is the sort of character Mollà likes to play, who moves easily from warm to frightening (Casanova, 2005: 44). And sinister overtones to Samuel's personality soon emerge from beneath the surface. The suggestion of menace behind his cheerful demeanour is implied from the moment they leave their old home for the suburb: as Samuel drives through the summer sunshine he responds happily to Julia's determination to make the best of her new life ahead. She smiles back at him and adds the coda, ominous even at this stage, that he never gives up and that he has what he wanted. This hints at Samuel's forcefulness for all his cheer.

Once in the new home Julia's fears of nothingness focus increasingly upon Samuel as he refuses to accept her perception of their new life, to the extent that eventually she accuses him of being behind the horrible place, the woman (María) and the cats. In parallel he adopts a more overtly threatening attitude towards her and confrontations between the two increase. Although initially he discourages her from continuing with her medication, eventually he is injecting her himself. The fact that when previously Julia handled her own medication we saw no syringe subtly underscores the violence behind Samuel's attitude as he injects her. Indeed, this form of penetration replaces sexual penetration. In a scene that parallels their earlier lovemaking, Samuel lays Julia down on their bed only to inject her with the syringe. Samuel also commits physical violence against Julia, as he grabs the top of her head and pushes her savagely down on to a nearby sofa. Julia's increasingly drugged state positions her in a period of imprisonment: she watches Samuel and the children leave the house through the window blinds (a common image of imprisonment) and subsequently Samuel locks her in her room. The growing menace of Samuel has its counterpart in María's ability to draw near, enter the house and approach Julia. She enters the house for the first time after the serious quarrel between Samuel and Julia over hitting Luis, and her entrance occurs after a cut from a scene in which Samuel watches over Julia threateningly as she washes up. Later, on Julia's discovery that Samuel has locked her in her room, she turns to find María in the room with her, telling her she will soon get used to it, an indication that Julia should not resist what is happening to her and that she should accept her entrapment. But Julia does not accept it, instead taking her resistance to the utmost by running Samuel down in the family car that originally brought her to this suburban hell, then chasing after Félix with a knife. At the end even her family appear to be invisible to Julia: we cut from a shot of her wrapped in a blanket as the crowds flow past, to another of her dripping wet as if she has just emerged from the pool, newborn. The camera circles round her gently (in contrast to some of its earlier tense and rapid circles) as she looks round her at the empty estate where not even her own family appear in shot. From the point of view of the suburb around her, Julia appears lost, isolated and pathetic, soaking wet and wrapped in a blanket. But when the scene cuts to her own perception there is greater ambiguity, with a beatific note to the *mise-en-scène*, a sense of peace and freedom – that will then contrast with the final close-up on the family photo.

## The horror of the ideal environment

The other ideal apparently embodied by Julia's world is the pleasant suburb to which she and her family have moved, the perfect backdrop for the bourgeois family, with spacious houses and gardens where the sun always shines. The setting contrasts greatly with the industrial wastelands of the Basque trilogy in particular, and to the fast pace of life in Madrid in *Asfalto*, but as in the previous films the setting has a crucial part to play in the film. Mollá observes in interview that the suburb is itself a character, that may or may not exist but around which everything revolves (Casanova, 2005: 43). Indeed, we could arguably perceive the suburb itself as the embodiment of the nothingness that comes to haunt Julia. It, too, is a monster.

As Calparsoro observes on the DVD commentary, if the place is so idyllic why is nobody there? The more pleasant setting is in addition no guarantee against marginalisation: industrial grime is not the essential landscape for this. The greenery is still a hostile territory for Julia, comparable to the alienation of the Spanish troops in the fields and woods of Kosovo in *Guerreros*. Although Calparsoro claims not to

16   Tension in the idyllic landscape

have wanted to make any comments on depopulated urban areas and the isolation of them, he notes that so many of those living in housing complexes similar to the one in the film are living there imprisoned and in torment because their money cannot stretch till the end of the month (Estrada, 2005).

Calparsoro offers a marked break between the office blocks where Julia wants to belong (themselves shot as objects of beauty in the opening credit sequence) and the suburb through a bridging long shot of a skyline of tower blocks, a pylon in the foreground, in which the camera pans away to reveal trees, then a road along which a solitary car is driving (that of Julia and her family). At the end of the sequence in the car the camera pans away again to reveal the empty suburb. Although both the office landscape and the suburb prove to be equally devoid of people, it is the former with which Julia identifies, and, as they travel away from it in the bright sunshine, Julia is in fact descending into her own personal hell.

While there are no people visible, the suburb takes on a life of its own through the security cameras that menacingly track the movements of the family. Similarly, in the maintenance room Julia finds no one there, but the suburb is nonetheless watched: the bank of TV monitors includes one that displays her sons playing. The cameras and screens become the eyes of the suburban monster. The link of the security cameras to the sense of the horror within Julia's mind is hinted at when she comments to Samuel that she does not like being watched like that, to which he responds that the cameras are protecting them and not watching them – a discrepancy of opinion that marks their different perspectives. The cameras serve as another form of imprisonment for Julia. Calparsoro notes that this overly protected and overly watched place, with no outside influences, entraps the characters and confronts them with their own fears and ghosts ('Daniel Calparsoro habla de "Ausentes"', 2005), and the cameras add to this ambience, as if Julia were in a prison camp (and prefiguring her actual imprisonment later by Samuel). Security cameras and their grainy images also function as a conduit for other forms of horror, in particular the first shots of María as she arrives at the house and rings the doorbell.

The maintenance building which Julia visits also has the Gothic appearance of a fortress, looking like a distorted small castle with gates. Within the building Julia encounters a series of doors along the corridor. As she stands uncertain in the maintenance room, these doors begin to swing open by themselves in sequence and she takes fright at a presumed approaching menace and runs away through the streets. On meeting Samuel she insists that there was nobody in the building (which he contradicts) and the doors opened on their own. He responds by talking about the doors they shut and those they opened to move here, implying that this is a new opportunity for them. But while the moves to the suburb may have opened up new vistas for Samuel, the symbol of the open door represents horror for Julia. Her own house, too, becomes an alien entity for her, even before it acts as her own cell. The first arrival of María at the house prompts Julia to step outside and scrutinise it and the street around it from all angles (as suggested by the many editing cuts in this sequence).

## Minimalism

Mollà observes of *Ausentes* that what attracted him to the story was that so much could be done with so little (Casanova, 2005: 43). This perception of minimalism was also noted by Calparsoro himself, remarking that he has already filmed with far too many guns, but that this time he achieved tension and suspense with very few elements (Estrada, 2005). Much of this minimalism we have considered already: the absence of people throughout most of the film (so that the final switch to the crowded poolside comes as a shock to us if not to Julia, who never knows they are there), the emphasis on the everyday, the lack of the more obviously grotesque horror elements. The minimalism, while employed in a very different setting, harks back to the earlier films with their small casts and location settings. It also extends to the use of black-and-white security camera footage. While the earlier films looked this way partly because of a very small budget and lack of experience, the sparse style of *Ausentes* is more carefully crafted, suggesting that Calparsoro, too, has learnt his art just as other directors of the '95 generation have while nonetheless retaining some measure of stylistic consistency. It is useful in this context to compare the opening shots in the car of *Salto al vacío*, clearly and crudely faked, with the smoother depiction of Julia and Samuel's conversation in their car – yet both scenes contribute to a sense of claustrophobia, isolation and entrapment for the central female character. As in *Guerreros*, the opening credits provide different images – cutting back from the office blocks of the opening scene to the suburb, the images fading into each other or superimposed on top of each other. In both cases the credit sequences suggest a smoother sophistication that contrasts to the cruder montage of images in the openings credits of *A ciegas*.

We have also considered another, and distinctive, aspect of style in the film: shooting in full daylight, which effectively adds to rather than diminishes the horror. While the suburb provides plenty of greenery the overwhelming impression of the film is that of whiteness, until in the penultimate shot the whole screen fades to white. White comes to stand for horror, with the white walls of the house or the milk that reappears mysteriously on the kitchen table. The clinical coldness of the white light differs from the warm brightness of the sunlight of *Asfalto*'s Madrid. Into this whiteness other colours occasionally intrude, not only the green of the foliage but bluey tones such as in the early interview scenes, or the greens of Samuel's night-time search of the garden captured on camera. Again, however, these are cold colours, similar to all the other films except *Asfalto*, and again suggesting alienation. The brief glimpse of the red door is one of the very rare occasions the colour is used, almost as if we had briefly glimpsed the monster itself. The only other comparable use of red was the bridge of *Pasajes*, suggesting the illusion of escape; so, too, here, as the open door is a symbol of hope for Samuel but of horror for Julia. The black-and-white sequences that derive from the security cameras serve to counteract the notes of colour and bleach the film once more.

As in the previous two films, the music comes from Carlos Jean. The electronic sounds with piano motif switch to slow strings as Julia appears in shot after her interview, and these strings include a slight modulation that provides a discordant note as Calparsoro cuts to the interview itself. The music includes conventional horror elements such as fairly quick strings that increase in intensity to convey suspense as Samuel searches outside the house at night after hearing noises or as he chases Julia and Luis in the car, the use of throbbing electronic pulses as Julia runs in terror from the maintenance building, or a brief touch of discordant strings as Julia finds cats in the laundry room. But rather than conforming to horror conventions the music conforms to the minimalism, providing for the most part muted touches of sound that only occasionally become prominent. Camerawork, too, is for the most part unobtrusive to conform to a genre that is less expansive than the previous war film, which required more long shots and steadycam movements paralleling those of the soldiers. But nor do we have the insistence on close-up that echoed the tensions of the central

trio of *Asfalto*. Instead we find a fairly even mixture of different shots
from different angles and distances that again does not for the most
part intrude, only becoming noticeable with the circling shots such as
at the poolside and at the end of the film (and, even then, these shots
do not obtrude in the same way as the circling and weaving shots of
*Salto al vacío* do).

Calparsoro is by now fitting the style to the genre, and thus *Ausentes*
continues with the change in style that we have previously noted for
the preceding two films. We can also detect a thematic shift in his
attention to a middle-class milieu, though even here the thread of
marginalisation, so prominent in *Salto* and *Pasajes*, reappears. The
director returns to the strong focus on female subjectivity that marked
the Basque trilogy but reformulates his focus in order to coincide
with – if not, indeed, extend – the boundaries of horror. And he
provides a new variation on the notion of landscape as the embodiment of alienation. Critical reception proved more negative on this
occasion, however, and reveals a mismatch in perception, castigating
recycling of older horror when this has become a commonplace of
the genre. *Ausentes* also provides an occasion for Huerta's outburst
against Spanish cinema as a whole as acquiescent, false and lifeless,
a comment that lies at the extreme end of the spectrum of critique
but which provides a sense of the crisis which some critics at least felt
pervaded Spanish cinema.

## Notes

1  In conversation with the author, 17 May 2006.
2  Willis is drawing on the ideas of J. Collins (1993), 'Genericity in the
   nineties: eclectic irony and the new sincerity', in J. Collins, H. Radner
   and A. Preacher Collins (eds), *Film Theory Goes to the Movies* (London:
   Routledge), pp. 242–64.
3  In conversation with the author, 17 May 2006. At the time of writing, the
   American remake of *Ausentes* has been slated for production in 2009,
   according to the websites IMDbPro and www.comingsoon.net (both
   consulted 12 September 2007).

# 9

# Conclusion

In my introduction to this study of Calparsoro, I proposed a twofold purpose in carrying out the study. In the first place, I intended a detailed close analysis of the director's six feature films. The ensuing chapters should have served to open up Calparsoro's work to further study and debate: the discussion therein is not exhaustive but functions to posit the films as a coherent corpus. Secondly, I hoped to place this corpus in its wider context, examining it not as a hermetically sealed unit but a porous one within which negotiation and confrontation with the surrounding industry can be detected. In my examination of the films I have considered the ways in which critics approached the films themselves and also the way in which critique of Calparsoro's films informs wider debates on Spanish and Basque cinema. I suggested that, using this two-pronged approach, it would be possible to understand Calparsoro as an auteur, both in the older sense of a unique individual vision that derives from the initial conceptualisations of the auteur; but also in the more recent sense of a construct that lays bare and destabilises the surrounding cinematic context, as theorised by Timothy Corrigan.

In terms of older conceptions of the auteur, we can easily discern that Calparsoro fits such conceptions readily enough, particularly within the Spanish context. He reveals consistency in theme even across the move towards genre cinema, thus providing a coherent worldview that strongly implies an auteurist vision, while nonetheless beginning to move on from his original points of departure. The director's overall vision is a bleak one, in common with many films about marginalised young people and the underside of society; but he is unusual in his constant focus on women as subjects of the narrative rather than objects of desire. Even in the one possible exception to

this, *Guerreros*, Calparsoro demonstrates a commitment to the revisu-
alisation of women in contemporary cinema ironically through his
low-key presentation of Balbuena wherein her gender is for the most
part left unstressed. The persistence of a female viewpoint may have
stemmed in the first place from Calparsoro's collaboration with Najwa
Nimri, so that the move to a primarily male ensemble in *Guerreros*
may have arisen in part at least because of the end of the couple's
marriage and Nimri's development of her acting portfolio further
afield. With *Ausentes*, however, the director continues once more his
preference for female protagonists. While, as Jordan and Morgan-
Tamosunas observe (1998: 100–1), the cinema of Spain's democratic
era has favoured the use of stories centred on women, in the past ten
years no director from the upsurge of 1995 has matched Calparsoro in
a filmography that repeatedly insists on female subjectivity even if, as
we have seen, this subjectivity can be problematic. Only Almodóvar,
from an earlier era, surpasses him. If Spanish cinema has opened
up conceptions of contemporary women, then Spanish critique has
certainly not noticed this in Calparsoro's case, pursuing Nimri with
their pens as they argue Calparsoro does with his camera. If Spanish
cinema has changed in terms of women, Calparsoro exposes the
possibility that Spanish critique has not adjusted.

Also consistent throughout Calparsoro's oeuvre is his sense of
characters as at odds with their environment, so that the landscape
comes to figure the alienation of the characters from their surroundings. This applies regardless of the nature of the landscape. While the
first three films stress the underside of the urban Basque Country –
decaying factories, bleak tower blocks, claustrophobic passageways –
the later films hop from the buzz of Madrid to the tranquil greenery of
Kosovo and then to the sunny suburbs; but in each case the protagonists cannot feel at home where they are, and the resulting tensions
in their lives give rise to the violence that plays an integral part of
each plot. The insistence in each film with which Calparsoro brings
out this antagonistic relationship between people and environment
implies once more the unity of vision that exemplified the classic
conception of the auteur. Initially, his landscapes also alienated some
critics, who refused to recognise the settings as real despite location
filming. This may suggest a discomfort with the grubbier realities of
the Basque Country, underlined by the relief with which the sunny
Madrid of *Asfalto* was hailed.

In addition, Calparsoro's cinema is violent, this being the characteristic for which it is probably most noted. Perhaps too much so, for a close examination of the films reveals that violence, though visually powerful, is intermittent. Unequal power relations always carry the possibility of violence; and much of the violence that occurs within Calparsoro's work reflects this. The violence of urban youth has formed a regular part of social realist cinema in Europe, while with his move to genre cinema Calparsoro has so far picked on specific genres that tend to violence. Violence is obviously inherent in the war film; and an ever-present possibility with horror, lurking beneath the surface of *Ausentes* until manifesting itself at the film's climax. The motif of violence continually cited in early reviews corresponds to some extent to the films themselves, but it also indicates tensions that would continue to surface during the resurgence of Spanish cinema concerning violence as a marker of US-style cinema, neglecting the precedents of both Spanish and European social-realist cinema. When Calparsoro turns to the war and horror genres the critique of violence is more muted. By the time the director immerses himself into genre film he has to some extent already been pigeonholed as the violent *enfant terrible* of Spanish cinema and critics are able to pigeonhole the violence of the films in exactly the same way: they make use of an auteurist conceptualisation to dismiss more detailed consideration of the representation of violence in Spanish cinema.

Calparsoro's vision thus remains fairly unified across his work in terms of theme and narrative structure. In terms of *mise-en-scène* his work shows more variation as the frenzied camerawork of *Salto al vacío* and the unusually angled shots of *Pasajes* give way to more conventional shooting, while the alternation between heavy rock and choral chords of the early films is displaced by, firstly, the upbeat music of *Asfalto* and, then, the more reflective music of the genre films. The most noticeable changes across Calparsoro's work, then, comes with changes in *mise-en-scène* from *cine social* to genre; and this shift coincides with changes in collaboration (in particular Nimri's retreat from full participation, the addition of scriptwriting assistance and new composers and a new director of cinematography). The director maintains a consistency of vision thematically despite working with a variety of collaborators on different films: this may simply indicate that he collaborates with those whose cinematic vision and thematic and narrative interests most closely resemble his own, but it does tend further to support the notion of Calparsoro as auteur in the traditional sense. This applies to some extent even to the most prominent of collaborations, with Nimri. While the collaboration with Nimri seemed to be the most powerful driving force within Calparsoro's first four films, to the extent that critics saw these films as a homage to Nimri, he maintains interest in similar thematic points even though she no longer embodies these themes. The original theme, centred on the female protagonist of *Salto al vacío*, was conceived prior to Nimri's casting, so it both predates and outlives her. This implies difficulties with the star framework used to interpret Calparsoro's work: the presence of Nimri in the films is not a negligible factor, but it may not be the overriding one that some critics have perceived.

Calparsoro's work implies a continuum with older styles of Spanish filmmaking that predate the upsurge in the industry in 1995. Although that was the year that Calparsoro made his breakthrough, his case provides one example to suggest that the upsurge did not mean a total break with the past. The commitment to *cine social* maintains the tradition of such cinema in both Spain and Europe more generally. The greatest change in Calparsoro's work has been the move towards genre cinema, though the continuity with earlier themes suggests a smoother blurring of cinematic approaches between genre and *cine social*. Ironically, he began to make this move at the very time critics claim the crisis in Spanish cinema began, turning to the very areas they now dislike, just as they look back with nostalgia at the cinema that he leaves behind. Calparsoro's trajectory is virtually the opposite to that of critical perceptions of the Spanish film industry in that the latter acknowledge the strength of the upsurge of 1995 at the very time Calparsoro continues the tradition of *cine social* (although his appearance as a new director in 1995 gains him some critical benefit from the perception of a new generation of filmmakers) and later, at the time of crisis, lament the loss of older styles of filmmaking while Calparsoro turns towards genre.

This move against the grain does not itself necessarily destabilise the context within which the director works: we might ascribe this to originality, perversity, unawareness or simply a desire to follow his own path regardless. But his cinema is exactly the sort that Carlos Losilla lamented as lacking in his article of 1997 (considered in the introduction), the solitary dissident auteur making war; yet Losilla did not perceive the similarity of Calparsoro to the ideal he was looking for. In this sort of guerrilla cinema there is little room in the early films for the smooth and polished style that in fact many critics looked for and usually failed to find in the director's trilogy. Yet the themes and plotlines of his films suggest the style as of a piece with a notion of the world as alienating and threatening. The style is meant precisely to disorientate us. Later films are smoother at a time when the commercial vein had been found wanting. This, too, might arguably function as a form of cinematic dissidence in that breaching the divide between *cine social* and more commercially orientated genres problematises an over-simplistic divide between Spanish, European and Hollywood cinemas. Many Spanish directors do in fact utilise different genres and styles, while those who stick to one style or genre are less common. Industrial constraints in Spain prevent too much dependence on specialisation (horror may be an exception), while some directors, including Calparsoro himself, prefer to experiment in any case. Examples might be Amenábar's move from thrillers such as *Tesis* to a biopic like *Mar adentro*; while Juanma Bajo Ulloa shifted from the dark tones of *Alas de mariposa* and *La madre muerta* (The Dead Mother, 1993) to the comedy of *Airbag* (1997) (see Allinson, 2003).

In the introduction I suggested the director as a crossing point of interrelated threads that go to make up the contemporary Spanish film scene. In Calparsoro's case the interrelations of these threads reveal tensions at the heart of the Spanish film enterprise that result from conflicting pressures to make films that are commercially viable, attract audiences, attract funding and have pretensions to art. In the introduction I also reviewed Corrigan's theory of the contemporary auteur, which I argued could be applied to the Spanish context notwithstanding the different connotation in Spain and the USA of what commercial cinema is. Corrigan talks of auteurism as 'part of an agency that culturally and socially monitors identification and critical reception' (Corrigan, 1991: 105), and Calparsoro achieves this by revealing some of the faultlines in critical reception of Spanish cinema. Corrigan also argues for the potential of some auteurs to destabilise the field within which they work (107), and Calparsoro achieves this as well by laying bare and by problematising the prevailing critical and interpretative structures through which the canons of Spanish and Basque cinema are formed; the auteurist framework brings the difficulties and contradictions of these structures into relief. Calparsoro functions as an auteur in terms of Corrigan's monitoring of identification and critical reception. Critics function as a conduit between directors, stars, the industry and audiences, although their impact on all of these is never predetermined. They also participate in the debate about Spanish cinema as a whole, providing guidelines at the cutting edge as to how to talk about it. Critics frequently use an undefined criterion of 'good' cinema with which to judge films (it often includes a good screenplay while other cinematic elements might be neglected); and Calparsoro's work does not always pass this vague test. They do, however, talk of Calparsoro in implicitly auteurist terms (in the older sense), contradicting Losilla's fear (1997a: 40) that auteurist cinema is disappearing in the contemporary era to some extent, since critics still impose such a framework for discussion.

Calparsoro's work brings into prominence some of the assumptions that undergird this framework, and above all the concept of the auteur itself. When I asked Calparsoro if he thought of himself as an auteur, he replied that he did not think he was one yet.[1] His response raises the question as to when the auteur comes into being. Yet the assumption of the auteur guides much of critical reception in Spain whether the label of auteur is merited or not; in Calparsoro's case I think it is (*pace* his own caveat), but the point may in fact be moot, as his place within the Spanish cinema scene revolves around this assumption. Heredero's entire conceptualisation of the '95 generation rests on the director as its guiding figure, which does not in itself automatically presume auteurism but definitely heightens its use as a concept in the older sense while playing down the more fluid approach in the concept's later incarnation that takes into account the collaboration of others. The other major assumption in critique of Calparsoro is the need for quality, particularly as regards the plot and screenplay. Calparsoro ironically appears an auteur for many Spanish critics precisely in that he consistently ignores their markers of quality in terms of screenplay and plot. In fact, the majority of Calparsoro's films are reasonably well plotted, although the early use of *cine social* with its stress on realism more overtly coincides with what appear at first blush to be episodic films. This produces a contradiction at the heart of Calparsorian critique: the auteurist framework used implies an indication of arthouse quality, a throwback to earlier forms of Spanish filmmaking, an insistence on a certain standard of filmmaking which Calparsoro then fails to live up to in the eyes of the reviewers because their standard of a good film is not his. For Calparsoro, as we saw in the introduction, screenplay and plot are not nearly as important as character and emotion. The contradiction is complicated still further by the simplistic equation of contemporary Spanish cinema with Hollywood-style violence; and since violence is one of the elements that most struck reviewers with Calparsoro's films, a further framework is imposed over the top that ignores the long-standing use of violence in Spanish cinema. It is in this sense above all that the director works as a cultural nexus, not solely in terms of a consistent vision of contemporary Spanish society but also of a consistent misperception of how he conveys that vision.

In terms of Basque cinema, Calparsoro's work highlights the difficulties of the very narrow conceptualisation of the idea posited by Jaume Martí-Olivella and Joseba Gabilondo, as outlined in the introduction. Basque cinema as a concept appears to have a strong tie to wider concepts of Basque national identity; and this in turn reveals that some cinematic realities are more acceptable than others (thus potentially replicating wider Basque problems) and automatically excluding some issues and some people as properly Basque. While Calparsoro has not been alone among directors in refusing to be confined to a narrow definition of Basque cinema, preferring to question the concept rather than subscribe to it, he is a rarer example of depicting Basque realities that are less welcome than the preferred rural arcadias. Basque nationalism has in the past had problems in coming to terms with the working class and underclass (indeed, it arose in great part in reaction to and against the presence of such groups within the Basque Country). Martí-Olivella's accusation that Calparsoro ignores Basque realities hints that such conceptions of Basque nationalism may still apply today. In addition, the use that both Martí-Olivella and Gabilondo make of the concept of home and homeland prove irrelevant for both the underclasses and women, as the trilogy demonstrates. The question of exile and the uncanny haunting of home proves moot when the characters cannot get away from a home that is in fact a trap; such conceptualisations also ignore the very different resonances that home may have for women, tied in as the latter concept is with a private sphere often neglected in Basque nationalism. The value of the term 'Basque cinema' may be debatable (and for all my unease with the hypotheses of Gabilondo and Martí-Olivella, such hypotheses have their place within this debate), but certainly we need to find some convenient way to refer to films that derive from Basque issues but that do not define them within too narrow a framework. Basque cinema shares with other national cinemas the need to recognise that not all problems can be defined solely in nationalist terms. Calparsoro's extension of his themes from the trilogy to genre films indicates as much. The theories of Basque cinema offered to us run the risk of ignoring relevant contributions of films and directors that fall outside of a current remit that may well prove too narrow to be sustainable. Indeed, they raise the question of whether there can be such a thing as an auteur within Basque cinema and how we should perceive and interact with such cinema if Basque auteurs cannot exist within it.

The case of Calparsoro, then, shows the misapplication of four critical frameworks: the star as the director's muse, the auteur as provider of arthouse cinema, the use of violence as simply reflective of US practice (itself a possible reductive understanding of US cinema), and the overly narrow conceptualisation of Basque cinema. To point out the poor fit of these interpretative frameworks is not to claim a director such as Calparsoro as a misunderstood genius; whether or not this is true, such a notion returns us too readily to the original concept of the director as artist. What I would like to highlight is that Calparsoro's case demonstrates the fact that the more fluid movement between arthouse and genre cinema indicated by Allinson (2003) has undermined the contemporary critical enterprise within the Spanish film industry. It has recognised the changes on the Spanish cinema scene of the last decade or so but it has not adapted, so that it perpetuates the older forms of auteurist debates, led by Heredero's framing of contemporary cinema precisely in terms of the director. The relation of the director to the Spanish cinema scene via the review process is in danger of becoming anachronistic. How much does this matter? As James Naremore comments, the study of the director continues to be necessary (Naremore, 1990: 21), while on the other hand the auteur debate leaves untouched the question of audience interactions with contemporary Spanish film. But the increasing (and welcome) emphasis on the audience that scholars of Spanish film are providing should not mean the neglect of the critical corpus of reviews and scholars themselves in their attempt to shape the critical discourse on contemporary Spanish cinema. Critics are not infallible any more than directors are, but they are the interface between the different elements within the Spanish cinema scene, and as such they demonstrate what is at work in the articulation of a Spanish national cinema that discourses of plurality such as the generational one have, as Triana-Toribio puts it, disavowed (Triana-Toribio 2003: 147). Calparsoro's oeuvre and its reception indicate that what is at work is not so much a crisis in the industry but a crisis in its interpretative frameworks.

## Notes

1  In conversation with the author, 17 May 2006.

# Filmography and synopses

*Salto al vacío* (Jump into the Void) 1995, 85 mins
Produced by: Daniel Calparsoro, Fernando Colomo
Executive Producer: Enrique Fernández Ayuso
Director of Photography: Kiko de la Rica
Editor: Pite Piñas
Screenplay: Daniel Calparsoro
Leading players: Alex (Najwa Nimri), Javi (Roberto Chalu), Esteban (Alfredo Villa), Toño (Ion Gabella), Juáncar (Karra Elejalde), Alberto (Kandido Uranga), Luis (Saturnino García), Fati (Carla Calparsoro), María (Mariví Bilbao), Eva (Noemí Parra)

Alex and fellow gang members Javi, Toño and Esteban drive to a waste dump with a policeman they have kidnapped after a robbery that goes wrong. On arrival at the dump, Javi and Esteban argue; Toño shoots the policeman dead. The gang drive off; the bickering continues in the car until Toño, who is driving, crashes the car in sheer rage. The gang go their separate ways but not before Javi and Alex share a kiss. At home, Alex listens to the different demands of her family. Her mother tells her that Javi would find her more attractive if she made more of an effort with her looks: subsequently Alex goes to the bathroom and begins to apply make-up. Alex's uncle Alberto comes to the family flat to ask her to work for him as a bodyguard at a meeting; he and her father Luis argue violently, and Alex intervenes by pointing a gun at her father. The gang meet in Esteban's caravan; two men subsequently arrive to carry out a gun deal with Esteban. The three men fight, and Esteban's finger is cut off; the rest of the gang intervene. Later, Alex carries out a series of drug deals before meeting her brother Juáncar and talking to him of her hopes with Javi. She then meets with her uncle at a dogfight, shooting dead two men who beat him up. She meets Javi at a party; the two begin to kiss but then Javi reveals he is impotent. Subsequently, Esteban – now working for the gun runners – shoots Juáncar dead. Alex vows revenge, paying no attention to Javi, who is now proposing they go away together and set up a bar. Javi walks away and leaves her alone in the gathering mist.

*Pasajes* (Passages) 1996, 90 mins
Produced by: Agustín Almodóvar
Director of Photography: Kiko de la Rica
Editor: José Salcedo
Music: Alberto Iglesias
Screenplay: Daniel Calparsoro
Leading players: Gabi (Najwa Nimri), Carmina (Charo López), Manu (Alfredo
    Villa), Butano (Ion Gabella), Gema (Carla Calparsoro)

Gabi and Gema carry out an apartment robbery. The police are alerted; Gabi
escapes the apartment building but Gema is shot dead. Manu and Butano
wander round the dockside discussing Butano's hopes of boxing success.
At their squat they find Gabi, who tells them of Gema's death. Butano is
distraught, while Manu accuses Gabi of using people. As Gabi walks the
streets, she catches sight of a woman, Carmina, walking in high heels. Gabi
begins to stalk her, following Carmina to her home and subsequently to her
job as a hospital cleaner, from which she is fired. Gabi moves into Carmina's
flat, begins an affair with her and induces her into the world of crime. But
when the couple rob a fish warehouse, Gabi is jealous at Carmina's flirtation
with the warehouse watchman and the two women quarrel. After a subsequent house robbery Gabi takes Carmina to buy the green marbled shoes
about which Gabi has fantasised. The couple then meet with Manu and
Butano, and the four plan the robbery of a bar. As the robbery is carried out,
Gabi abandons Carmina and goes with the two men to their hideout, where
she attempts to persuade Manu to leave Butano and go abroad with her. The
police arrive and Manu dies in a shoot-out; Gabi departs, leaving Butano to
weep over Manu's body.

*A ciegas* (Blindly) 1997, 92 mins
Produced by: Juan Alexander
Director of Photography: Gonzalo F. Berridi
Editor: José Salcedo
Music: Mario de Benito
Screenplay: Daniel Calparsoro
Leading players: Marrubi (Najwa Nimri), Mikel (Alfredo Villa), Clemente
    (Ramón Barea), Aitzpea (Elena Irureta), Paquita (Mariví Bilbao), Taxista
    (Javier Nogueiras), Eneko (Vidal Fernández), Andoni (Víctor Peñas),
    Reporter (Santiago Ugalde)

Marrubi works in a laundry, watched over obsessively by her boss Clemente.
At the end of her shift she goes with her partner Mikel to carry out an ETA
assassination at a house in the country. However, instead of shooting dead the
owner of the house she shoots her comrade Eneko in the knee, and the house
owner subsequently seizes a gun and shoots him dead as well as threatens
her. Mikel drives her away to a safe house, where he reports her actions to

Aitzpea. He takes away the son of himself and Marrubi. The safe house is raided by police; Marrubi escapes and seeks refuge with Clemente. He holds her hostage and forces her to fellate him; in the process she bites his penis and holds him at gunpoint. Mikel comes to Clemente's home looking for Marrubi; Marrubi hides in fear that he has come to kill her, but in fact he has not. Marrubi imprisons Clemente and his housekeeper in bubble wrap and then leaves the flat; she wanders the streets as a riot takes place in response to the death of Eneko. Marrubi subsequently meets Mikel in a station; the two make love but Mikel refuses to leave with her and their son. Meanwhile, Aitzpea waits with the son in the station café. Mikel is ambushed and shot dead by police on the station platform; a shoot-out begins in the café. Aitzpea flees with the son; Marrubi sees them and follows. As she approaches Aitzpea, the latter points a gun at her but then lets it fall; she allows Marrubi to leave with her son.

*Asfalto* (Asphalt) 2000, 90 mins
Produced by: José María Lara
Director of Photography: Josep M. Civit
Editor: Julia Juaniz
Music: Nacho Mastretta, Najwajean
Screenplay: Daniel Calparsoro, Frank Palacios, Santiago Tabernero
Leading players: Lucía (Najwa Nimri), Charly (Juan Diego Botto), Chino (Gustavo Salmerón), Antonio (Alfredo Villa), Clarita (Antonia San Juan)

Charly and Chino meet Lucía, Chino's girlfriend, and take her back to Charly's place where Chino and Lucía make love. Chino invites her to help in the raid they are about to carry out; Charly is annoyed and the trio argue. They go to the flat of a Frenchman; Chino attacks the Frenchman and thinks he has killed him. He runs off while Charly and Lucía raid the flat for drugs. The trio agree to meet up later, but Chino does not arrive. Charly begins to show a sexual attraction towards Lucía. He and she go to his home and start to make love, but Chino interrupts them and realises what is going on. Lucía then initiates a sexual threesome. Afterwards Chino is not happy and calls his brother Antonio for help; Antonio, a policeman, organises a raid that results in Charly going to prison. On his release from jail Charly is met by Lucía, who tells him that she and Chino are setting up home together and do not want to see Charly again. Chino has meanwhile joined the police. He wants Lucía to stop dealing in drugs. She agrees to carry out one final deal before quitting, but as she does so she is robbed of her money. Chino subsequently realises that the theft was a setup organised by Antonio. He meets with Charly, and the two then find Lucía, but Antonio catches up with them and starts a quarrel with all three. As they drive along in Chino's car, the argument causes Chino to crash. The trio stagger out of the car, steal another and head away from Madrid into the country. But Chino stops the car, embraces Charly and Lucía

and then starts to walk back towards the city, while Lucía and Charly head in
the opposite direction.

### Guerreros (Warriors) 2002, 96 mins
Produced by: Fernando Bovaira, Enrique López Lavigne
Director of Photography: Josep M. Civit
Editor: Julia Juaniz
Music: Najwajean
Screenplay: Daniel Calparsoro, Juan Cavestany
Leading players: Vidal (Eloy Azorín), Alonso (Eduardo Noriega), Rubio
    (Rubén Ochandiano), Balbuena (Carla Pérez), Ballesteros (Jordi Vilches),
    Lucas (Roger Casamajor), Gómez (Iñaki Font), Mónica (Sandra Walhbeck),
    Marceau (Olivier Sitruck)

In the middle of a battle in a Kosovan town, the power is cut. Meanwhile,
Spanish soldiers are working to restore a church near a refugee camp in
another part of Kosovo, when one solider, Vidal, goes to rescue a man being
tortured. The other soldiers have to intervene and Vidal is reprimanded by
Lieutenant Alonso. The troop is then sent to restore power to the Kosovan town
of the opening sequence; on the way the peacekeeping forces are ambushed
and the Spanish troop retreats. One soldier, Gómez, dies, Rubio is injured,
then the interpreter, Mónica, is seriously injured by a landmine. Vidal is sent
to rescue her, but smothers her instead. Another soldier, Lucas, dies. The
remainder of the retreating soldiers arrive at the town and are imprisoned.
Balbuena is raped. Vidal, Balbuena, Rubio and Marceau escape; on the run,
they kill a soldier and a farmer, and are then nearly buried in a mass grave.
They return to the town just as the light is restored; panicked by gunfire, they
are quickly surrounded by the townspeople. Alonso comes to tell them their
mission is over.

### Ausentes (The Absent) 2005, 91 mins
Produced by: Juan Alexander
Director of Photography: Josep M. Civit
Editor: Iván Aledo
Music: Carlos Jean
Screenplay: Daniel Calparsoro, Ray Loriga
Leading players: Julia (Ariadna Gil), Samuel (Jordi Mollà), María (Mar
    Sodupe), Félix (Nacho Pérez), Luis (Omar Muñoz)

Julia, who has failed in her attempt to find a new job, moves to a suburban
development with husband Samuel and children Félix and Luis. The
suburban development is apparently empty. Julia's unease in her new home
is exacerbated by the occasional mysterious appearance of a ghostly woman
called María in the house. When Julia visits the maintenance block and a
supermarket, she is struck by their emptiness and appears to be pursued

in both by unknown beings. The more she grows uneasy, the more Samuel and Félix treat her as if she were unwell, until eventually Samuel starts to inject her with drugs and lock her in the house. Eventually, Julia attempts to run away with Luis; Samuel pursues them, and María seizes Luis. Julia then runs Samuel down in their car and chases Félix to the local swimming pool; appearing to be attacked once more by unseen beings, she lashes out frenziedly with a knife. From Félix's point of view, however, we see that she is in fact lashing out at a crowd of bathers. Finally, she falls into the pool. Subsequently, María brings the children to be reunited with their wounded father while Julia stands to one side, isolated. A cut to her point of view reveals that she still sees nobody around her.

# Bibliography

Some of the references listed below were consulted in the archives of the Filmoteca, Madrid; not all the material stored there carried full bibliographical information, and page numbers are often not available. This material can be consulted in the Filmoteca's collection of press clippings.

'A ciegas' (1997), *Fotogramas* L/1947, 108.

Aldarondo, R. (1996), 'Relámpagos sobre el agua', *El diario vasco* (25 November).

Allinson, M. (1997), 'Not matadors, not natural born killers: violence in three films by young Spanish directors', *Bulletin of Hispanic Studies* 74 /3, 315–30.

Allinson, M. (2003), 'Is the auteur dead? The case of Juanma Bajo Ulloa', *International Journal of Iberian Studies* 15/3, 143–51.

Andrew, D. (1993), 'The unauthorized auteur today', in J. Collins, H. Radner and A. Preacher Collins (eds), *Film Theory Goes to the Movies* (New York: Routledge), pp. 77–85.

Ángulo, J. (2000), 'Najwa Nimri', *Cinemanía* 53, 33.

Ángulo, J. and J. L. Rebordinos (2005), *Contra la certeza: el cine de Julio Medem* (San Sebastián/Huesca: Filmoteca Vasca/Festival de Cine de Huesca).

Arocena, C. (2003), '¡No encuentro el punto de giro! El papel de los guionistas en la crisis del cine español', in L. Alonso García (ed.), *Once miradas sobre la crisis y el cine español* (Madrid: Ocho y medio), pp. 75–95.

Asúa, A. (2002), 'Eduardo Noriega', *Cinerama* 94, 24–6.

Ballesteros, I. (2001), *Cine (ins)urgente: textos fílmicos y contextos culturales de la España postfranquista* (Madrid: Fundamentos).

Barredo, I. (2002), 'Piedras', in Equipo Reseña (eds), *Cine para leer 2002: enero-junio* (Bilbao: Mensajero), pp. 283–6.

Benavent, F. M. (2000), *Cine español de los noventa: diccionario de películas, directores y temático* (Bilbao: Mensajero, 2000).

Brooks, P. (1995), *The Melodramatic Imagination: Balzac, Henry James, Melodrama, and the Mode of Excess* (New Haven: Yale University Press).

Casado, M. (2002), 'Daniel Calparsoro baixa als inferns de Kosovo', *Avui* (21 March), www.avui.es/avui/diari/02/mar/21/410121.htm, accessed 23 May 2003.

Casanova, M. (2000), 'Daniel Calparsoro', *Cinemanía* 53, 46.

Casanova, M. (2002), 'El pacifismo imposible', *Cinemanía* 79, 86–91.

Casanova, M. (2005), 'Jordi Mollà', *Cinemanía* 121, 42–4.

Castro de Paz, J. and J. Cerdán (2003), 'La crisis como flujo', in L. Alonso García (ed.), *Once miradas sobre la crisis y el cine español* (Madrid: Ocho y medio), pp. 23–39.

C. L. (2000), 'Asfalto: sobra el thriller', *Cinemanía* 53, 80.

Clover, C. (1992), *Men, Women and Chain Saws: Gender in the Modern Horror Film* (Princeton: Princeton University Press).

Comas, J. (1995), '"La realidad es todavía peor en Barakaldo"', *El País* (19 February).

Corral, R. (s.d.), 'Guerreros', www.labutaca.et/films/7/guerreros1.htm, accessed 23 May 2003.

Corrigan, T. (1991), *A Cinema Without Walls: Movies and Culture After Vietnam* (London: Routledge).

Cortijo, J. (1996), '"Dos películas no bastan para juzgarme como director"', *ABC del ocio* (21 November 1996).

Costa, J. (1997), 'Fruitopia "jarrai"', *Avui* (15 September).

Creed, B. (1993), *The Monstrous Feminine: Film, Feminism, Psychoanalysis* (London: Routledge).

Crumbaugh, J. (2001), 'An aesthetic of industrial ruins in Bilbao: Daniel Calparsoro's *Leap into the Void* (Salto al vacío) and Frank Gehry's Guggenheim Museum Bilbao', *International Journal of Iberian Studies* 14/1, 40–50.

Cueto, R. (1998), 'Introducción: de los toros a la coca', in R. Cueto (ed.), *Los desarraigados en el cine español* (Gijón: Festival Internacional de Cine de Gijón), pp. 7–16.

'Daniel Calparsoro habla de "Ausentes"' (2005), www.aullidos.com, accessed 18 July 2005.

'Daniel Calparsoro se pasa al suspense con "Ausentes"' (2005), *ABC* (13 September), www.abc.es/abc/pg050913/actualidad/espectaculos/cine/200509/13/ausentes.asp, accessed 27 September 2005.

'Daniel Calparsoro: "Ya se me han pasado las ansias de ser protagonista"' (2005), *Canarias7.es* (28 August), www.canarias7.es, accessed 24 October 2005.

Davies, A. (2003), '*La voz de su amo*: male noir angst in a rural Basque landscape', unpublished paper given at the Hispanic Cinemas Conference, London.

Davies, A. (2005), 'Roads to nowhere: how Basque terrorists cross space and place in cinema', *Bulletin of Hispanic Studies* 82/3, 343–55.

Davies, A. (2007), 'Spanish neo noir', in A. Spicer (ed.), *European Film Noir* (Manchester: Manchester University Press), pp. 210–35.

Demicheli, T. H. (1997), 'Calparsoro: "Un terrorista es un fascista disfrazado de romántico o idealista"', *ABC* (26 August).

'Directores: los que gritan "¡Acción!"' (2005), *Cinemanía* 121, 204–10.

Doane, M. A. (1987), 'The "woman's film": possession and address', in C. Gledhill (ed.), *Home is Where the Heart Is: Studies in Melodrama and the Woman's Film* (London: British Film Institute), pp. 283–98.

Elsaesser, T. (1987), 'Tales of sound and fury: observations on the family melodrama', in C. Gledhill (ed.), *Home is Where the Heart Is: Studies in Melodrama and the Woman's Film* (London: British Film Institute), pp. 43–69.

Estrada, J. (2005), 'Terror entre adosados', *El mundo* (14 September), www.elmundo.es/metropoli/2005/09/16/cine/1126821606.html, accessed 27 September 2005.

Evans, P. W. (1999), 'Introduction', in P. W. Evans (ed.), *Spanish Cinema: the Auteurist Tradition* (Oxford: Oxford University Press), pp. 11–17.

Evans, P. W. (2004), *Bigas Luna: Jamón jamón* (Barcelona: Paidos).

Fecé, J. L. and C. Pujol (2003), 'La crisis imaginada de un cine sin público', in L. Alonso García (ed.), *Once miradas sobre la crisis y el cine español* (Madrid: Ocho y medio), pp. 147–65.

Fernández Santos, A. (2005), 'Una extraña y apasionante jornada de cine español', *El País* (19 February).

Fernández-Santos, E. (1997), 'Daniel Calparsoro retrata en "A ciegas" la confusión de una terrorista arrepentida', *El País* (24 August).

F.M. '*Pasajes*', *Cine para leer 1996* (Bilbao: Mensajero, 1997), 500–1.

Freixas, R. (2005), 'Ausentes: el espanto surge de la nada', *Dirigido* 349, 24.

Gabilondo, J. (2002), 'Uncanny identity: violence, gaze and desire in contemporary Basque cinema', in Jo Labanyi (ed.), *Constructing Identity in Contemporary Spain: Theoretical Debates and Cultural Practice* (Oxford: Oxford University Press), pp. 262–79.

Galindo Frías, D. (2005), 'Daniel Calparsoro', http://barcelona.lanetro.com/canales/, accessed 18 July 2005.

Gates, P. (2005), '"Fighting the good fight": the real and the moral in the contemporary Hollywood combat film', *Quarterly Review of Film and Video* 22/4, 297–310.

Girard, R. (1972), *Deceit, Desire and the Novel: Self And Other in Literary Structure*, trans. Y. Frecerro (Baltimore: Johns Hopkins University Press).

Gómez, L. (1995), 'La Fuerza de la persuasión', *El País Babelia* (30 December), 2

Gómez Cascales, A. (2002), 'Eduardo Noriega planta cara', *Shangay Express* 185 (21 April), 21–4.

'"Guerreros", retrato de unos soldados españoles en la guerra de Kosovo' (2002), *El mundo* (23 March), www.elmundo.es/elmundo/2002/03/20/cine/1016648634.html, accessed 27 September 2005.

Hamilton, C. (2000), 'Re-membering the Basque nationalist family: daughters, fathers and the reproduction of the radical nationalist community', *Journal of Spanish Cultural Studies* 1/2, 153–71.

Heredero, C. F. (1997), *Espejo de miradas: entrevistas con nuevos directores del cine español de los años noventa* (S.l.: Festival de Cina de Alcalá de Henares/Caja de Asturias/Filmoteca de la Generalitat Valenciana/Fundación Autor).

Heredero, C. F. (1999), *20 nuevos directores del cine español* (Madrid: Alianza).

Huerta, M. A. (2006), 'Ausentes', in Equipo Reseña (eds), *Cine para leer 2005: julio-diciembre* (Bilbao: Mensajero 2006), pp. 101–2.

Iturriaga, M. L. (1995), 'Rock terminal, ruidoso y salvaje', *El País de las tentaciones* (3 March 1995).

Jardín, R. (2006), 'Menos es nada: una aproximación al último cine negro español (1980–2005)', in J. Palacios (ed.), *Euronoir: serie negra con sabor europeo* (Madrid: Festival Internacional de Cine, Las palmas de Gran Canaria/T&B), pp. 389–401.

J.O. (2005), 'Ausentes', *Cinemanía* 120, 110.

Jordan, B. and M. Allinson (2005), *Spanish Cinema: A Student's Guide* (London: Hodder Arnold).

Jordan, B. and R. Morgan-Tamosunas (1998), *Contemporary Spanish Cinema* (Manchester: Manchester University Press).

Kinder, M. (1993), *Blood Cinema: The Reconstruction of National Identity in Spain* (Berkeley: University of California Press).

Kristeva, J. (1982), *Powers of Horror: An Essay on Abjection*, trans. L. Roudiez (New York: Columbia University Press).

Langford, B. (2005), *Film Genre: Hollywood and Beyond* (Edinburgh: Edinburgh University Press).

Larequi García, E. M. (2003), 'Un intento de cine bélico español: *Guerreros* de Daniel Calparsoro', www.lenguasecundaria.com/resenas/imprimir/guerrerc.htm, accessed 23 May 2003.

Larraguibel, C. (1999), 'Asfalto', *Cinemanía* 48, 106–7.

Leyra, P. (1995a), 'Daniel Calparsoro: "La violencia es un género que todo el mundo entiende"', *El semanal* (23 April).

Leyra, P (1995b), '"Mi película llega al estómago": Daniel Calparsoro', *Cambio 16* (20 March), 356–7.

Leyra, P. (1995c), 'Tarantino a la española', *Cambio 16* (20 March), 357.

Losilla, C. (1997a), 'Adónde va el cine español', *Dirigido* 257, 34–42.

Losilla, C. (1997b), 'A ciegas': cine español, suma y sigue', *Dirigido* 261, 14.

Luchini, A. (1996), 'Daniel Calparsoro: "El filme trata del capitalismo de las relaciones"', *Metropoli* (22 November).

Marinero, F. (1997), 'Contradictoria, incomprensible y caótica', *El mundo* (12 September).

Marinero, F. (2002), 'El espectáculo del drama', www.el-mundo.es/metropoli/paginas/critica_cine_p617e.html, 21 Mar, accessed 23 May 2003.

Martínez Montalbán, J. L. (s.d.), 'Salto al vacío', in Equipo Reseña (ed.), *Cine para leer 1995* (Bilbao: Mensajero), pp. 491–3.

Martí-Olivella, J. (1999), 'Invisible otherness: from migrant subjects to the subject of immigration in Basque cinema', in W. A. Douglass et al. (eds),

*Basque Cultural Studies* (Reno: Basque Studies Program, University of Nevada), pp. 205–6.

Martí-Olivella, J. (2003), *Basque Cinema: An Introduction* (Reno: Center for Basque Studies, University of Nevada).

Mazierska, E. and L. Rascaroli (2003), *From Moscow to Madrid: Postmodern Cities, European Cinema* (London: I. B. Tauris).

Montero, M. (1995), 'Calparsoro: "No tengo que ver con Tarantino"', *El Periódico* (31 May), 599.

Montero Plata, L. (2005), 'El guión ausente', www.filasiete.com/ausentes. htm, accessed 27 September 2005.

'Najwa Nimri' (2000), www.elmundo.es/magazine/num148/textos/naj1.html (31 Jan), accessed 27 September 2005.

Naremore, J. (1990), 'Authorship and the cultural politics of film criticism', *Film Quarterly* 44/1, 14–22.

Nowell-Smith, G. (1987), 'Minelli and melodrama', in C. Gledhill (ed.), *Home is Where the Heart Is: Studies in Melodrama and the Woman's Film* (London: British Film Institute), pp. 70–4.

Ocaña, J. (2005), 'Ausentes', *Cinemanía* 120, 94–5.

Palacios, J. (2000), 'Asfalto', *Fotogramas* LIII/1876, 14.

Palacios, J. (2002), 'Guerreros', *Fotogramas* LV/1902, 18.

Palacios, J. (2006), 'Ni rebeldes ni causa: delincuencia juvenile en el cine español de los noventa', in J. Palacios (ed.), *Euronoir: serie negra con sabor europeo* (Madrid: Festival Internacional de Cine, Las Palmas de Gran Canaria/T&B), pp. 369–83.

Pastor, C. (2005), 'Terror en el adosado', *El mundo* (13 September), www. elmundo.es/elmundo/2005/09/13/cultura/1126622825.html, accessed 27 September 2005.

Perriam, C. (2003), *Stars and Masculinities in Spanish Cinema: from Banderas to Bardem* (Oxford: Oxford University Press).

Prout, R. (2000), 'Femme foetal: the triple terror of the young Basque woman in *Pasajes*', in B. Jordan and R. Morgan-Tamosunas (eds), *Contemporary Spanish Cultural Studies* (London: Arnold), pp. 283–94.

Pujol Ozonas, C. (2005), '*Lucía y el sexo*: de la *intelligentsia* cinematográfica a las revistas femeninas', *Archivos de la Filmoteca* 49, 97–107.

Quintana, Á. (2005), 'Modelos realistas en un tiempo de emergencias de lo político', *Archivos de la Filmoteca* 49, 11–31.

Raussell, P. (2003), 'La guerra del cine', *El País* (18 February), www.elpais. es/articulo/elpepiautmad/20020109elpmad_20/Tes/La%20guerra%20 civil%20en%20el%20cine, accessed 8 Mar 2006.

Rodríguez, M. P. (2002a), *Mundos en conflicto: aproximaciones al cine vasco de los noventa* (San Sebastián: Universidad de Deusto/Filmoteca Vasca).

Rodríguez, M. P. (2002b), 'Female visions of Basque terrorism: *Ander eta Yul* by Ana Díez and *Yoyes* by Helena Taberna', in O. Ferrán and K. M. Glenn (eds), *Women's Narrative and Film in Twentieth-Century Spain: A World of*

*Difference* (New York: Routledge), pp. 155–67.

Rodríguez Marchante, E. (1995), '"Salto al vacío": puntadas de buen cine sin hilo argumental', *ABC* (5 March).

Rodríguez Marchante, E. (1996), '"Pasajes": gran salto, pero vacío', *ABC* (22 November).

Roldán Larreta, C. (1999), *El cine del País Vasco: de Ama Lur (1968) a Airbag (1997)* (San Sebastián: Eusko Ikaskuntza).

Rosal, C. (2002), 'Guerreros, de Daniel Calparsoro: cine bélico, ¿español?', www.miradas.net/criticas/2002/0204_guerreros.htm, accessed 23 May 2003.

Rozas, I. (1996), 'Calparsoro/Nimry: corriente iónica', *Devórame* [supplement to *El Diario Vasco*] (27 September), 12.

Rubio, A. F. (1996), '"El cine vasco no existe"', *El País* (9 May).

Sánchez M., Vicente (2005), 'Recopilando', www.lasemana.es/ocio, accessed 27 September 2005.

Sánchez Noriega, J. L. (2002), '*Guerreros*', in Equipo Reseña (ed.), *Cine para leer 2002: enero-junio* (Bilbao: Mensajero), pp. 179–80.

Santos Gargallo, A. (2000), '*Asfalto*', in Equipo Reseña (ed.), *Cine para leer 2000: enero-junio* (Bilbao: Mensajero), pp. 52–4.

Sojo Gil, K. (1997), 'Acerca de la existencia de un cine vasco actual', *Sancho el Sabio* 7, 131–8.

Stone, R. and H. Jones (2004), 'Mapping the gendered space of the Basque Country', *Studies in European Cinema* 1/1, 43–55.

Taberna, D. (2006), '"En un casting todos los actores son muy importantes, hasta el que sólo dice hola', *Eibar* 3/72, 36, www.egoibarra.com/Eibar/Revista_Eibar_aldizkaria/eibar_2006_07.pdf, accessed 20 September 2006.

Tasker, Y. (2005), 'Soldiers' stories: women and military masculinities in *Courage Under Fire*', in R. Eberwein (ed.), *The War Film* (New Brunswick: Rutgers University Press), pp. 172–89.

Torres, A. M. (1995), 'Irregular retrato femenino', *El País* (6 March).

Torres, S. (1996), '*Pasajes*: cuando fuimos perdedores', *Fotogramas* XLIX/1829, 127.

Trashorras, A. (1996), 'Pasajes', *Fotogramas* L/1837, 26.

Trasobares, A. (1999), 'Calparsoro se pega al "Asfalto" para dar un giro de 180 grados a su carrera', *Diario 16* (26 June).

Triana-Toribio, N. (2003), *Spanish National Cinema* (London: Routledge).

Verney, C. (1998), '*A ciegas*', in Equipo de Reseñas (ed.), *Cine para leer 1997* (Bilbao: Mensajero, 1998), pp. 95–7.

Willis, A. (2004), 'From the margins to the mainstream: trends in recent Spanish horror cinema', in A. Lázaro Reboll and A. Willis (eds), *Spanish Popular Cinema* (Manchester: Manchester University Press), pp. 237–49.

# Index